English Drama 1865-1900

Surendra Sahai

English Drama 1865-1900

Orient Longman

Upsala College
Library
East Orange, N. J. 07019

English Drama 1865-1900

© Surendra Sahai

First published November, 1970

Published by
W. H. Patwardhan
Orient Longman Ltd
3/5 Asaf Ali Road
New Delhi 1

Regd. Office
50 Sunder Nagar
New Delhi 3

Regional Offices
Nicol Road, Ballard Estate
Bombay 1

17 Chittaranjan Avenue
Calcutta 13

36 A Mount Road
Madras 2

3/5 Asaf Ali Road
New Delhi 1

Typography
Sangam Press

Printed in India
by S. J. Patwardhan
Sangam Press Ltd
17 Kothrud Poona 4

To my mother and father with love and gratitude

Acknowledgements

I should like to thank my kind friends who looked into some of the proofs of the book : Mrs. Ranjana Bhan, Harish Narang and Rakesh Gupta. To Professor Naresh Chandra of the Department of English, Lucknow University, I owe a special debt. He looked into this project from the very beginning: but for his kind guidance this book would not have been possible. My thanks are due to all those friends who helped me in many other ways and inspired me to go ahead with this work.

Surendra Sahai
University of Delhi

Foreword

In life, it is a virtue to have the courage of one's convictions; in criticism, it is a virtue to be able to substantiate one's generalisations by offering apt and first hand evidence in support of them. Dr. Sahai's study of English drama in the last four decades of the nineteenth century exhibits both of these virtues. He has the courage to challenge the widely-held assumption that the revival of drama during these years was due solely to the influence of Ibsen and the practice of Shaw, and to assert that its sources were more complex and are also to be sought in the work of T. W. Robertson, W. S. Gilbert, A. W. Pinero, H. A. Jones, and Oscar Wilde. He likewise has the knowledge and discrimination necessary to give currency and cogency to this revaluation, and readers of this book will derive a special pleasure from the light that he sheds on the dramatic thought and stage practice of the dramatists whose achievements he so warmly endorses. Robertson's endeavour 'to fashion heroes out of the actual, dull, everyday man' and Gilbert's reaction against the mercenary dramaturgy which aimed merely at 'striking situations for the end of each act' prepare the way for Pinero's creation of a drama which would stand the test of close reading as well as effective performance. Dr. Sahai's discussion of Jones is particularly valuable and gives warrant to his claim that 'the renascence of drama as it appeared in the nineties was no less the result of Jones' efforts in explaining to people his conception of modern drama and its requirements than it was due to Shaw's campaign for Ibsen'. I have great pleasure in commending Dr. Sahais' book to all readers who are interested in a fuller knowledge and more accurate understanding of later nineteenth century drama.

William A. Armstrong

Professor of English
Westfield College
University of London

Contents

	Foreword : ix
I	The English Stage : 1
II	English Drama : 19
III	William S. Gilbert : 34
IV	Arthur Wing Pinero : 67
V	Henry Arthur Jones : 95
VI	Henrik Ibsen and the Development of the Problem Play : 117
VII	George Bernard Shaw : 142
VIII	Oscar Wilde : 166
IX	English Stage 1865-1900 : 193
X	A Period of Achievement : 210
	Select Bibliography : 223

Read : 1865–1900 *for* : 1860–1900
in all *verso* page-headings

Chapter I

The English Stage
Beginnings of a Movement

> "There is no such thing in existence as an English Stage."
> —Henry James, *The London Theatres 1880*

> "Why, William," said Kemble, "it is no doubt a disagreeable part, but there is passion in it." —*Macready's Reminiscences*

> "Robertson invented stage management." —Gilbert

The eighteen nineties witnessed a great dramatic revolution whic changed the concept of drama, in its various aspects. Many favourable circumstances brought about this change towards the close of the nineteenth century but, roughly, the span of this movement could be said to begin from 1865. The restriction for production of plays only at the Covent Garden and the Drury Lane and the Little Haymarket Theatre, imposed by Charles II was removed in 1843. Other show houses ran under different names of animal or musical shows. Between the Restoration period and the last quarter of the nineteenth century English drama was at its lowest ebb, the only two redeeming names being those of Sheridan and Goldsmith.

1

English Drama 1860-1900

Preparations for the revolution began amid these conditions of general dissatisfaction. The Act of 1843 was the first step in the theatre movement. It, however, did not have an immediate effect because the long continued ban had stifled the dramatic genius in the country and the mere passing of an Act could not suddenly rejuvenate it. No improvements were made till twenty more years had passed and then in 1865 Marie Wilton and Squire Bancroft produced at the Prince of Wales' Theatre a play, *Society*, by a new playwright, Thomas William Robertson, which may be chosen as a convenient landmark for the beginning of our study. Between 1843 and 1865 various factors combined to form a new dramatic renaissance.

A true picture of theatre in the fifties appeared in *Mask and Faces*[1] by Tom Taylor and Charles Reade in 1852. Triplet, the young author, is talking to the leading lady Woffington:

Woffington	:	............Are you an author, Sir?
Triplet	:	In a small way, madam, I have here three tragedies.
Woffington	:	(looking down at them with comical horror). Fifteen acts, mercy on us.
Triplet	:	Which if I could submit to Mrs. Woffington's judgment.
Woffington	:	(recoiling) I am no judge of such things, Sir.
Triplet	:	No more is the manager of this theatre.
		... ...
Triplet	:	(aside) One word from this laughing lady, and all my plays would be read—

A little later she gives the reason for Triplet's failure: "Ah! now if those things were comedies, I would offer to act in one of them, and then the stage door would fly open at the sight of the author." Triplet, with determination, goes to write a comedy immediately.

---

[1] *Nineteenth Century Plays* Ed. by George Rowell, Oxford University Press

The English Stage

The new tendencies of this period were really present in an embryonic form in the 1800-1865 period. They only manifested their full possibilities when the conditions became favourable. Some trends of this period proved highly portentious for the dramatic revival in the later decades. The chief characteristics of change between the drama of 1800-1865 and 1865-1900 were these: the romantic tradition in playwriting and acting gave place to a realistic approach; the stage manager, director or producer now came to hold a more dominating position than before; the writer commanded respect and actors were sought for plays rather than plays for actors as in the past; new dramatists found opportunities which now were no longer restricted to the old and famous writers; the financial returns for writers greatly increased and came on par with what writers in other branches of literature received, particularly the novel; and what is most important, the audience of the later period was vastly different from that of earlier times.

All these changes were suitably shown in *Society* which may be said to symbolise the new consciousness among dramatists.

Marie Wilton and Squire Bancroft, managers of the Prince of Wales' Theatre at the Tottenham Road had asked H. J. Byron to give them a play but the writer failed to honour his promise. Instead he introduced a friend, hitherto unknown, as a writer. The management surprised the young author by accepting his play for the stage and produced it on 11th November 1865. *Society* was welcomed among all circles of theatregoers. The author, Thomas William Robertson, realised the needs of his time, and the managers helped him accomplish the revolution he had designed. Its importance was twofold: it forestated the great changes to come in the following period 1865-1900; and, it showed the weakness of the contemporary English drama, by its brilliance in practically all aspects of production.

Robertson's life at this time was later sketched by Arthur Pinero in *Trelawny of the 'Wells'*. Tom Wrench is a caricature of Robertson in the sixties. Here is Tom talking to the leading lady, Imogen, in the first Act of the play:

English Drama 1860-1900

Imogen : Aren't you trying to write any plays just now?
Tom : Trying : I am doing more than trying to write plays. I am writing plays. I have written plays.
Imogen : Well?
Tom : My cupboard upstairs is choked with 'em.
Imogen : Won't anyone take a fancy?
Tom : Not a sufficiently violent fancy.
Imogen : You know the speeches were so short and had such ordinary words in them, in the plays you used to read to me — no big opportunity for the leading lady, Wrench.
Tom : M'yes I strive to make my people talk and behave like people, don't I — ?
Imogen (vaguely) : I suppose you do.
Tom : To fashion heroes out of actual, dull, everyday men — the sort of men you see smoking cheroots in the club windows in St. James' Street; and heroines from simple maidens in muslin frocks. Naturally, the managers won't stand that.
Imogen : Why, of course not.
Tom : If they did, the public wouldn't.
Imogen : Is it likely?
Tom : Is it likely? I wonder!
Imogen : Wonder — what ?
Tom : Whether they would.
Imogen : The public.
Tom : The public.

Tom's speeches gave authentic information on the pre-Robertson drama. He gave a true picture of the writers about the year 1865. A beginners' condition was helpless both as a dramatist and actor; importance of swashbuckling knights and lachrymose heroines was tremendous, grandiloquent speechmaking was favoured and great romantic actors controlled the production of plays. The production of *Society* was a great event in the nineteenth-century theatre. A retrospective glance at the pre-Robertson period will relate the advance made by *Society*.

Managers of the Covent Garden and Drury Lane, as also of the Little Haymarket were punctilious to the minutest details in the

4

grandeur and spectacle of their productions. Poetic and romantic plays were the tests of the managers' skill and the scene designers' art. The hunger for spectacle was well fed. Shakespeare's plays offered such grand settings. Managers and shareholders of theatres patronised a few authors of their choice. Charles Macready, at Covent Garden, encouraged Edward Bulwer Lytton and Robert Browning. Henry Irving, the great romantic actor, had his own set of authors. He introduced Tennyson to the stage. Macready's successor at the Princess' Theatre in 1851, Charles Kean, started his series of magnificient productions of Shakespeare's plays. Samuel Phelps opened the Sadler's Wells Theatre at Islington on May 22, 1844 with the avowed purpose to "render it what a theatre ought to be—a place for justly representing the works of our great dramatic poets."[1] After 1843, when the remedial Licensing Act was passed the theatre came to specialize in different branches of drama. Minor theatres which were busy producing spectacular shows before 1843, now openly came into competition with the patent houses. Melodramas were the rage and extravaganzas in great demand. The Prince of Wales' Theatre was much in advance of its time, and while other theatres were enjoying the new-found liberty by producing all kinds of dramas, the new management decided to go a step further, and selected a play which, by virtue of its novelty, shocked and surprised every member of the audience.

The Bancrofts (Marie Wilton had married Squire Bancroft later) built a new stage for their plays. They completely renovated the little theatre at the Tottenham Road and, fully conscious of the appalling effect of the huge auditoriums of the reconstructed Covent Garden and Drury Lane theatres, made the Prince of Wales' Theatre a small cosy theatre, not meant for accommodating large crowds. Only those genuinely interested went there. The seats were comfortable and stalls were provided with carpets. The management encouraged young talented authors and introduced Wilkie Collins, William Gilbert and Arthur Pinero to the theatre-

---

[1] Thomas H. Dickinson: *The Contemporary Drama of England*, pp. 26-27

goers. This was very risky. Managers had upto this time trusted only authors of established reputation, sure of commercial success of the play and ready with the work at short notice. They needed cheap translations and adaptations of less known works. This was the usual practice.

The Prince of Wales' Theatre did not cater to the popular entertainment seekers by providing them with a night's programme, including various dramatic varieties, i.e. tragedy, comedy, farce, burlesque, etc. Even the curtain raisers were abandoned. An evening's programme consisted mainly of one single performance.

The pains which Robertson took in directing the production of his plays were great, in view of the fact that before his venture, great actors usually took to directing and controlling the production. Henry Irving was dreaded among actors for he took umbrage at the slightest interference in the compliance of his orders. Almost with similar strictness Robertson controlled direction of his plays. From Henry Irving to Robertson the power came to pass from the actor to the author. *Society* heralded the advent of a new development in stage direction. His contemporaries acknowledged the debt they owed Robertson. Gilbert wrote: "I frequently attended his rehearsals and learnt a great deal from his method of stage management", adding, "Robertson showed how to give life and variety and nature to the scene by breaking it up with all sorts of little incidents and delicate by-play".[1] Pinero, another great writer said: "It can scarcely be denied that Robertson was a man of vision and courage".[2]

Robertson's direction of *Society* was symbolic of another great change: the birth of a modern director or stage manager. The author and the director, now onwards, came to play a very important part. Usually authors suffered due to the prejudicial treatment of their work by actor-managers. Charles Dickens' novels were freely dramatized and more than one version was

---

[1] *William Gilbert*: *His Life and Letters* by Sidney Dark and Rowland Gray, p. 5

[2] The Theatre in the Seventies in *The Eighteen Seventies* Ed. by H. G. Barker, p. 142

made for different theatres. Other writers who were not concerned with the stage suffered the same fate. The stage directors and managers sacrificed the author for the pleasure of actors or for spactacle and showmanship. Robertson received the needed encouragement from the Bancrofts and was left completely in command of his productions.

Robertson's direction started a new movement and it had its effect on all the great English dramatists of the succeeding period. William Gilbert, Arthur Wing Pinero, Henry Arthur Jones and Shaw were very particular about the perfect stage production of their plays. Robertson's nearest contemporary, Gilbert, worked on plaster models of the stage at home to contrive an exact reproduction of his ideas on the real stage. Robertson's technique could only be matched with the extreme care Charles Kean took in managing his Shakespearian productions. But as Kean was concerned only with reproduction of Elizabethan magnificence, he had no influence on the English drama of the following period. Robertson did his best to replace magnificence with realism. The romantic tradition was on its last legs. The new theatre built by the Bancrofts forbade Elizabethan fantasies and reserved its stage for projecting a real, lifelike image of things. At the auditorium of the Prince of Wales "A rich and elaborate gold border, about two feet broad, after the pattern of a picture frame, is continued all round the proscenium, and carried even below the actor's feet — there can be no doubt that the sense of illusion is increased, and for the reason just given; the actors seem cut off from the domain of prose; there is no borderland or platform in front; and, stranger still, the whole has the air of a picture projected on a surface".[1]

Also the intimacy with the audience, the sense of closeness with those addressed, had a good effect on acting. Lack of intimacy at the Drury Lane and the Covent Garden stages had pernicious effects on acting. Besides this picture-frame stage, Robertson also wanted actual doors with locks to them on the stage. Tom Wrench in *Trelawny of the 'Wells'* says:

---

[1] Percy Fitzgerald: *The World Behind the Scenes*, pp. 20-21

"I tell you, I won't have doors stuck here, there and everywhere; no, nor windows in all sorts of impossible places!" and also, 'windows on the one side, doors on the other — just where they should be architecturally and locks on the doors, real locks to work and handles to turn.'

This craving for stage realism was one of the most curious signs of the times. The scenery on the stage came to receive great attention due to the minuteness of original details represented on the stage in productions of Shakespeare's plays. Charles Kean, noted for extreme conscientiousness regarding such intricate details, was proud of his position, and treated historical and fantastic plays with the same earnestness. Even where there was not much room for such illustrative and historical accuracy, Kean could find opportunity to show his punctiliousness. The best illustration of such care taken for stage production by managers is furnished by J. W. Cole who, writing about Kean, says that in *A Midsummer Night's Dream* there was not much scope for that kind of classical research, even then "he availed himself of the few opportunities afforded by the subject, of carrying out his favourite plan. So little is known of Greek manners and architecture in the time of Theseus, twelve hundred years before the Christian era, and so probable is it that the buildings were of the rudest form, that any attempt to represent them on the stage would have failed in the intended object of profitable instruction. Holding himself for these reasons, "unfettered with regard to chronology", Mr. Kean presented ancient Athens to us......"[1]

The need for spectacular shows was realised both by the producer and the audience. This brought popularity to the show, money to the producer and satisfaction to the entertainment-seeking spectators. This endless "succession of skilfully-blended, pictorial, mechanical and musical effects"[2] was the craze among the producers and the audience.

This magnificence and grandeur of historical plays was a gift of the romantic tradition. Besides this there was another mania

---

[1] *The Life and Theatrical Times of Charles Kean*, p. 382
[2] *The Life and Theatrical Times of Charles Kean*, pp. 11, 199

for spectacle, born out of the minor houses.[1] Animals were brought to the stage and played important parts in plays. As early as 1803 at the Covent Garden in Reynold's *The Caravan*, a real dog, Carlos, made its stage appearance to drag the heroine out of a tank of water. In 1811-12 an elephant appeared on the stage in a pantomime *Harlequin and Padmanaba*, an earthquake was produced on the stage in the opera *The Virgin of the Sun*, and horses and waterfalls appeared in Moncrieff's *The Cataract of the Ganges; or, the Rajah's Daughter*. Even as late as in 1874 in *Rachel the Reaper* (Qns. 1874) there were real pigs, real sheep, a real goat and a real dog, with real litter strewn all over the stage.

Spectacular productions required heavy expenditure and also necessitated a specific type of drama. It was realised that it was time to free the stage from the thraldom of the carpenter. Robertson had foreseen this state of things and in his productions introduced all the necessary changes. His efforts to introduce real doors with locks to them would have appeared ridiculous to those accustomed to seeing these spectacular shows.

Robertson endeavoured to introduce realism in all aspects of his stage productions. The spirit of realism entered into the dialogues of his plays. As Imogen complains in *Trelawny of the 'Wells'* "...the speeches were so short and had such ordinary words in them......no big opportunity for the leading lady". She was pleading for the stilted and declamatory style of the romantic tradition. Robertson wrote his dialogues in the easy, natural style with as few words as could convey the sense. The 'five shillings' episode in *Society* illustrates this most suitably:

Sidney (L)	:	I find I've nothing in my portmannaie but notes. I want a trifle for a cab. Lend me five shillings.
Tom	:	I haven't got it; but I can get it for you.
Sidney	:	There's a good fellow, do (Returns to seat).

---

[1] Minor houses, without legal permission, staged plays and presented animals and other such elements, to masquerade their plays as something different from those produced at the patent houses. The patent theatres also took to their ways.

English Drama 1860-1900

Tom	:	(to Mac Usquebaugh, after looking round) Mac, (whispering) lend me five bob.
Mac U.	:	My dear boy, I haven't got so much.
Tom	:	Then don't lend it.
Mac U.	:	But I'll get it for you (crosses to Bradley—whispers) Bradley, lend me five shillings.
Brad	:	I haven't it about me; but I'll get it for you (Crosses to O'Sullivan — whispers) O'Sullivan, lend me five shillings.
O'Sull.	:	I haven't got it, but I'll get it for you (Crossing to Scargil —whispers) Scargil, lend me five shillings.
Scarg	:	I haven't got it, but I'll get it for you (crossing to Makvicz —whispers) Doctor, lend me five shillings.
Dr. M.	:	I am waiting for change for a soveren; I'll give it yon when de waiter brings it me.
Crag	:	All right! (To O'Sullivan) All right!
O'Sull.	:	All right! (To Bradley) All right!
Brad	:	All right! (To Mac Usquebaugh) All right!
Mac U.	:	All right! (To Tom) All right!
Tom	:	(To Sidney) All right!

Almost a similar succinctness in dialogue appeared at its best in *School* where the school-girls discussed love. Robertson's characters spoke the language of everyday life.

Robertson's aim in writing *Society* was not to write a play of the popular romantic genre but one which dealt with feelings rather than passion. The first fifty years of the nineteenth century were full of plays dealing with a leading passion, one dominating mood. In fact the romantic tradition was kept alive not so much by playwrights as by great actors of this style, such as Macready, Kean, Phelps, Henry Irving and Martin Harvey. Plays were accepted not on their merit but for presence in it of any dominating passion. Very early in the nineteenth century Joanna Bailie's *Plays on the Passion* started this type of play which, for the opportunities it offered to players, soon found favour with managers and the leading actors. *The Apostate* by Richard Sheil disappointed Macready but the consolation he received from Charles Kemble restored his confidence. "Why

William", said Kemble, "it is no doubt a disagreeable part, but there is passion in it".[1] *The Apostate* was performed as early as 1817, but Charles Kemble's words apply to all romantic plays and actors. With such a strong predilection for passion among managers and actors till late in the century, Robertson's *Society* flew in the face of strong opposition. It was an episode from common life and had telling effects on the standards of acting. The Bancrofts favoured individual artists and not schools. The star system was abandoned in favour of the individual merit system.

Robertson's aim was "to fashion heroes out of actual, dull, everyday men — the sort of men you see smoking cheroots in the club windows in St. James' Street, and heroines from simple maidens in muslin frocks". This was contrary to the established traditions of the romantic actors. Plays were written with certain great actors in view and the other parts were sacrificed for it. Even Shakespeare's plays[2] had to be recast to suit actors. This was true of all romantic actors, who delayed the efflorescence of realistic drama till the audience itself cooperated with the author to throw off this dead weight. Also, this star system was highly detrimental to young actors who could only appear and disappear at the star-actor's convenience. Robertson's contribution in this direction was great. New and young actors could only dream of appearing on the London stage before the producer-director of *Society* launched a revolution.

In the new school of acting, parts were written in proportion to their importance in the play, and not as concession to the players' talent and popularity. A completely fresh attitude towards actng, adopted by the Bancrofts at the Prince of Wales' Theatre, "was the result of a most praiseworthy stand against the absurd arti-

---

[1] *Macready's Reminiscences and Selection from his Diaries and Letters*, Ed. by Sir Frederick Pollock, Vol. I, p. 145

[2] Writing of Macready, George Vandenhaff says, "When he played *Othello*, Iago was to be nowhere!......The next night, perhaps he played Iago and lo! every thing was changed, Othello was to become a puppet for Iago to play with: But the tendency, alas! was dominant whatever his surroundings". William Archer: *W. C. Macready* (1890), pp. 210-11

ficialities and conventionalities then in vogue on the stage...... How delighted fashionable audiences were with a system which replaced the grossest caricatures of themselves, their manners and customs, with the closest and most faithful reproduction, was at once proved by the rapid bounds by which the theatre at which that system first saw the light progressed in public esteem... Still as the popularity of the Prince of Wales' flourished unabated so also flourished and increased the new school of actors"[1].

Robertson did not favour big roles and great stars. The new actors he selected were very well trained and rehearsed to perfection. This preference for young and inexperienced talent over the great stars proved a good experiment. Robertson's closest contemporary, Gilbert, also followed in his footsteps and he selected new talents. Gilbert engaged an inexperienced actor, Rutland Barrington, for a key role in one of his plays. Questioned on the choice, he replied: "He's a staid, stolid swine, and that's what I want"[2]. The choice of Mrs. Patrick Campbell for the role of Paula Tanqueray in Pinero's famous play *The Second Mrs. Tanqueray* completely changed her fortune, and that of the author. Besides, because he did not create type characters and the 'stars' had their own 'type' roles written specially for them, Robertson treated individual roles as studies in human life. His characterisation demanded a new approach to acting and the old ways could not also be carried on.

Robertson's reforms were in all those directions which affected the author-director. In his stage directions, in the accomplishment of realism on the stage, in his training of actors and founding a new school of acting, and in other practical aspects of theatrical production, Robertson made new strides in the development of English drama in the sixties. His achievements praised, his contribution acknowledged, this glorified picture of Robertson's achievements should not make us neglect the main basis of all his greatness.

---

[1] *The Saturday Review*, LXVI, Dec. 22, 1888, pp. 741-2.
[2] Hesketh Pearson: *Gilbert and Sullivan*: *A Biography*, p. 102

The English Stage

The audience of the nineteenth century saw the rise and fall of two different types of dramas and the part it played in shaping the form of drama was significant. The gradual change in the behaviour of the audience of the early decades to that of the later decades was symbolic of many social and political changes. In 1865, when *Society* was first played at the Prince of Wales' Theatre, English theatregoers were in a transitional period, and changed from an unruly and indisciplined crowd to a set of restrained and controlled people. Two things greatly affected the audience, the Licensing Act of 1843 and the Great Exhibition in 1851. The audience of 1865 was not very different from the audience of earlier decades, except that its behaviour was adjusting itself to the corresponding change in the tone of drama.

The monopoly over the stage prevailing since the days of Charles II was abolished in 1843. When the nineteenth century began, theatres were few, and visited mostly by lower middle-class spectators of debased character and obnoxious manners. Theatre was regarded as a place of entertainment. This was one of the many reasons for the failure of realistic drama in the early decades. Audiences at the patent houses consisted of rakish members of the city, and free-fights in the auditorium were a common feature. Bottles and peeled oranges were freely thrown on the stage at the slightest provocation. The population increased by leaps and bounds and the patent houses, despite their huge reconstructed auditoriums, could not accommodate the large number of persons eager to pass their evenings there.

The railways came to London in 1828, and the railroad system was laid in 1843. These facilities for easy communication also contributed to the gathering of this huge mass of humanity. The Great Exhibition of 1851 was a symbol of the material prosperity of the people. Greedily attracted by stage productions, specially the unauthorized minor houses' shows of spectacle, the populace crowded the theatres. To young men it became a fashionable amusement and an evening rendezvous. Theatres became the main social centres of the city dwellers. But whereas theatres were filled with people, bourgeois opinion was very much against them, and respectable people despised actors and other theatre-folk. This state of affairs continued till late in the nineteenth century.

But this capricious behaviour of the audience also underwent a change, and during the sixties, it was completely transformed. Great actors like Macready, Phelps and Henry Irving dominated the stage. They commanded great respect. The Queen herself had a considerable impact on the audience. She frequently visited the Princess, the St. James and the Little Haymarket late in the century. She attended a few Gilbert and Sullivan operas.

There was a widespread consciousness that the public should seek to improve its theatrical taste, and discipline its response in the auditoriums. With the changing times the audience also realised its responsibilities. Changes were apparent. The behaviour was now more controlled and the expression of disapproval subdued. In 1865 when Robertson produced *Society* there were not many disturbances during the performance.

A new outlook was more and more perceptible. Many new factors contributed to this changed attitude of the audience: increase in the number of theatres, popularity of the novel as a force distracting a large crowd to another popular form of literature, attitude of the Church and critics of the stage.

After 1843, managers were given freedom to open theatres. The major theatres, the Covent Garden and Drury Lane were put on par with the hitherto illegitimate theatres. New theatres specialised in particular forms of drama. Notable among such enterprises were St. James' and the Court Theatre which specialised in farce, Adelphi in melodrama, Opera Comique in opera. The unruly crowd, loving spectacle, was pandered to at various houses, thus, freeing the main theatres of the obligation to mingle spectacle with serious themes.

Entry of respectable people in theatres was symbolic of the favourable attitude towards the histrionic art. At this time two forms of literature were popular, poetry and drama. Poetic plays were written mainly by poets. Nearly all great poets of the nineteenth century wrote dramas. Those interested in literature now found in the novel a new entertainment. This gave a tinge of seriousness to the drama. Many persons absented themselves from the theatres because they found better means of entertainment.

The new conditions changed the position of authors. Even in 1866, W. Allingham observed: "The question of some importance to the English drama, is this, how shall a writer outside theatrical circles bring a play under the eyes of managers without the risk that should it contain anything of value for stage purposes, this will be appropriated without the smallest acknowledgment"[1]. This was the general condition and the most notable play of the last years, *Society*, was first turned down as rubbish by Buckstone before being accepted at the Prince of Wales', where too, he got a chance due to H. J. Byron's inability to fulfil his engagement. Many managers returned new plays without even reading them. William Gilbert met with embarrassing treatment when he submitted a blank verse burlesque of Tennyson's poem 'The Princess' to Horace Wigan, manager of the Olympic, "with the middle pages carefully gummed together." A few days later Wigan handed it back to him with the remark that it was unsuitable.

> 'Did you read it?' queried Gilbert.
> 'Of course' Wigan replied in a hurt tone of voice.
> 'By gum, you didn't!' said Gilbert, displaying the pages and the adhesive substance which proved the fact.[2]

There were even cases when plays once rejected and returned were later produced with little alterations and a changed name. W. Allingham in 1886 wrote to *The Athenaeum* complaining of *The Lord Harry* produced at the Princess' Theatre which was based entirely on his own, once rejected, play *Ashby Manor*. This created "a not unimportant question. In 1883 I sent my play in print to Mr. Wilson Barrett, and had, at his request, an interview with that gentleman, and a second one in 1884. He said he was 'much struck' with *Ashby Manor*, but it was not suitable for his company, and in any case would require 'a great deal of pulling about.' He made no proposal but asked if I had anything else to show him.

---

[1] *The Athenaeum*, No. 3045, March 6, 1886, 338
[2] Hesketh Pearson, *op. cit.* p. 51

Since then I have heard nothing. Mr. Barrett has now produced *The Lord Harry*, not only the germ of which is unquestionably in *Ashby Manor*, though there has been extensive 'pulling about' and much addition of sensational incident and scenery, unconnected with any plot—but also—the personages in each are essentially identical."[1]

This neglect of fresh talent in favour of stage popularity accounted for the decline of the drama. But as the 1843 Act was passed and new theatres were built,[2] young authors were given opportunities to show their talent. Few young writers of real talent appeared on the stage. There were various reasons for this. But the most important factor was the greater opportunities and money offered by other forms of published literature, particularly the novel. During the nineteenth century drama was closely associated with poetry in the earlier decades and with the novel in the later decades. Scott and Dickens were freely adapted for the stage and sometimes novels like *Bride of Lammermoor* and *A Tale of Two Cities* ran at six or seven theatres simultaneously. Dickens was very much affected by these adaptations, as many of his editions were pirated in America where they were played with a great commercial success. Thackeray also had his influence. Robertson in *Caste* was influenced by both Dickens and Thackeray. The character of old Eccles seemed to be modelled on the 'Dolls' dress-maker' in Dickens' *Mutual Friend*. Also the influence of Thackeray is manifest in the similarity between George in *Vanity Fair* and George D'Alroy in *Caste*.

The monetary return from drama compared poorly with the returns of a published novel. This was why many men with a genius for

---

[1] *The Athenaeum*, No. 3045, March 6, 1886, p. 338

[2] Between 1860 and 1870 seven theatres were built, Royalty, Gaiety, The Charming Cross, The Globe, The Holborn, The Queen's and the Prince of Wales'. Between 1870 and 1880: The Court, The Opera Comique, The Vaudeville, The Criterion, The Philharmonic and The Imperial. Between 1880 and 1890: The Comedy, The Savoy, The Avenue, the Novelty, Terry's, The Lyric, The Shaftesbury, The Prince's, The Empire and The Garrick. Between 1890 and 1900: The Duke of York's, Daly's, Her Majesty's and Wyndham's.

story-telling took to the novel instead of drama. The popularity of the novel deprived the English stage of many talented people. But even then, many English writers were given opportunities. Gilbert, Pinero and Jones were fortunate in their brief apprenticeship period. It became a fashion to say, looking at the vast number of adaptations of French and other foreign works, that foreign talent was preferred to English. But Bancroft observes in a letter that "this is not at all the case"[1]. Above all, it has to be acknowledged that the neglect which English authors had to suffer before Robertson, was gradually given up and actually there was little difficulty for men of talent to find their way.

The gradual change that was slowly manifesting itself was much aided by criticisms and reviews of various stage performances by experts of this art. The notice that critics took of the stage was helpful in making, certain authors popular, certain plays successful and some actors, well-known.

A retrospective look at the English drama before 1865 shows what a sea change the drama of the later period had undergone. It will not be too much to say that the person chiefly responsible for this was Robertson. The Bancrofts aided him in all possible ways to procure for him conditions which helped him bring about a revolution on the English Stage. Robertson's direction of his plays, his founding a new school of acting based on 'realism', his reform of stage scenery, and all other aspects of theatre-craft connected with production of plays, ushered a new era in the English drama

---

[1] *Mr. and Mrs. Bancroft on and off the Stage Vol. I*, P. 158:

"At the Prince of Wales's theatre; since 1865, twenty two pieces have been produced, thirteen were new works written by English authors — *Society, Ours, Caste, Play, School* and *M.P.* by Mr. Robertson; *How She Loves Him* by Mr. Boucicault; *War to the knife, A Hundred Thousand Pounds* and *Winkle* by Mr. Byron; *Man and Wife* by Wilkie Collins; *Sweethearts* by Mr. Gilbert; and *Tame Cats* by Mr. Edmund Yates. Revivals of the following six plays, all English, have been given........."

Bancroft recounts a number of plays to prove the baselessness of arguments wrongly accusing of the neglect of English talent.

of the late nineteenth century. This is not to suggest that he alone was responsible for all this, because movements rarely begin with a single person. The audience helped him, his contemporaries prepared the ground for his appearance. Robertson made the best use of his capabilities to redeem the theatre from utter decrepitude, and revolutionised the contemporary stage traditions which cleared the way for a new drama.

Chapter II

English Drama
The Beginnings

> "*Society*.........a queer out of the way thing, almost monstrous in its disregard of the conventions...produced at the little Prince of Wales Theatre on the night of November 11th 1865; and that night a New form of drama took root."
>
> *The Theatre in the Seventies*
> A. W. Pinero

> Tom: To fashion heroes out of actual, dull every day men...... and heroines from simple maidens in muslin frocks. Naturally the managers won't stand that.
> Imogen : Why, of course not.
>
> *Trelawny of the Wells*
> A. W. Pinero

Society (1865) initiated a new dramatist. The play itself had not much to offer. It was based on a multitude of circumstances: lost child, mistaken identity, bought notes, arrest for debt, lachrymose lovers and merciless moneylenders. Not only were these parts of the story familiar to the audience but also the tricks of language, puns and long asides were well known to them. Despite all these apparent weaknesses *Society* marked a new beginning in stage realism.

Whereas many critics knew Robertson's limitations as a dramatist, they did not cry him down. For a beginner in the dramatic art *Society* was good and was soon followed by better plays wherein Robertson gained confidence in his art and in his role as a 'new' dramatist.

Ours, 1866, appealed to the patriotic feelings of his countrymen in their affection for soldiers in the Crimean War, and displayed good craftsmanship.

All his tentativeness ended with *Caste*, 1867, a satire on the prevailing class distinctions in society. *Caste* had a well-defined purpose, and, whereas it was in compliance with the growing need for thought-provoking plays, it showed Robertson as a great 'force' in contemporary drama. *Caste* dealt with the stratification in society which "among the Brahmins is masked by express law, and which among the most western representatives of the great Aryan race is drawn by a prejudice which has scarcely less than legal force."[1] Hon'ble George D'Alroy, rich and aristocratic, falls in love with a dancing girl, Esther. Theirs is the predicament of an ill-matched union. The rich aristocracy stands against the poverty-stricken people.

Hawtree	:	The girl is a nice girl, no doubt; but as to your making her Mrs. D'Alroy, the thing is out of question.
George	:	Why? What should prevent me?
Hawtree	:	Caste! — The inexorable law of Caste! The social law, so becoming and so good, that commands like to mate with like, and forbids a giraffe to fall in love with a squirrel.
George	:	But, my dear Bark—
Hawtree	:	My dear Dal, all those marriages of people with common people, are very well in novels and in plays on the stages because the real people don't exist ......and so no harm's done, and it's rather interesting to look at; but in real life with real relations and real mothers, and so forth, it's absolute bosh. It's worse — it's utter social and personal annihilation and damnation.

Clearly enough, it is not Captain Hawtree haranguing on the question of marriage and its problems but Mrs. Grundy addressing

---

[1] *The Times*, 11th April, 1867, in *The Specimens of English Dramatic Criticism*: Ed. by A. C. Ward, p. 133

the audience. Characters, like Hawtree, were developed into *raissoneurs* in plays of Pinero, Jones and Shaw. They expound the opinions of society or serve as a mouthpiece to the author.

But George is not to be so easily moved. Having decided to act of his own accord, and flouting the dictates of the 'grand Brahmin Priestess' his mother the Marquise de St. Maur, George and Esther are married. The stiff-necked mother-in-law is set against this marriage. George leaves for India with his regiment and disappears in a frontier skirmish. The young widow and her little child return to her father's place. The drunken old man, Eccles, is introduced as if to counterbalance the marchioness. The whole Eccles family is in dire financial straits. The old man, given to drinking, in a piece of realistic satire, steals the necklace from Esther's son.

> Eccles : ...Milk — for this young aristocratic pauper. Everybody in the house is sacrificed for him! ......That there coral he's got round his neck is gold, real gold! Oh, Society! Oh, Government! Oh, Class Legislation! Is this right? Shall this mindless wretch enjoy himself, while sleeping with a jewelled gawd and his poor old grandfather want the price of half pint? No! it shall not be! Rather than see it, I will myself resent this outrage on the rights of man! and in this holy crusade of class against class, of the weak and lowly against the powerful and strong — I will strike one blow for freedom...

Eccles steals the necklace, and when the affairs of the Eccles' family have reached an impasse owing to utter penury, the hero returns and with him happiness returns to the poverty-ridden household. *Caste* ends on this happy tableau.

Caste was Robertson's best play, and also his most representative as it was in this play that he pronounced most unreservedly his opinion on a social problem. His strong bid to attain realism on the stage was fulfilled in the production of the play. Mrs. Bancroft, who produced *Caste*, wrote: "It was in *Caste* that we made a distinct stride towards realistic scenery. The rooms for the first time had ceilings, with such details as locks and doors and similar matters had never been seen upon the stage".[1] Bernard Shaw writing about it in 1897, observed: "After years of sham heroic and superhuman balderdash, *Caste* delighted everyone by its freshness, its nature, its humanity".[2] With the production of *Caste* in 1867, Pinero quoted a critic, "the reformation is complete, and Mr. Robertson stands pre-eminent as the dramatist of this generation".[3]

Other plays of Robertson were written on the same lines. *Play* followed *Caste* in 1868. *School* appeared in 1869 and proved the most successful of Robertson's plays. It ran for three hundred and eighty-one nights. As Dickinson observes, *School* was "something of a tour de force, in that the entire psychology of the play is school girl psychology". The nineteenth century does not afford another example of such a "play for adults being constructed out of the playful, elusive, but immature materials of girlish character"[4] The subtle penetration into the young minds has a freshness about it. Here in this scene young girls are busy finding out what love is:

Tilly	:	Everybody knows what love is.
Clara	:	Then what is it?
Naomi	:	Who's got a dictionary? You're sure to find it there.
Tilly:	:	My eldest sister says it's the only place in which you can find it.
Hetty	:	Then she's been jilted.
Milly	:	My pa says love is moonshine.
Naomi	:	Then how sweet and mellow it must be.
Milly	:	Particularly when the moon is at the full.
Naomi	:	And there's no eclipse.
Tilly:	:	It seems that nobody knows what love is.
Hetty	:	I despise such ignorance.
Clara:	:	Then why don't they teach it us? We've a music master to teach music, why not a love master to teach love?
Naomi	:	You don't suppose love is to be taught like geography or the use of the globes, do you? No; love is an extra.

---

[1] *Mr. and Mrs. Bancroft: On and off the Siage, Vol. I*, p. 230
[2] *Plays and Players*, p. 252
[3] *The Eighteen Seventies, op. cit*. p. 141
[4] *op. cit.* p. 47

In the rest of *School* Robertson shows how Naomi gets this 'extra' and Bella, her prince lover. But before the end is reached, Dr. Sutcliffe and Farintosh agree on the necessity of a school.

Dr. Sutcliffe	:	So many things are required for the composition of the real thing. One wants nobility of feeling.
Farintosh	:	A kind heart.
Dr. Sutcliffe	:	A noble mind.
Farintosh	:	Modesty.
Dr. Sutcliffe	:	Gentleness.
Farintosh	:	Courage.
Dr. Sutcliffe	:	Truthfulness.
Farintosh	:	Birth.
Dr. Sutcliffe	:	Breeding.
Mrs. Sutcliffe	:	(coming between them) and above all — School !

Robertson's other plays include *M.P.*, *Home*, *Dream* and *War*.

Robertson's real contribution to English drama lies not so much in his new themes but in his boldness in having written plays quite different from the staple stage productions.

Success was no chance occurrence, it came of his genius and originality. His determination to create the new audience, and an understanding of the drama was successful. He had decided not to yield to popular demands. Plays that could 'make 'em laugh, make 'em cry' were in great demand. There were many playwrights waiting with such plays. The inevitable followed. The condition of drama became worse with every decade. Various factors contributed to this decline.

Upto 1843, when the Theatre Licencing Act was passed, only three theatres were officially permitted to stage plays. The great rush at theatres was uncontrollable and unmanageable. To cope with the new audience many minor show houses came into existence and worked as music and animal shows to escape the rigorous discipline of the Lord Chamberlain's law. These were the conditions before the stage production of *Society* in 1865. Such conditions encouraged the production of plays of the mixed variety; in comedy, farce and burlesque were used freely, and in tragedy poetic plays had a fair amount of melodrama. Generally an all-round performance was given. The main varieties of plays that filled the stage during the period prior to Robertson's comedies, were the following:

(1) **Verse Plays:** Nineteenth Century drama began with the production of poetic plays written in imitation of Elizabethan playwrights. The Romantic poets were the chief supporters of and contributors to this form of play. In fact all the great poets of the Romantic School had written plays. Wordsworth and Coleridge, Scott, Godwin and Lamb wrote dramas which failed on the stage. Among the successful poet-dramatists, Byron was the most important. Although soaked in an Elizabethan spirit, his plays had an originality and force in their action that made them successful on the stage. *Manfred* (1817) and *Sardanapalus* were his important plays. Shelley's *The Cenci* was startling in its theme, but was for various reasons rejected as 'untheatrical'. Browning's *Stratford* (1837) and *A Blot in the Scutcheon* (1843) were psychological in essence. Poetic plays continued to be written till late in the nineties when Tennyson wrote *Becket* (1893).

Reasons for the failure of poetic plays are not far to seek. First, the poets were too subjective in their treatment of grand themes to give a free hand to the natural development of theme. Secondly, their extreme dependence on the Elizabethan playwrights as models crippled their own originality. Grandiloquent speeches and philosophical platitudinizings filled plays whereas the audience hated ideas. It wanted action on the stage but the poetic plays offered little in this direction. Thirdly, there was overcrowding at the newly-constructed auditoriums of the Drury Lane and Covent Garden. Huge crowds, noisy atmosphere, shrieks, cries and catcalls—almost all varieties of rowdyism and disturbances were the order of the day. The actor on stage would begin his soliloquies and keep shouting out his thoughts. The sense of intimacy required for the performance of the poetic play was missing. The Elizabethan theatres had a platform projecting out of the main stage like a tongue into the very midst of the groundlings and the actor spoke with a touch of intimacy with the audience. That intimacy could not be obtained in the nineteenth century theatres. The caprices and prejudices of theatre managers and the dominating actors like Macready, Kean, Phelps and Henry Irving were to a great extent responsible for making true poetic plays an impossibility on the stage. It is a paradox that poetic plays were written for such actors only. Plays full of passion, were in vogue. Joanna Bailie's *Plays on the Passions* revived a tradition which continued throughout the century.[1] Substantial parts for the chief actors were the deciding factors in the acceptance of certain plays for the stage. Actors usually toured with such plays. One reason for the production of Shakespeare's historical plays in the nineteenth century was the opportunity they afforded to the leading player for displaying his talent. The roles were practically a challenge to the great actors of the day.

The sacrifice of other characters for one major role was most common on the stage and even Shakespeare's texts were changed to suit 'stars' of the stage. On many occasions 'everything was sacrificed to one character'[2]

With the Bancrofts this tradition of romantic acting got a rebuff and the star system was revoked. Even in his first comedy at the Prince of Wales, *Society*, parts were distributed on the basis of talent and not on reputation. Squire Bancroft acknowledged Robertson's obligation when he said: "As the part I first played in *Society* was a very important one to entrust to so young an actor as I then was, bearing, as it does, much of the burden of the play, I would like to note how much the success I was fortunate enough to achieve was due to the encouragement and support I received from the author, who spared no pains with me, as with others to have his somewhat novel type of characters understood and acted as he wished".[3] The point about Robertson's novelty of characters is very important since indirectly it contributed to the growth of a new school of drama and acting.

---

[1] See *supra* Ch. I

[2] Dr. Doran: *Their Majesties' Servants—Annals of the English Stage, Vol. II From Betterton to Edward Keene*, p. 515

[3] *Mr. and Mrs. Bancroft on and off the Stage, Vol. I*, p. 202

(2) Another important and popular variety of stage fare was melodrama. J. R. Planche in *The Camp at the Olympic* (Olympic 1853) gave a good account of the prevailing forms of drama. In this play a stage manager's problem is solved by the British Dramatic forces. Burlesque 'a vice of kings: a king in shreds and patches!' English opera with a foreign band, Ballet, Melodrama, Pantomime, Hippo-Drama and Spectacle. Mr. Wigan, the manager, is in a fix about which of these to choose.

Mrs. Wigan : In each of them there's some thing that's good.
Without committing ourselves here to fix 'em.
Let's take the best and mix 'em.

Mr. Wigan : Mix 'em!

Mrs. Wigan : Mix 'em!

Mr. Wigan : Like pickles? or like physic? What a notion!
D'ye think the town will swallow such a potion?
Why, Tragedy's a black dose of itself!

Mrs. Wigan : Who talks of taking all, you silly elf?
I mean an extract of each spirit Tragic,
Comic, Satiric, Operatic, Magic, Romantic,
Pantomimic, Choreographic, Spectacular, Hip.

Mr. Wigan : Spare that tongue seraphic
Such vain exertion — for they would but call
Your mixture melodrama, after all.

Mrs. Wigan : With all my heart, I say, I don't care what
It's called.

A better picture of mid-nineteenth century drama can hardly be drawn. Melodrama was in great demand. The influence of German plays, specially of Kotzebue, appeared in the love of sentimental and sensational elements, of pathos and surprise in plays. But melodrama did one service to drama in having brought the playwright down from the aristocratic world of the poetic plays to the middle-classes. Domestic plays with maudlin sentimentality were in vogue. Sentimentality and excitement usually meant exaggerated sentiments full of tearful tosh, sensational discoveries, helpless hero, distressed heroine, ruthless villain, poisoned hero, lost heirs, thrilling fights and the conclusion in which the languishing heroine breathed her last in the arms of her lover. Musical accompaniments were provided to move with the electric movement of the plot.

The popularity of melodrama rose following the popularity of illegitimate playhouses before 1843. Isaac Pocock, D.W. Jerrold and Bayle Bernard contributed to melodrama. Among contributors to melodrama only Dion Boucicault deserves mention because of the ingenuity of his plots. His main contribution lies in having given a picture of real life on the stage. From the princely characters of the poetic plays, he changed over to middle-class characters. His acute eye for oddity and eccentricity in characters, his tragedies of domestic interiors and presentation of the conditions of real life on the stage were highly helpful in the evolution of drama in the late nineteenth century. *The Collean Bawn; or, The Brides of Garry-Owen* (Adelphi 1860), *The Octoroon; or Life in Louisiana* (Adelphi 1861) and *Arrah-na-Pogue; or, The Wicked Wedding* (Princess' 1865) were melodramas with the usual hair-raising incidents, and maudlin love affairs. These melodramas exercised a great influence over the dramatists in the eighties and nineties. Bernard Shaw's *Devil's Disciple* owed a complete scene design to Boucicault's *Arrah-na Pogue*. This was one of the many examples where later writers imitated their predecessors and at the same time criticised them for the same qualities.

(3) **Comedy:** The sentimental and the sensational elements in the popular melodrama almost polluted all forms of plays. This love for melodramatic elements had its most telling effect on pure comedy. Except by Goldsmith, since Sheridan no genuine comedy was written till Robertson.

(*A*) *Farce, Burlesque and Extravaganza*: The most baneful effect of the minor houses' productions manifested itself in the popularity of depraved comic forms. Generally written in one-act form, farces aimed at producing mirth in the audience. Burlesque, based on eighteenth century operas, and extravaganzas, full of topsy-turvy humour and music, were popular and had very many good writers as contributors including J. R. Planche. William

Gilbert in the seventies brought it to a level of unexcelled craftsmanship.

(B) *Domestic Plays:* Sentimental tales with all sorts of turns and twists in the fortunes of the hero and heroine, fortuitous appearances and disappearances of characters at the required moments, and all the other usual tricks of appeal to the broad mass of theatre-goers were quite popular.

In domestic plays lay the germs of the realistic play of the nineties. As these dealt with characters who were largely drawn from the middle classes, drama came to have a likeness to the life of the people. Its relation to common humanity which was lost in the early nineteenth century was restored. In domestic dramas mainly two themes dominated; first, scenes from married life and the relation of husband and wife; secondly, the classification of social classes on the basis of money, and wealth versus humanity. In the drama of the last three decades the question of the position of women in society attracted much attention. Plays were written about emancipation of women from the thraldom of household, falsehood of marriage ideals, hypocrisy of husbands and what is most important, of women with a past. Robertson's comedies did not touch this aspect of life, but the most important playwrights of the eighties and nineties, Pinero, Jones and Shaw and Oscar Wilde, wrote on the theme of women with a past and seemed to begin a new movement. The real beginning of the women's movement had started there decades earlier, in the fifties.

How passion destroyed family happiness and led to catastrophe was shown in *Retribution* (Olympic 1856) by Tom Taylor. In another play, *Still Waters Run Deep* (1855) Taylor touched upon a very serious theme. An aunt controls the household; the young neglected wife is engaged in an affair with a rascally captain but the affair is discovered by the aunt, and the captain is no other than a former companion of the aunt. The aunt is Mrs. Strenhold and the cuckold is Mildmay. The villain is sent to the galleys for forgery and the hero is united with the heroine. In *The Second Mrs. Tanqueray* (1893) of Pinero, Paula marries Aubrey. Her stepdaughter is engaged to a Captain Ardale, who had an affair with

Paula before her marriage to Aubrey. Their past is discovered. The Captain is moved out of the way. It is almost a redramatization of *Still Waters Run Deep* in its theme. In excellence of construction *The Second Mrs. Tanqueray* made an immeasurable advance in drama. Despite the obvious sentimentality of its theme of domestic happiness and marital felicity Taylor's play had a striking originality in days when 'originality' was at a discount. Mrs. Mildmay's final reconciliation to her husband shows the atter's courage which was lacking in Ibsen's *A Dolls House* which is 'advanced' only from the woman's point of view. Torwald appears a coward and cramped by tradition and position in comparison to Taylor's Mildmay. Pinero only succeeded in sending the Captain away and in the heroine's suicide as a woman with a past could not be tolerated by polite society. Taylor deserved credit for his frank treatment of the question of sex and domestic happiness. Writing as early as 1855, he produced a piece of great originality. Pinero, Jones and Shaw, in a sense only walked on the track cleared by Taylor. It takes away much glory from Ibsen as a 'leader' in the movement for dramatic liberation.

In *Victims* (1857) Mrs. Merry Weather, is for some time "flattered and fluttered by the attentions of the poetaster Fitzherbert and where the husband proves himself the magnanimous hero".[1] This presaged *Candida* by Bernard Shaw in which the hero wins the game because the ties of a husband-wife relationship were too fast to break for the heroine. An almost similar situation was taken up in *Cyril's Success* where the heroine neglected by the hero, leaves, but is later reconciled to him. H. J. Byron's play was written in 1868, a time when full five acts in plays and originality were rare commodities on the stage. Byron's aim was "to remind any who may care to collect the fact that *Cyril's Success* is original, and a comedy—and even in these vicious dramatic days—in five acts! there!" While five-act plays were rare, plays with acts divided into scenes were even rarer. Robertson wrote the rarer type. In his plays acts were broken into scenes.

Other plays on married life included *To Oblige Benson* (1854)

---

[1] Nicoll: *Late Nineteenth Century Drama*, Vol. I. p. 10

by Tom Taylor, *A Novel Expedient* (1852) by Ben Webster and Henry Lewes' *A Cozy Couple* (1854). The second oft-recurring theme in the drama of the period prior to Robertson was the testing of human values on money. Money as the touchstone of real sincerity had formed the theme of many plays portentous of a new dramatic 'problem' to be developed in the later plays. The first and the most important of such plays, was *Money*, a comedy by Bulwer Lytton in 1840. Alfred Evelin loves the poor Clara, but as she does not want to aggravate Alfred's poverty, refuses to marry him. Alfred acquires a fortune but, stung by Clara's refusal, he proposes to the worldly-wise Georgina, only to discover her motive when she transfers her affections to another suitor. To test her feelings, he pretends to have lost money. Clara comes forward. True lovers are united. *Money* was handicapped by the faults of the age: Sentimentality, artificial characterisation and stilted speech-making. Yet *Money* marks an important break from the line of sensational shows that filled the stage. It was a step in the development of realism on stage.

Another play on this theme was *Second Love* (1856) by Palgrave Simpson. Attracted by the blind girl Elinor's fortune, Colonel Dangerfield makes passionate advances to her, but as she is cured of her affliction, reality dawns upon her and the real lover Ralph gets Elinor and also her fortune. Many other plays were written on the same theme with only a slight variation in treatment. Robertson's *Caste* (1867) was an indirect attack on the rich aristocracy hating the class which provides them their earnings. Marquis de St. Maur and Eccles are two representatives of classes opposed to each other. It must be noted that in Robertson's Comedies, there is discernible, a clear note of departure from the popular way of thinking. In *Society*, *Ours*, *Caste*, *War*, Robertson almost excelled all contemporaries in having written thought-provoking comedies. He infused into his plays a tinge of irony and moral purpose. Apparently any motive of social reformation is absent, The real cause of delay in the efflorescence of realistic comedies was the Victorian way of thinking. Conventionalism of opinion, and fear of offending respectable society restricted playwrights to conventional values. But Robertson was not a leader and professed no claims to advanced thinking which is clear from one of Sam's speeches in *Caste*: "People should stick to their own class. Life's a railway journey, and Mankind's a passenger—first class, second class and third class. Any person found riding in a superior class to that for which he has taken his ticket will be removed at the first station stopped at, according to by-laws of the Company". Robertson has only taken a customary stand that society is governed by similar by-laws and the middle-classes are supposed to stay with the middle-classes and the nobility with the nobility, in order to prevent a 'marriage of giraffe to a squirrel.' Critics like Perry[1] who look for a satisfactory answer to the problem in Robertson are obviously on the wrong track when they insist on a thing which is not there.

What limits his achievements to only technical aspects of playcraft is Robertson's strict adherence to principles of realism. Robertson was not a revolutionary dramatist and when he could have made a clear breakthrough he has only taken a standing opinion, thus ignoring the writing on the wall which was later to appear more striking and was in turn caught by Shaw.

Boucicault said: "Robertson differs from me, not fundamentally, but scenically; his action takes place in lodgings and drawing rooms—mine has a more romantic scope".[2] The *Times* assessed *Caste* as showing "an epigramatic tendency, which not only shows itself in the dialogue, but points the entire fable; a predilection for domestic pathos which is ever kept in check by a native abhorrence of twaddling sentimentality, a firm, steady hand, and a freedom from convention in the delineation of character, an eye to picturesque efforts...and a connection with realism.[3]"

Robertson's characters were nearly all drawn from middle-classes, different from the early nineteenth century aristocratic

---

[1] *Masters of Dramatic Comedy*: "The answer is not so satisfactory as his treatment of the problem", p. 359.

[2] *Mr. and Mrs. Bancroft*: *On and Off the Stage*, p. 118

[3] *op. cit.* p. 132

characters of poetic plays. The way in which Robertson presented them was original, otherwise as Shaw pointed out about *Caste*, they are "old stagers very thinly humanized".[1] Marquis de St. Maur was "simply a ladyfication of the conventional haughty mother", while Eccles and George together epitomize "mid-century Victorian shabby genteel ignorance of the working classes". But on the whole his characters were drawn from the ordinary folk which Tom Wrench in *Trelawny of the Wells* describes as an attempt to "to fashion heroes out of actual, dull, everyday men—".

When all is said about Robertson and his contribution to drama, it must be acknowledged that his greatest contribution lies in having infused a purpose — central unifying motive — into plays. Prior to him Lytton's *Money*, Byron's *Cyril's Success* and only a few others had this quality. But after Robertson this factor became the salient feature of plays. The thought-provoking element was further developed to its full possibilities in the 'Problem' play of the last decade.

Robertson was the first English dramatist, between the Goldsmith-Sheridan and Gilbert-Pinero periods, who infused new life into drama. His plays started a revival of critical and general interest in the native dramatic talent.

The pre-Robertson drama in the nineteenth century reveals two striking features: first, the gradual decline of the Romantic drama and its ultimate downfall, suggesting the beginning of a new drama based on realism and concerned more with common humanity; second, the growth of realistic drama following *Society* by Robertson.

Also, compared with plays of the earlier part of the century, plays written in the fifties and sixties show a dexterity in plot-construction. Robertson, Byron and Lytton took their work seriously and wrote plays with a purpose. This technical triumph was due in a large measure to the French influence of Scribe and Sardou. 'Well-made-plays', as these came to be called, were

---

[1] *Plays and Players*, p. 253

later perfected by Arthur Pinero and Henry Arthur Jones. In Robertson, the unity of motive lends uniformity to the whole play. Sentimental tale, cleverly-contrived plot and dexterous arrangement of events with puppet-like characters comprised this 'fool-proof technique'[1]. The demand of managers and of the audience and the necessity of making a success each time, demanded from the writer a subscription to the popular ingredients of appeal. This 'well-made-play' was later infused with a serious problem. This problem, only vaguely suggested in plays like *Money, Married in Haste, Caste* and *Cyril's Success,* developed to become the chief object of a dramatist. The success that these plays had on the stage, and the writers' intentions were symbolic of the incipient revolution that burst forth in the nineties. The audience in the sixties, more well behaved than in the earlier part of the century, listened to the stage with intent. This helped writers to attempt tentatively this new form of thought-provoking purposeful drama. The air of domesticity in themes, of respectability in the audience, of purpose instead of entertainment and of an overall seriousness in tone of the drama prepared the way for greater achievements in the last decade. This is the greatest factor leading to the growth of realism. Robertson appeared when everything appeared pliable and ready to be moulded into newer forms. In a transitional staget he only succeeded in contributing his share without any grea, achievement. But he prepared the ground for others. This was the beginning of a great movement.

---

[1] Nicoll: *World Drama*, p. 488

Chapter III

William S. Gilbert

> (i) "Yet: although not being problem drama, Gilbert's work contains germs of problem drama."
>
> *The Initial Stages in the Development of the English Problem Play* Von Martin Ellehauge.
>
> (ii) "Without Gilbert moreover we would not only not have had precisely the Wilde of *The Importance of Being Earnest;* we would not have had Shaw himself in quite the form we have him."
>
> *The Thread of Laughter*
> Louis Kronenberger

After Robertson's endeavours to revive English drama William Gilbert was the first to take new strides in this direction. Gilbert was known to readers as the author of *Bab Ballads* (1869) and *More Bab Ballads* (1873). He was a prolific writer and tried his hand at sentimental drama, extravaganza, burlesque and 'operas' on which rests his reputation as a dramatist. He made his debut on the stage with *Ruy Blas* in 1866. Before we study the Savoy operas it will be rewarding to look at the other forms of drama which interested Gilbert. Even the titles of certain plays are illustrative of the contents:

Dulcamara, or, the Little Duke and the Great Quack (Dec. 1866), *Hush-a-Bye Baby* written in collaboration with Charles

Millward, *Robinson Crusoe; or The Injun Bride and the Injured Wife* written in collaboration with H. J. Byron, T. Hood, H. S. Leigh and A. Sketchley (July 1867), *Highly Improbable* (Dec. 1867) and *Harlequine Cock Robin and Jenny Wren; or Fortunates and the Water of Life, The Three Bears, The Three Gifts, The Three Wishes, and The Little Man Who Woo'd the Little Maid* (Dec. 1867). Any attempt to enlist his miscellaneous stage plays would be necessarily otiose as before 1875 when with *Trial by Jury* he broke new ground, Gilbert had already written thirty-eight plays of which three were Fairy plays, seven burlesques, four extravaganzas, two pantomimes, two musical comedies and twenty other hybrid theatrical pieces. His fecundity was simply amazing in view of the large number of plays he wrote.

Gilbert had a serious interest in his sentimental plays and thought they were his best. Some of these plays offer a good picture of the contemporary drama in England.

In *Palace of Truth* (1870) Gilbert uses 'loud thinking' as a technique of revealing the inner character. Anyone who enters the palace of truth cannot tell a lie and unwittingly comes out with the truth:

Philamir : ......I beg your pardon, but the furniture has caught your dress.

Azema : (rearranging her dress hastily) Oh, I arranged it so that you might see how truly beautiful my foot and ankle are : (As if much shocked at the exposure).

Similar use of irony was made in *Pygmalion and Galatea* (1877). The tragic love of Pygmalion for the beautiful statue of Galatea, her coming to life and the bitter experience in this mortal world which compels her to resume her stony silence are good evidence of Gilbert's skilful handling of plot and a delicate theme. Galatea's experience makes an indirect indictment on the selfishness of people and the cruelty of human institutions.

In *Sweethearts* (1874) Gilbert hits at the vanity of the human mind. In the first part of the play the coquettish beauty, Jenny, sneers at her lover's feeling but later on languishes in his memory. Spreadbrow has, however, in the meanwhile forgotten her. The sapling he had planted before leaving for India has grown into a tree under which the lovers are reunited. Gilbert's characteristic touch captures the spirit of time and growth in the dramatic symbol of the growing sycamore and the surroundings, at one time barren. The fickleness of love and the irony of circumstances gave *Sweethearts* a striking novelty.

Sentiment reigns in the next play: *Tom Cobb; or, Fortune's Toy* (1875), a farcical comedy. Here Matilda's love affairs are used by her father as opportunities for borrowing money from her suitors. This shows Gilbert's understanding of the many facets of love in this world and his disdain for the nonsense made of such a practical feeling by poetic conceits.

In *Broken Hearts* (Dec. 1875), Gilbert made another attempt to write a verse play in the Elizabethan fashion. But even the island setting, lachrymose and tragic love affairs, disguise and music failed to produce any favourable impression of Gilbert as a poetic playwright. Prince Florian, on an island, meets two ladies in love with him. His veil is the source of complications but in the end he marries Lady Hilda as Lady Vavir dies love-sick.

Dan'l Druce Blacksmith (September 1876), may be mentioned to illustrate Gilbert's desperate effort to catch the spirit of the serious in playwriting. Dan'l Druce, living with his own daughter Dorothy, is unaware of the fact. She, as a child, was left by Sir Jasper Combe in his cottage, being the daughter of Dan'l's wife who had eloped with Sir Jasper. All ends well in this play after all popular ingredients have been exhausted: lost children, unknown parentage, property, countryside setting, innocence and villainy. Gilbert's predilection for domestic themes and sentiments appeared lifeless in *Dan'l Druce*.

The same stock-in-trade situations are used in *Engaged* (October 1877), in which the hero, Cheviot Hill, falls in love with every girl he comes across. A melodramatic farce, *Engaged* consists of elopements, train accidents and legacies. Each new situation reveals Cheviot Hill in a new romance. Money here, as in *Tom Cobb*, plays an important role in deciding the fate of love-affairs. Miss Treherne abandons her admirer Belvawny because of his uncertain ncome but mourns in "all the anguish of maiden solitude, iuncared for, unloved and alone". Gilbert, aware of the sentimental, wanted it to be produced with extreme earnestness and sincerity. *Engaged* is actually a burlesque on the sentimental and romantic.

Engaged is an important play as it has in embryo, many features which later developed into higher forms of comedy. The farcical complications of *Engaged* anticipate many incidents of Oscar Wilde's *The Importance of Being Earnest*.

This earlier group of plays reveals Gilbert's irresolution on the use of verse or prose as medium of dialogue. *Bab Ballads* gave Gilbert fond hopes of poetic skill but the popularity of the ballads was more due to their human interest than poetic excellence. For Gilbert it was difficult to believe. Another lesson which was unpalatable for him was the failure of these serious and sentimental plays. He could have continued in this way but for circumstances and luck which brought him into contact with Richard D'Oyly Carte and Arthur Sullivan the famous musical composer. Gilbert had written a short play which D'Oyly Carte found interesting and decided to produce. Earlier Sullivan had worked with Gilbert in 1871, when he scored the music for *Thespis*, a little play about a group of actors temporarily relieving the Gods at the mount Olympus to create a precious muddle all round. *Thespis* failed at the Gaiety Theatre which was known for its burlesque shows. Gilbert and Sullivan parted and four years later came back to work together in the new play by the former.

The story of *Trial by Jury* was suggested by the notorious current Tichborne trial[1]. A legal trial in actual life was being watched

---

[1] The Tichborne trial was the most protracted trial ejecting Colonel Lushington from Tichborne house, Hampshire, which had been let to him by a person named Orton who came from Australia and claimed to be Sir Roger Charles Doughty Tichborne, feared to have been lost at sea in the

with great interest and so Gilbert, who always had an eye on public taste, decided to present one on the stage. It has two features. First, it treated a case of breach of promise, the plaintiff with her 'blind adoration' claiming damages from the defendant whose bosom once 'welled with joy' at the sight of the plaintiff.

Love and its ridiculous aspects had been the object of Gilbert's satire in his earlier serious plays. Secondly, Gilbert himself having spent four fruitless years as a barrister found an opportunity of bringing on the stage men of the same profession under his very eyes. He combined his cynical view of love with a cynical view of the legal profession and turned this dull and sordid affair of a breach of promise trial into a supremely funny play. The miraculous blend of legal fact and operatic fancy contributed to its great popularity among theatre-goers. The most important feature of *Trial by Jury* was a number of witty songs full of irony and music. The typical Gilbertian element consisted in the arguments at the law court and the topsy-turvy humour, which was his forte. The defendant pleads that he should be allowed to change his love, because it is not:

> The act of a sinner
> When breakfast is taken away
> To turn your attention to dinner.

If such a change-over is the rule in other affairs of life, why should it not be countenanced in love as well? He agrees to marry the other the following day. This subtlety is one of Gilbert's important qualities. But the Judge in *Trial by Jury* is the most engaging character for his humour and simplicity. In self-revealing songs, the Judge innocently discloses the hollowness of his profession, and blandly gives away the fact that his right to hold that eminent position is doubtful. His confession.

> I fell in love with a rich attorney's
> Elderly, ugly daughter

'Bella' in 1851. The question was whether the claimant was or was not identical with the young man who was for so long believed to have been lost with the 'Bella'! That law suit broke all records so far as time and money were concerned.

leads to many other interesting revelations. The judge who should decide the case for others, announces "I will marry her for myself", because as he himself felt

> Though homeward as you trudge,
> You declare my law is a fudge,
> Yet of beauty I'm a judge.
>
> ALL:
> And a good judge too.

This is a subtle way of saying that many an honourable gentleman on the Queen's Bench owed his position to mere accident, and that a judge who tried another for a legal offence might be guilty of it himself.

The novelty of theme, irony of love-affairs, and music of the opera captivated the audience. Originality placed Gilbert in the front rank of new dramatists.

Two years were to pass before Carte again brought Gilbert and Sullivan together. Carte inaugurated the Comedy Opera Company with *The Sorcerer* on November 17, 1877.

The Sorcerer has a rather far-fetched and complicated plot. Alexis is going to marry Aline, a descendant of the family of Helen of Troy. Alexis believes in the equality of all classes in love. He invites a sorcerer from London to administer a magic potion with tea. Under its spell, all pair off with the most unsuitable partners. Sir Marmaduke, Alexis' father, falls in love with Dame Partlet and Aline is fascinated by Dr. Daly. Alexis fears disaster and following the only way out persuades the sorcerer, Wells, to sacrifice his life. Normalcy returns.

Mr. Wells, a 'paragon of middle-class respectability' appears to be the descendant of Henry Fielding's Mr. Hen (*The Historical Register*, ii, 1). Auction scenes were popular in the eighteenth as also in the nineteenth century, and Gilbert in *The Sorcerer* presented an auctioneer who sells 'true French' modesty, one bottle of courage, a clear conscience, a very considerable quantity of interest at Court, and all the cardinal virtues. Both modesty and conscience were left unbidden for. For the contemporary *beau monde*, modesty was out of fashion and they would sooner pay to get rid of a conscience than purchase it. Even the cardinal virtues disappoint the purchasers.

Fielding's aim in *The Historical Register* was to satirize the contemporary society and he made no attempt to hide his satire. Gilbert in *The Sorcerer* was more concerned with stage virtues of an auction scene as productive of humour and laughter. Hence the portrait of Mr. Wells is less crude and the articles he sells are curiosities and have very little to do with satire.

Mr. Wells: "Yes Sir, we practise necromancy in all its branches. We've a choice assortment of wishing caps, divining rods, amulets, charms and counter-charms."

The Song of Wells:

> Oh! my name is John Wellington Wells
> I'm a dealer in magic and spells,
> In blessings and curses,
> And everfilled purses,
> In prophecies, witches and knells.

proved very popular. *The Sorcerer* showed the absurdity of the idea that love is above social classes. The hero believing that by administering the love potion he can produce harmony among his fellow-beings discovers the foolishness of the idea when the Duke falls in love with Dame Partlet and Lady Sangazure falls in love with Mr. Wells. Even Aline is fascinated by Dr. Daly. Alexis, fearing to lose Aline, realises his folly and admits that the Duke should only marry Lady Sangazure and not the village dame. Thus *The Sorcerer* stresses the theme of class distinctions and satirizes the idea that love levels ranks. "The naturalness and ease with which these quaint things were said and done",[1] was amazing.

H. M. S. Pinafore; or The Lass that Loved a Sailor was produced on May 25, 1878 at the opera Comique. In its theme it is not very different from *The Sorcerer* as it also deals with class distinctions. Writing in an age when the social position of a man was of great significance, and social hierarchy was an established institution,

---

[1] Herman Klein: *Musicians and Mummers*, p. 199

William S. Gilbert

Gilbert perceived tremendous possibilities of ridiculing it on the stage by turning this established institution upside down. The alternative title of *H. M. S. Pinafore* is *The Lass that Loved a Sailor* The lass in question is Captain Concoran's daughter Josephine, and the Sailor, Ralph Rachstraw, a British Sailor on H. M. S. Pinafore. Sir Joseph Porter, First Lord of Admiralty wants to marry Josephine, though she occupies a station in the 'lower middle class'. He believes that 'Love is a platform upon which all ranks meet.' The tables are turned when a discovery about his parentage is made. Ralph is high-born and Sir Joseph low born. Uniforms are changed and the characters pair off according to the dictates of the heart, Josephine with Ralph, Captain with Buttercup and Sir Joseph with his first cousin Hebe.

H. M. S. Pinafore is Gilbert's first opera in which he made any topical allusion and a tentative attempt at political satire. The appointment of W. H. Smith as the First Lord of Admiralty was discussed everywhere. Gilbert opposed this in indirect satire and ridicule. The song of Sir Joseph Porter almost settled the suspicion that the singer was no other than a stage caricature of W. H. Smith. Within a few weeks of the production Disraeli was referring to 'Pinafore Smith'. Sir Joseph's song is in line with the Judge's song in *Trial by Jury*:

> I grew so rich that I was sent
> By a pocket borough into Parliament
> I always voted at my party's call,
> And I never thought of thinking for myself at all.
> I thought so little, they rewarded me
> By making me the Ruler of the Queen's Navee!

Sir Joseph advises:

> If you want to rise to the top of the tree
> ×　　×　　×　　×　　×　　×
> Stick close to your desk and never go to sea,
> And you may all be Rulers of the Queen's Navee!

Unless Sir Joseph can show by his behaviour that he knows his position, he will be treated with scant regard save that which his office commands. To the Concorans he is 'that little jumped up lawyer' and he is ridiculed even in the garb of official welcome.

H. M. S. Pinafore is a burlesque on the jolly-jack-tar them from the moment the curtain rises with the honest fellows singing:

> We sail the ocean blue
> And our saucy ship's a beauty;
> We're sober men and true,
> And attentive to our duty—,

until that splendid moment when the crew acclaims Ralph Rackstraw with the cry: "He is an Englishman".
The burlesque in the dialogue and the unexpected frankness on the part of Ralph Rackstraw are all illustrative of Gilbert's concealed motive of burlesquing the Navy.

Sir Joseph	:	You're a remarkably fine fellow.
Ralph	:	Yes, Your honour.
Sir Joseph	:	And a first rate seaman. I'll be bound.
Ralph	:	There's not a smarter topman in the Navy, Your honour, though I say it who shouldn't.

Even in the exchange of compliments between the Captain and his crew, there is an unmistakable air of burlesque.

Captain	:	My gallant crew good morning.
All : (Saluting)		Sir, good morning.
Captain	:	I hope you're all quite well.
All : (as before)		Quite well, and you, Sir?
Captain	:	I am in reasonable health and happy, To meet you all once more.
All	:	You do us proud, Sir.

Gilbert also ridicules the growing selfish sort of patriotism. In the sublimely logical burlesque:

> He is an Englishman
> And it is greatly to his credit,

which climaxes on the heights of irony:

William S. Gilbert

> But in spite of all temptations
> To belong to other nations,
> He remains an Englishman.

Gilbert has poked fun at the complacency with which the British people feel proud of their nationality. Gilbert was an expert in saying most serious things with apparent meaninglessness and here in *H. M. S. Pinafore* he hit at the preposterousness of false pride in being an Englishman. The Chorus in *H. M. S. Pinafore* formed an important character and was not treated as a group of mere visiting singers. The male chorus introduced themselves:

> We sail the ocean blue
> And our saucy ship's a beauty
> We're sober men and true
> And attentive to our duty.

The chorus consisted of Sir Joseph's sisters, cousins, and aunts.

In *H. M. S. Pinafore* Gilbert used a few ballads from *Bab Ballads*. The highly humorous and paradoxical ballads provided him with material ready for the stage. Chesterton suggests that in his attempt to use the *Bab Ballads* for the stage Gilbert "came back with the wrong idea, because he had forgotten the right one".[1] 'The Bumboat-Woman's story' anticipates Little Butercup in the *H. M. S. Pinafore* to the minutest details. The oft-repeated tale of two babies exchanged at birth was used in the simple *Private James and Major General John*. The holy spirit of nonsense that pervades the *Bab Ballads* was lost in the process of dramatizaion. The point in the ballad was, as Chesterton suggests, the outrageous abruptness with which James comes to know the truth by intuition, entirely unsupported by reason:

> A glimmering thought occurs to me
> (Its source I can't unearth),
> But I've a sort of notion, we
> Were cruelly changed at birth.

---

[1] Chesterton, G. K. *Gilbert and Sullivan* in *The Eighteen Eighties* Ed. by Walter de la Mare, p. 141

The absurdity of this intuition is matched by the abruptness and thoughtlessness with which it is accepted:

> So General John as Private James
> Fell in Parade upon:
> While Private James, by a change of names
> Was Major General John.

Chesterton appears right when he says that Gilbert missed the pointlessness of the *Bab Ballads* in dramatization. But Gilbert was not always dramatizing the ballads. In *H. M. S. Pinafore* Gilbert was writing a comedy and he wanted to use these ballads in the new context; also, he knew his limitations when writing for the stage.

The Pirates of Penzance; or, The Slave of Duty was Gilbert's next opera. The 'slave of duty' is Frederic, the Pirate apprentice, who on his twenty-first birthday wants to leave that profession as he had only joined it because of a mistake committed by the nurse Ruth. The Pirates have a strange way of not attacking a weaker party, particularly orphans. They meet the daughters of Major General Stanley and want to marry them. The Major General declares himself to be an orphan so the Pirates free him. Frederic leaves, determined to work for the extermination of the Pirates as he no longer belongs to them. Frederic plans an attack on the Pirates, when it is revealed that because he was born on 29th February in the leap year, according to calculations he was only five and a half years and not twenty-one. He returns to the Pirates and with the same sense of duty tells them that the General is not an orphan. The play ends as the Pirates of Penzance get the Stanley girls and the slave of duty, his beloved.

The Pirates of Penzance has for its setting "a rocky sea shore on the coast of Cornwall". In such a weird setting any inconsistency may be condoned, as Darlington observes: "We are in a world of fantasy". The autobiographical pattersong of Major General Sanley:

> I am the very pattern of a modern Major General
> I've the information vegetable, animal and mineral

became popular for is rattling metre. But unlike other operas this was not received with expansive gaiety and broad indulgence by the audience. Some even regarded it as offensive. The Judge in *Trial by Jury*, Mr. Wells in *The Sorcerer*, and Sir Joseph Porter in *H. M. S. Pinafore* were received with great enthusiasm but the General's song did not arouse much interest. The reason was very clear. The song of the General:

> For my military knowledge, though I'm plucky and adventury,
> Has only been brought down to the beginning of the century.

failed to get applause for its crude humour. It made too obvious an attack on the army. Also, another joke in the play was regarded as disrespectful by the throne. When the Police say to the Pirates, "We charge you yield in Queen Victoria's name." the Pirate King replies.

> We yield at once with humbled mien,
> Because with all our faults, we love our Queen

Immediately afterwards it is revealed that:

> They are no members of the common throng;
> They are all noblemen who have gone wrong!

and the General exclaims :

> No Englishman unmoved that statement bears,
> Because with all our faults we love our House of Peers

Here Gilbert erred in making the satire, on an institution of which every Englishman was so proud, too apparent. Very soon the writers with an imperialistic creed, like Kipling, were to show that the wrecking of the British Empire was the result of the lukewarmness of the Englishman's faith in the British army and navy, and the inherent right of Englishmen to rule. In his attempt to point at the contemporary evils Gilbert for a few moments forgot his higher aim of being a pure 'comedian'. Perhaps this was due to Sullivan's association with the higher circle and their contempt for his association with Gilbert. Besides, Gilbert himself felt a little unsuited for the job. But business kept them together.

Patience; or Bunthorne's Bride followed *The Pirates of Penzance*. This 'Entirely New and Original Aesthetic Opera' dealt with a poet, an aesthete, Bunthorne, who is followed by Lady Angela, Saphir, Ela and Jane — all madly in love with him. Bunthorne loves Patience — the milkmaid. He is faced with a rival in another 'aesthete' — Grosvener. Grosvener now becomes the centre of attraction. The play ends with Patience going to Grosvener, the ladies to the army officers and Bunthorne standing with a lily.

This is the story of the *Patience* which was staged. The original plan was different. Gilbert's earlier satire in the ballad form ridiculed the affectations of kindness by parsons. He disliked the way ladies were generally crazy about them. His scorn of parsons was notorious.[1] Gilbert dramatized a ballad 'The Rival Curates' from *Bab Ballads*. In this, Rev. Clayton Hooper is a mild curate who, hearing of an even milder curate, sends two hired assassins to threaten the other with death unless he agrees to change his ways. The other milder Curate Rev. Hopley Porter hears about the new changes — dancing, smoking, scents, playing, pleasure, curling the hair and winking at every passing girl. In a characteristic Gilbertian way, Rev. Porter has a greater surprise in store when he says :

> For years I've longed for some
> Excuse for this convulsion;
> Now that excuse has come —
> I do it on compulsion.

In *Patience* Bunthorne asks Grosvener for a "complete change at once. Your conversation must henceforth be perfectly matter-of-fact. You must cut your hair, and have a back parting. In appearance and costume you must be absolutely commonplace".

---

[1] Pearson records that "Staying in some provincial hotel, he once found himself the only layman among a number of divines who were present for a conference in the town, one of whom addressed him with quiet irony: "I shall think, Mr. Gilbert, you must feel slightly out of place in this company". "Yes", answered Gilbert, "I feel like a lion in a den of Daniels" *Gilbert and Sullivan: A Biography* pp. 125-26.

William S. Gilbert

To this the aesthete, Grosvener, replies, "I do cheerfully. I have long wished for a reasonable pretext for such a change as you suggest. It has come at last. I do it on compulsion". Grosvener repeats the words of Rev. Hopley Porter of *The Rival Curates*. Gilbert owed much to *The Rivel Curates* for the material of *Patience*. In *The Sorcerer*, Dr. Daly's song describing a 'Pale Young Curate',

> Time was when love and I were well acquainted.
> ×   ×   ×   ×
> Time was maidens of the noblest station,
> Forsaking even military men,
> Would gaze upon me, rapt in adoration,
> Ah me! I was a fair young curate then!

had in embryo the chorus of the rapturous maidens, who have forsaken Heavy Dragoons — the military men in *Patience*. Gilbert had no particular parson in mind. Only the idea of a kind man ready to kill another man because he was kinder than he himself, appealed to him. Mr. Hopley Porter is the rival. Clayton Hooper summoned straight away his sexton and his beadle and orders

> To Hopley Porter go,
> Your fare I will afford you —
> Deal him a deadly blow
> And blessings shall reward you.

The Victorians had as great a regard for their Church as they had for the House of Lords and the Queen. The joke about the Church could pass on merrily on paper but on the stage it could not be allowed. Gilbert was a practical man of the stage. He saw the possibilites of such a theme on the stage but decided that it would be far better to change the form. The people were still not prepared to see the clergy ridiculed on the stage. Aesthetes were substituted for the clergy. The original idea of a paradox still retained its humour. And so the fact that Gilbert changed from "one form of pretentiousness to another makes it an attack on pretentiousness in general."[1]

---

[1] Darlington: *The World of Gilbert and Sullivan*, p. 80

The aesthetic movement was dominant at that time. Oscar Wilde was the most noted supporter of this cult which "sought relief from the standards of the prosperous, respectable and self-satisfied society of the time in a deliberately cultivated archaism which aimed at being simple but achieved an exaggerated artificiality".[1] The aesthetes manifested their artistic temperament in their dress and other external symbols[2]. The change was symbolised in the picture of a poet holding a lily, rapt in contemplation in utter disregard and contempt for the average man.

Gilbert was quick to perceive in this aesthetic attitudinizing an excellent opportunity to ridicule. "This extraordinary rig, the loose collar and flowing tie, the black braided velvet jacket, the velveteen knickerbockers and silk stockings? It aroused horror."[3] The curators of the ballad were substituted for the aesthetes. The satire in *Patience* is not a satire on 'aestheticism' in particular, it is a satire on any 'ism' which is carried to extremes. Oscar Wilde was supposed to have provided the model for Bunthorne. The exaggerated traits of aesthetic philosophy were personified in Bunthorne, hence it was not necessary to look for an individual as a model.

Patience is an important opera for another reason also. It contains many beautiful lyrics. It is a story of two poets and their rivalry; so Gilbert could use the theme to display his poetic

---

[1] Darlington: *op. cit.* p. 76

[2] "The Aesthetes in general and the early Wilde in particular seemed to feel their admiration of lovely rarities in itself a sufficient mark of temperament, a sound guarantee that they had achieved the requisite sensibility... they saw in the pale lily, the radiant sunflower, the blending poppy, symbols of their salvation from middle class vulgarities". Jerome Hamilton Buckley, *The Victorian Temper*, pp. 217-18.

In 1881 Richard D'Oyly Carte issued a circular on the subject matter of *Patience* which aimed at ridiculing the outpourings of a clique of professors of ultra-refinement who preach the gospel of morbid langour and sickly sensuousness, which is half real and half affected. *Patience* did not attack the true aesthetic spirit but only "the unmannerly oddities which masquerade in its likeness". Leslie Baily : *The Gilbert and Sullivan Book* p. 179·

[3] William Gaunt: *The Aesthetic Adventure*, p. 105

capabilities. The song with which the Colonel introduces himself is one of the most famous:

> If you want a receipt for that popular mystery,
> Known to the world as a Heavy Dragoon,
> Take all the remarkable people in history
> Rattle them off to a popular tune

Bunthorne's song is more beautiful because he is a poet. It attacks the hypocrisy of aesthetic poets and is a satire on their exaggerated behaviour:

> If you are anxious for the shine in the high aesthetic
> line as a man of culture rare,
> You must get up all the germs of the transcendental
> terms and plant them everywhere.
> You must lie upon the daisies and discourse in novel
> phrases of your complicated state of mind
> The meaning does not matter, it's only the idle chatter
> of a transcendental kind.
> And if you walk down Piccadilly with a poppy or lily in
> your medieval hand
> And everyone will say, as you walk your flowery way.
> ×　　　×　　　×　　　×
> Why, what a most particularly pure young man this pure
> young man must be.

Bunthorne's song is one of the wittiest lyrics of Gilbert and the most trenchant satire on the affected aestheticism in nineteenth century literature. Besides showing his proclivities for satirizing social institutions, *Patience* also illustrates Gilbert's heartless ridicule of ladies getting old. Little Buttercup in *H. M. S. Pinafore*, and Ruth with her 'middle aged way' in *The Pirates of Penzance* were the first old ladies delineated. In *Patience* it was Lady Jane who,

> Year by Year
> Sees, one by one, her beauties disappear.

49

There are contradictory opinions about the merit of *Patience*, because in action and plot construction this is comparativery slow and feeble but in the use of irony and lyrical expressions *Patience* is undoubtedly one of the best operas of Gilbert.

Iolanthe; or The Peer and the Peri was the next Gilbert and Sullivan opera, produced on November 25, 1882. Iolanthe, the fairy, married a human being, the present Lord Chancellor. As a penalty for this she is suffering seclusion. Strephon, her son, half mortal and half fairy, living on earth, wants to marry Phyllis, whom many Lords and Peers, including the Lord Chancellor himself, want to marry. Fairies intervene in the affair and a strange medley of fantasy and matter-of-factness in the true Gilbertian style is the result. Iolanthe reappears and is reunited with the Lord Chancellor. Fairies wed Lords and Peers. The Fairy Queen selects the Guard Sentry for her husand. Strephon is united with Phyllis.

Like many other operas of Gilbert, *Iolanthe* was also the dramatic version of a ballad. *The Fairy Curate* provided the material. Here is the opening verse of the ballad:

> Once a fairy
> Light and airy
> Married with a mortal;
> Men, however,
> Never, never
> Pass the fairy Portal.
> Slyly stealing
> She to Ealing
> Made a daily journey,
> There she found him
> Clients round him
> (He was an attorney).

In these lines lie the essence of *Iolanthe*, the fairy, young and immortal, and the attorney, dry and mortal, are the two incongruous beings united together. The scenes alternate between the 'Arcadian Landscape', which is the setting for fairies and the

'Palace Guard, Westminister'. the dwelling of mortals, the Lords and Peers. The atmosphere is so far removed from daily life that reality cannot obstruct the path of fantasy. The Gilbertian keynote is struck with the chorus:

> Tripping hither, tripping thither,
> Nobody knows why and whither.

In *Trial by Jury* Gilbert had poked fun at the jury. The skill with which he extracted laughter even out of the dull and dry judiciary was highly commendable. In *Iolanthe* he repeats that feat. Gilbert always laughed at the absurdities of established institutions, which, at heart, he loved and respected. As the mirth was without malice and prejudice it could be accepted by the Victorians. The institution in question here is the House of Lords. The House of Lords even in Gilbert's time was only an assembly of aristocrats who claimed high titles and privileges by virtue of their high birth alone. The procession of Peers 'superbly robed and caronotted' is irresistibly comic. For the audience which does not know that except on very formal occasions the aristocracy would not consent to dress so extravagantly, half the joke of the Peers stalking the stage is lost. But as in *Trial by Jury* and in *Iolanthe* again, the dispenser of justice is highly susceptible. The Lord Chancellor sings:

> The Law is the true embodiment
> Of everything that's excellent.
> It has no kind of fault or flaw,
> And I, my lords, embody the law,
> The constitutional guardian I
> Of pretty young wards in Chancery,
> All very agreeable girls — and none
> Are over the age of twenty one.
> A pleasant occupation for
> A rather susceptible Chancellor!

This susceptible Chancellor, embodiment of faultless law, is like the judge whose law was fudge. Giving agreeable girls away, the Chancellor is sorry not to have

> A one for me which is exasperating for
> A highly susceptible Chancellor!

Perhaps he would have decided the case, like the Judge in *Trial by Jury*, in his own favour, had not his fairy wife Iolanthe reappeared on the scene.

Iolanthe has three distinctive features. First, the fairies and the mortals who give to the story its unique character; secondly, the Peers and their behaviour, which give Gilbert an opportunity to mock at their comical demeanour and refer to their visits to the countryside which could not be for sparrows alone; and thirdly, the class distinctions of the rich and the poor. The last aspect is only a possible interpretation of *Iolanthe*. Gilbert always kept away from serious social criticism.

The song of the Lord Chancellor 'When I went to the bar' is a good example of Gilbert's felicity with word music. The nightmare song in particular is superb:

> When you're lying awake with dismal headache, and
> repose is taboo'd by anxiety,
> I conceive you may use any language you choose to
> indulge in without impropriety.

In his next play *Princess Ida, or, Castle Adamant*, Gilbert made 'a respectful operatic perversion' of Tennyson's *The Princess*. He maintained a close parallel with Tennyson's poem in theme. Princess Ida has, with a band of women, shut herself in a lonely country house to devote herself to stern philosophy. The women's university does not admit any male within its precincts. Prince Hilarion, Ida's husband, betrothed to her in childhood, and his two friends Florian and Cyril, come disguised as ladies. There is strange confusion when the identity of the Prince is disclosed. Fathers of the Princess and the Prince arrive to settle the dispute and Princess Ida realises her folly:

> I built upon a rock
> But ere Destruction's hand
> Dealt equal lot
> To court and cot,

William S. Gilbert

> My rock had turned to sand !
> Ah, faithless rock,
> My simple faith to mock !

In *Princess Ida* Gilbert took up the question of higher education of women, an issue of immediate importance in Victorian England. Tennyson, while dealing with this subject affected an equivocating attitude which satisfied the liberal and the conservative alike. There was in Victorian England behind much mock chivalry and sublime male prostration, a very material view prevalent on the place of women in the home. The old king in *The Princess* held that "the bearing and the training of a child is woman's wisdom". Florian in *Princess Ida* says, "A woman's college! maddest folly going". Gilbert, like the Prince's father, regarded women as little better than helpless fair skinned prey of the bold male animal.

Women's education in the last quarter of the nineteenth century made rapid progress and women were admitted to college[1]. The times did not yet encourage authors to deal with political and social questions on the stage — a fact which to a large extent accounts for the delay in the arrival of the renascence of drama. Without his humorous self Gilbert appeared dry and off colour in *Princess Ida*. The failure of *Princess Ida* on the stage showed the difference between the limitations of a stage and liberties of a poet. The satire on women's education in *Princess Ida* outweighed other good qualities of the play which included a considerable number of songs.

The Princess, a mock-heroic poem, presented a transformation in Ida's nature on a grand scale. Ida first appeared in an epic posture:

> There at the board by tome and paper sat.
> With two leopards couch'd beside her throne.

---

[1] M.G. Fawcett, agreeing with the general opinion in his support of new movements demanding equality for women wrote on 'The Future of English Women'. He urged "......remove the artificial restrictions which debar women from higher education and from remunerative employments..." *Nineteenth Century Opinion*, Edited by Michael Godwin, p. 96.

In the last section she is seen nursing the convalescent Prince:

> Glowing all over noble shame; and all
> Her falser self slip't from her, like a robe,
> And left her woman............

The discovery of her womanhood made Ida's previous unwomanly appearance false and ludicrous. This insistence on the role of women as circumscribed within the walls of the house accounts for the apparent backwardness of Gilbert's contemporaries. In *Princess Ida*, thus, Gilbert only succumbed to the popular prejudice. From the beginning Gilbert was steeped in Victorian traditions, but by making a premature attempt at introducing social questions on the stage Gilbert showed courage.

The Mikado was produced on 14th March, 1885. The story centres on Nanki Po, son of the Mikado, who has run away from his court because an old and elderly lady, Katisha, wants to marry him. He comes to the town of Titipu, sees Yumkum, and falls in love with her. But she is already betrothed to Koko. The Mikado orders Koko to execute at least one man within a month as a long time has passed since an execution has taken place in Titipu. Koko persuades Nanki Po to agree to get hanged after a month on the condition that he will allow Yumkum to marry Nanki Po. Katisha follows Nanki Po and is about to reveal his identity but Nanki Po and Yumkum cry aloud and she is hissed out. The plan of Koko is going to fail when Yumkum learns that she will have to die after her husband. But Koko and Pooh Bah, seeing no way out, allow them, Nanki Po and Yumkum, to run away and get married. The Mikado comes to Titipu. The identity of Nanki Po is revealed and Koko is charged with the crime of having murdered the heir-apparent. But because Nanki Po is still alive, he reappears and is restored to the Court.

The Mikado ingeniously contrived to incorporate humour and entertainment, unhampered by satire as in *Patience* and *Princess Ida*. But the fantastic and poetic character of the Mikado was in many quarters interpreted as offending, while "Queen Victoria thought its plot rather silly".[1] The Japanese ambassador really objected to the piece, regarding it as ridiculing the sanctimonious seat of the Japanese ruler. *The Mikado* stood all tests of adverse criticism. Act I, which opens with a chorus, strikes the keynote of the play.

> If you want to know who we are
> We are gentlemen of Japan:
> On many a vase and jar —
> On many a screen and fan"

The Mikado was the representative of a stage when "Europeans thought of her (Japan's) inhabitants as quaint and amusing little people, with their fans and paper houses and a topsy-turvy view of life."[2]

The Mikado has an imaginative setting as other plays of Gilbert had. It has no connection with the Island of the Rising Sun except that the characters are Japanese. Darlington regards this opera as "simply being humorous" with "no satirical intent". But Chesterton regards *The Mikado* as a studied criticism of English life. "There is not, in the whole length of *The Mikado*, a single joke that is a joke against Japan. They are all, without exception, jokes against England, or that Western Civilization which an Englishman knows best in England".[3] Chesterton's thesis is that Gilbert has only criticized the England of his time in *The Mikado*. Gilbert satirized the idea of guardians marrying pretty wards and the government's favouritism in the distribution of offices, and instances were not rare when one single individual was assigned various positions on greater emoluments. Pooh Bah is the Lord High Everything Else in Titipu. He is First Lord of the Treasury, Lord Chief Justice, Commander-in-Chief, Archbishop of Titipu, and he dines and dances with the middle-classes

---

[1] E. Wingfield Stratford: *The History of English Patriotism*, *Vol.* I, p. xxii

[2] Darlington: *op. cit.* p. 116

[3] Chesterton: *op. cit.* p. 152

at a very low fee. He can also sell state secrets unhesitatingly. Without particularising, Gilbert put on the stage a picture of Victorian England. In *The Mikado* Gilbert displayed again his tendency to ridicule social institutions. The queer Japanese people and their delightful ways interested him.

The Mikado shows Gilbert's humour at its best. It is unequalled in its sheer high spirits, invention and melody. Honours are equally shared by the Librettist and the composer. A few lyrics are very beautiful. Nanki Po's song—

> A wandering ministrel I —
> A thing of shreds and patches,
> Of ballads, songs and snatches
> A dreamy lullaby

is simply captivating. Yumkum's 'three little maids from school are we", and The Mikado's

> A more humane Mikado never
> Did in Japan exist"

are delightful compositions. The subtlety, variety and the refinement of the lyrics are wonderful. The whole of England was Mikado mad. For its excellence *The Mikado* ranks very high in light opera, as high as *Pickwick Papers* in comic fiction and *The Importance of Being Earnest* in high comedy.

Ruddigore or the Witch's Curse was a burlesque on melodrama and was produced on January 22, 1887. It deals with Robin who is the heir to the baronetcy of Ruddigore which allows its owner to live only so long as he continues to commit a crime every day. He lives disguised as a bashful farmer who does not express his love to Rose Maybud and conveys his sentiments through Richard, who himself falls a prey to her charms. Sir Despard Murgatroyd, younger brother of Robin and the present baron, comes and Richard clears his own way to Rose by revealing Robin's identity to him. Robin assumes his new responsibilities but fails to commit one crime daily. He succeeds by his logic in bringing about a typical Gilbertian climax:

Robin	:	I can't stop to apologize—an idea has just occurred to me. A Baronet of Ruddigore can only die through refusing to commit his daily crime.
Roderic	:	No doubt.
Robin	:	Therefore to refuse to commit a daily crime is tantamount to suicide!
Roderic	:	It would seem so.
Robin	:	But suicide is, itself a crime, and so, by your own showing, you ought never to have died at a !
Roderic	:	I see — I understand! Then I'm practically alive!

Gilbert's aim in *Ruddigore* was to laugh at the absurdities of popular melodrama. Sir Despard is a wicked baronet, Rose Maybud the pure village maiden is so innocent and sweet that she even introduces herself as "Sweet Rose Maybud", Richard, a breezy sailor and Mad Margaret "an obvious caricature of theatrical madness". *Ruddigore* has not much relation to life, its values being only stage values.

Ruddigore has very rich music. The song of Richard 'The Bold Mounseer' created a little fuss. A British 'revenue sloop' slights a French merchantman and makes fun.

> ...To fight a French fallal—it's like hittn' of a gale.
> It's lubberly thing for to do
> For we, with all our faults,
> Why, we're sturdy British salts,
> While she's only a Parley-voo,
>   D'ye see?
> A miserably Parley-voo!

The humour of the play was not well received and for the first time in the history of Gilbert and Sullivan operas a 'Boo' was heard as the curtain fell. Frenchmen felt offended at this 'Darn'd Mounseer', and Gilbert received many challenges to duels. *Ruddigore* has many other delightful lyrics. The chorus of professional bridesmaids with their working hours from ten to four is a deliberate caricature of bridesmaids in the regular melodramas. The male chorus is formed by the ghosts of the dead Murgatroyd ancestors who live within the frames of their pictures in the Ruddigore picture gallery.

Ruddigore failed on the stage, because Gilbert's irony and satire weighed too heavily on the audience. The caricature, the farcical situations and meaningless broad laughter were getting mixed with seriousness and the Savoy operas appeared to be losing their hold on the popular taste.

Gilbert made amends for his heavy satire and lack of humour in the next play *The Yeomen of the Guard* which received a tumultuous welcome. The plot is laid in the sixteenth century and the Tower provides an excellent setting. Colonel Fairfax is to be hanged, but is saved in time by his friend Sergeant Maryll, who with his daughter Phoebe changes the dress of the Colonel. In order to save his property, the Colonel marries the blindfolded Elsie, a strolling player. Wilfred the keeper of the prison is arrested for the Colonel's escape.

It is given out that the Colonel is shot dead by Wilfred. The Colonel, now free, makes love to Elsie who does not recognize him. She rebuffs his advances considering herself a widow. Phoebe, who so far pretends to be his sister, is troubled to see the Colonel making love to Elsie. Leonard, the real brother of Phoebe under whose name the Colonel has been masquerading arrives with the news of the Colonel's reprieve. Tragedy occurs in Point's life who is deprived of his love — Elsie.

The Yeomen of the Guard had for its setting Sixteenth Century England. Except for strolling players, guards on the towers and tricks of disguise, it had no other similarity with the said period. The illusion is well maintained in a plot which deals with sentiments and feelings with a sincerity rare in Gilbert.

Gilbert showed his powers of dramatic characterisation in handling the pathetic disappointment of Jack Point. It is generally felt that Gilbert "put a great deal of what he thought was his essential self into the character of Jack Point."[1] All the remorse which Gilbert had in his heart for the failure of his serious plays found vent in Point.

> See, I am salaried wit; and is there aught in nature
> more ridiculous? A poor, dull, heartbroken man, who
> must needs be merry, or he will be shipped; who must
> rejoice, lest he starve; who must jest you, jibe you,
> quip you, crank you, wrack you, riddle you............

Point is really bitter for the forced occupation of a Jester and Comedian. Gilbert himself was greatly grieved by the failure of his serious and sentimental plays. *The Yeomen of the Guard* has a few beautiful songs but the finest is:

> If life a Boon?
> If so, it must befall
> That Death, when e'er he call,
> Must call too soon.
> Though four score years he give,
> Yet one would pray to live
> Another moon!

This lyric is written in a true Elizabethan vein and is evidence in favour of Gilbert as a lyricist. *The Yeomen of the Guard* is free from any tinge of satire and was designed as a sentimental story with a poetic touch.

The Gondoliers or The King of Barataria was produced in December 1889. It deals with Marco and Guiseppe. One of the two is supposed to be the son of the king of Barataria, and married to Casilda, daughter of the Duke and Duchess of Plaza Toro. Marco and Guiseppe go to the state of Barataria and rule as one person. They govern happily on a socialistic pattern, without ever using the word and are romantic rather than realistic in their principles of government. But it is discovered that neither of the

---

[1] Pearson: *op. cit.* p. 181

two is the Prince of Barataria. The real Prince is Luiz, Casilda's attendant and lover.

Gondoliers ridicules the idea of social and political equality. In the eighties when the play was written, magazines occasionally published articles on socialism. Bernard Shaw and H. G. Wells were the two writers generally talked about. But they talked of principles. Gilbert, highly critical of the popular views on socialism, had his own ideas on this issue and to him a change in human nature was the first essential for the change that socialism was supposed to bring about. So the scene is eighteenth-century Venice, not a modern socialist state but an old-fashioned monarchy. The chorus informs us:

> In Barataria you may see
> A Monarchy that's tempered with Republican Equality
> This form of government we find
> The beau ideal of its kind —
> A despotism strict combined with absolute equality!

Gilbert was not ridiculing the republican form of government but the doctrinaire equalitarians wherever they might be found. He was not a politician and did not know much about State and Government. It was good for the play that he did not, because soon he busied himself sorting out the matrimonial tangle of two husbands and three wives. *Gondoliers'* irony and satire are genial.

The characters of the Duke and Duchess of Plaza Toro are very interesting, besides being representative of the poverty-stricken aristocrats, ready to sink pride and sell aristocratic privileges for whatever they will fetch. It was indeed characteristically Gilbertian to imagine man capitalising his social position in right earnest by turning himself into a public company, the Duke of Plaza Toro Limited. In a long duet the Duke and the Duchess explain what services they render to their shareholders. The duet is about the activities of politicians and their corruptions — how men in high positions use their privileges to advantage. The Duke uses his rank to fetch small titles and orders for Mayors and Records, gets insignificant M.P.'s baroneted, lays foundation stones and speaks at charity dinners where he gets cent per cent of the takings, and allows his name to be used by cheap tailors who are so bad that even Robinson Crusoe would not have cared to look at them. The Duchess also has her share in the activities. She presents only ladies whose conduct is shady in first-rate society, recommends bad dressmakers, soap advertisements, and attends parties on payment. The duet ends thus:

> In short, if you'd kindle
> The spark of a swindle,
> Lure simpletons into your clutches —
> Yes: into your clutches,
> Or, hoodwink a debtor,
> You cannot do better
> Than trot out a Duke or a Duchess.

The duet expresses Gilbert's feelings on decadent aristocracy which found in shooting, sporting and fashionable parties, its only occupation. The contemporary allusions show his indignation at certain issues. He was severe on the aristocracy. *The Gondoliers* is one of the wittiest operas of Gilbert and Sullivan. Gilbert fully admired the individual brilliancy of Sullivan in this play.

Utopia Limited or The Flowers of Progress was produced at the Savoy on 7th October, 1893.

King Paramount rules over Utopia. He has sent his elder daughter Zara to learn the English ways and she comes back with a few 'flowers of progress', experts who help her govern the Utopia. The management by the 'flowers of progress' is so good that Party government is established so that there may be disturbances and the condition may not remain awfully peaceful. *Utopia Limited* failed to capture the old Savoy spirit. It was an open attack on English manners and traditions. Queen Victoria felt offended at the way the Court was presented in the play. The first Cabinet Council meeting of King Paramount is held 'in accordance with the practice at St. James' Hall'. Really the Court scene on the stage was modelled on the famous Christy Minstrels, the black-faced comedians, implying that the Queen and the Cabinet were no better than them. Also, the imitation of the Court by the 'flowers of progress' was more a satire than anything else.

Gilbert's criticism of the old-fashioned English manners shows his contempt of time-worn customs. He was a little too conservative in his ideas about women. Lady Sophy has been ridiculed for her teaching English manners to the two young princesses, Nikaya and Kalyba, and using her pupils as models in a lecture on the behaviour of young English ladies receiving the advances of a pushing Englishman. What is still more absurd is the ironical hint:

> The lecture's ended. In ten minutes' space
> 'Twill be repeated in the market place.

A little later the girls try their demure ways on Lord Dramaleigh and Mr. Goldbury. The latter bursts into a song about the behaviour of a real English girl:

> Her soul is sweet as the ocean air,
> For prudery knows no haven there;
> To find mock modesty, please apply
> To the conscious blush and the downcast eye.

Goldbury's song, then called 'the outdoor girl' is very satirical and expresses Gilbert's views on women. Gilbert was delighted by naturalness of behaviour in women, but disliked and opposed any idea of providing them with higher education.

The 'flowers of progress' have so well managed the Utopia that there is dull perfection all around. What should be done?—they are busy finding the solution and Zara realises:

> Government by Party! Introduce that great and glorious element — at once the bulwark and foundation of England's greatness — and all will be well! No political measures will endure, because one party will assuredly undo all that the other party has done; and while grouse is to be shot, and foxes worried to death, the legislative action of the country will be at a standstill. Then there will be sickness in plenty, endless lawsuits, crowded jails, interminable confusion in the Army and Navy, and in short, general and unexampled prosperity.

William S. Gilbert

The decision is reached shortly as the king announces:

> From this moment Government by Party is adopted, with all its attendant blessings; and henceforward Utopia will no longer be a Monarchy (Limited), but, what is a great deal better, a Limited Monarchy !

Utopia Limited, apart from these weaknesses had another defect also. The love interest present in previous operas was missing in this. Zara and Captain Fitzbattleaxe have already decided to marry before their stage appearance. Nikaya and Kalyba are only mechanical, absurd, incapable of arousing interest. The romantic tangle in the play is solved by logic. Scapho and Phantis are two claimants of Zara's hand. The Captain is in a dilemma as to how to hit upon the right way to clear his way and hence this intelligent suggestion of doing it in the English fashion:

Scapho and Phantis: The English fashion? What is that?

Fitz : It's very simple. In England when two gentlemen are in love with the same lady, and until it is settled which gentleman is to blow out the brains of the other, it is provided by the Royal Admirer's Clauses Consolidation Act, that the lady shall be entrusted to an officer of Household Cavalry as stakeholder, who is bound to hand her over to the survivor in a good condition of substantial and decorative repair.

Scapho : Reasonable wear and tear and damages by fire excepted?
Fitz : Exactly.

Obviously the two wise men decide to live without Zara.

Utopia Limited ends on a patriotic note when Gilbert leaves the king to regenerate his land on the lines of great Britain, which is:

> That monarchy sublime,
> To which some add (but others do not)
> Ireland Such at least is the Tale Ireland etc.

Utopia Limited was very different from the early Savoy operas. It was a serious play openly attacking the English customs and manners. Gilbert attacked the contemporary structure of capitalism. Old family firms tended to be replaced by limited liability companies run by salaried managers. Limited liability companies were made possible by legislation of 1855-6. Concentration of capital and encouragement of larger undertakings promoted by the Companies Act of 1862, were satirized by Gilbert:

> Seven men form an Association
> (If possible all Peers and Baronets)
> They start off with a public declaration
> To what extent they mean to pay their debts.
> That's called their Capital.

But the rise of these joint stock companies and limited liability companies gave rise to a number of bogus companies. Earlier in *The Gondoliers* the Duke said:

> I sit, by selection, upon the direction
> Of Several Companies' bubble!
> ×   ×   ×   ×
> As soon as they are floated
> I am freely bank noted —
> I'm pretty well paid for my trouble.

The last flicker of the Savoy lamp was 'The Grand Duke', a fling at authority in general.

The Grand Duke of Pfenning Halb Pfenning, for his meanness and standoffishness has infuriated his subjects. The rest of the play is occupied by the attempts of the conspirators to instal the manager of a theatrical company in his place. *The Statutory Duel*, which also gives the play its alternative title, is the source of this change brought about with great ingenuity of argument in the usual Gilbertian way. Tables are turned upon the conspirators whose attempt to instal the manager are foiled by a new interpretation of the Statutory Duel. The Duke is reinstated in his position when the curtain falls finally to close *The Grand Duke*, and also, the long successful partnership of William Gilbert and Arthur Sullivan. *The Grand Duke* was extremely mechanical in plot and lacked life. It was "the final flash in the pan; in fact it was only a spark; and the most famous association in theatrical history fizzled out like a damp squib".[1]

---

[1] Pearson, *op. cit.* p. 227

William S. Gilbert

Much has been said on the comparative importance of Gilbert and Sullivan. Both persons were greatly different from each other in their natures. Sullivan was a musical genius and it was repeatedly said that he would do better if he devoted himself entirely to music and washed his hands of light opera. Similarly Gilbert also regarded his serious and sentimental plays as better than the Savoy operas. But as luck would have it comic opera proved most successful and both had to bow before commercial success. Who contributed more to the success of the Savoy operas? Undoubtedly it was Gilbert who was mainly responsible for the texts, stage direction and presentation. Sullivan only scored the musical compositions. Illustrations are not wanting of occasions where Gilbert helped Sullivan. It was Gilbert who created the haunting melody of 'I have a song a sing, Oh!' in *The Yeomen of the Guard*. It has been accepted that Sullivan in spite of having genuine talent lacked the dominant force. "His best music was", Pearson says, "the medium whereby another man's personality was expressed".[1]

Two points are very significant about the plays of Gilbert: first, his originality, and secondly, his characterisation. Writing in days when the popular theatrical fare consisted of melodrama, burlesque, sensational and comical plays, Gilbert had the wonderful gift of originality. His dominant personality had its own expression and on all that he wrote Gilbert left the indelible impression of originality. One feature of his originality was the vast majority of characters who peopled his plays. Gilbert's experience of life was varied and very widespread. He had served in the Forfar and Kincardine Militia, at the Bar and also in some Government Offices. The impressions he gathered about life and about persons were used to great advantage in his plays. Of course, in the serious and sentimental plays, characters are not varied, they are limited. But in the Savoy operas in each play he dealt with representatives of different classes, the judges, the lords and aristocrats, military men, poets, heroines — love-sick and sentimental. As Huchinson observes — "these professions and these professors became

---

[1] Pearson, *op. cit.* p. 235

grist to that slowgrinding mill of ironies which was subconsciously on the twirl all the while in Gilbert's brain. The men of the sword, the men of the gown, the men of the office stool, all come in for his satire and for our entertainment in their turn 'They'll none of them be spared' to parody his own words".[1]

The actors he selected for the roles also gave Gilbert no trouble. Generally dramatists depended on great and successful actors but Gilbert never favoured the star system. When he selected George Grossmith and Rutland Barrington for *The Sorcerer*, the company was horrified. When questioned by some one regarding his selection of Barrington for a singing part, Gilbert answered, "He's a staid, stolid swine and that's what I want". This is the key to Gilbert's attitude towards the star system. Later dramatists, even Shaw, depended on successful actors for their plays, but Gilbert never cared for them.

Gilbert thus proved to be the most successful dramatist of the Eighties only by virtue of his forceful personality and originality of approach to different issues. The Savoy operas are the best illustrations of what originality could achieve.

---

[1] Horace C. Huchinson, *Portraits of the Eighties*, p. 256

Chapter IV

Arthur Wing Pinero

(i) Pinero brought " the English stage into the European dramatic movement with which it had no relation a short time before."

Barrett H. Clarke

(ii) Pinero's stylers. " nothing but the lowest and most piteous kind of journalese."

Max Beerbohm

(iii) *The Second Mrs Tanqueray* "is in the opinion of the best critics, the most remarkable work in the history of the British Drama during the second half of the nineteenth century."

M. Charles Hastings in
' Le Theatre Francais et Anglais', Paris 1900

(iv) "......a real wicked Pinerotic theatre."

G. B. Shaw

Arthur Wing Pinero infused new spirit in drama with his farces. He was a man with wide experience of the theatre including the histrionics, and won acclaim as one destined "to take a good position as a dramatic author".[1] It was Pinero's feeling for the 'social' on the stage that earned him critical appreciation. In *The Money Spinner* (1880) and *The Squire*, he showed his grasp of the 'social' issues of the time although his plays were not unaffected

---

[1] Henry Irving on Pinero, quoted by Hamilton Fyfe in Sir Arthur Pinero's *Plays and Players*, p. 16

by popular taste. The Court Theatre farces, *The Magistrate* (1885), *The School Mistress* (1886) and *Dandy Dick* (1886) secured him an important position on the stage and his replacement of 'incident and situation' by 'character' earned him recognition as a talented dramatist. Realism in details and bold characterization were new to the contemporary London Stage.

Following his new position as a dramatist Pinero wrote comedies with a strong predilection for sentimentality and satire. In the first group 'comedies with an undertone of seriousness' are *Hobby Horse*, *Lady Bountiful*, *The Times* and *The Princess and the Butterfly*. The second group of plays about 'social problems and new ideas, consisted mainly of *The Profligate*, *The Second Mrs. Tanqueray* and *The Notorious Mrs. Ebbsmith*.

Pinero first showed signs of a new spirit in theatre with *Hobby Horse* (1886), a play about 'slumming' — a fashionable amusement. It was a mild satire on the 'boredom' among the rich and mixed the serious with the comic. Shaw did not fail to notice that the *Hobby Horse* "had character, humour, observation, genuine comedy and literary workmanship."[1] On the comic side the play portrayed a rich lady going on to live among the poor as an unmarried girl. The romantic interlude that followed gave *Hobby Horse* its novelty.

In *Lady Bountiful* Pinero was serious with his characters in as much as the play ridiculed the able-bodied men living as parasites on the rich. Camilla — the rich lady supports both father and son. Dennis the son, is shocked by Camilla.

Camilla : Dennis, it isn't great men women love dearest, or even fortunate men; often, I tell you, their deepest love goes out to those who labour and fail. But for those who make no effort, who are neither great nor little, who are the nothing of this world!
Dennis : Who are the Dennis Herons of the world!
Camilla : For those a true woman has only one feeling — anger and contempt.

---

[1] Shaw, G. B. *Plays and Players*, Ed. A. C. Ward, p. 232

The frustrated lover leaves and takes up employment as riding master in the stable of a former groom of the family and marries Margaret who dies conveniently to let Dennis go back to Camilla. They are, of course, married.

The plot of *Lady Bountiful*, though marred by maudlin sentimentality, had satire and irony of a kind different from the usual stage plays. It is representative of the old school plays "before Ibsen yeast has leavened the English lump".[1]

A similar strain of satire runs through another comedy, *The Times* (1891) which exposed people's craving for high society. It dramatised the efforts of Mr. and Mrs. Egerton Bompass to reach out for the aristocracy. They have amassed wealth and mastered some of the 'tricks' of their betters. Their character is discovered when Lady Ripstow and Lord Lurgashall visit their place. Lord Lurgashall is in love with Beryl, daughter of the Bompasses.

Lady R.	:	I think Mrs. Egerton Bompass will see me.
Manservant	:	I'm sure she will, m'lady, if she's at home.
Lady R.	:	She is not 'at home' this afternoon, I know, but she may be indoors.
Manservant	:	I'll ask Codrington, m'lady.
Lady R.	:	Codrington!
Manservant	:	My mistress's maid's woman, m'lady. (He goes out).
Lady R.	:	'My mistress's maid's woman!' The wives of drapers have their comforts, Denham.
Lurgashall	:	My dear mother!
Lady R.	:	Is not Mr. Bompass a draper?
L.	:	Mr. Egerton-Bompass—
Lady R.	:	Egerton!
L.	:	Mr. Egerton-Bompass is a draper on a large scale.
Lady R.	:	He has a dozen shops all in a row, you mean.
L.	:	Fourteen, as a matter of fact.
Lady R.	:	Surely that makes him fourteen times a draper.
L.	:	At any rate Beryl is not a draper!

*   *   *   *

Lady R.	:	Beryl is cotton, you are silk; each material in itself is estimable, but cotton and silk beget satinet.

---

[1] Chandler, F. W. *Aspects of Modern Drama*, p. 189

This sham aristocracy does not make the daughter happy.

Lurgashall	:	I shall be at Mrs. Cathew's about eleven.
Beryl	:	A trifle early for us.
Lurgashall	:	Early?
Beryl	:	We used to go very early to such places and stay right through, but now that Papa has 'got on' we arrive late everywhere and murmur an apology. (Lurgashall laughs). Ah, don't laugh! If you realised as I do the sham, the falseness of this sort of thing you wouldn't, you couldn't, laugh — you'd cry. One's life seems to be made of parade and pretension.

The happiness of the Bompasses is soon shattered when it is revealed that their son has married an Irish landlady's daughter. Trimble, a family friend, suggests that Mrs. Hooley and her daughter should stay with the Bompass family as Mrs. and Miss Mountrafford till they are sufficiently educated to have the ceremony of marriage once again publicly. The veneer of respectability and aristocracy cannot hide the truth. It breaks out and the deception of the Bompass family is known. But the Bompasses have one consolation. Lurgashall still wants to marry Beryl, his sentiments having got over the vulgarity of her father's mind.

The Times was a satirical comedy unhampered by sentimentality. In his Preface to the published edition, Pinero said that he "laid bare no horrid social wound, wrangled over no vital problem". What he gives, instead, is "a mimic castigation of the lighter faults of humanity in the hope that it might prove entertaining, nay, more, to certain minds instructive". Pinero held that "there may be still those who consider that the follies, even the vices, of the age may be chastised as effectually by a sounding blow from the hollow bladder of the jester as by the fierce applilcation of the knout; that a moral need not invariably be enforced with the sententiousness of the sermon or the assertiveness of the tract".

The Times asked: "Can the depths be sounded of ignorance' of vulgarity of mind, of vanity, and of self-seeking?" The answer is the Egerton Bompass tale. In Victorian society where materia-richness earned high positions for men, where men could descend to any depth of meanness to procure prestige and respectability and where the very foundations of real honour and happiness were ill-based, the position of men with genuine claims to these privileges was miserable. It was a social evil. *The Times* was one of the best light-handed satires on the evils of the contemporary society. In contrast to the thoughtlessness of the prevailing popular comedies, it left the audience with something serious to think over, and thus, made the audience take part in the general theme of the play. The passiveness with which the audience hitherto sought entertainment was beginning to change.

The trammels of sentimentality weaken the strings of seriousness, yet it will be unjust to say that it completely enervates the irony and satire involved in the Egerton Bompass story. The criticism of Victorian manners in *The Times* was the best done so far by any contemporary of Pinero. *The Times* unveiled a Victorian household's dexterously worked-out facade of respectability. Pinero's range of characters included typical representatives of both the new-rich classes and the decadent aristocracy. The councillor of the Bompasses is Mr. Montague Trimble, a parasite, a wicked and degenerate fallen from the old and established rich aristocratic class. Like the Duke of Plaza Toro (Gilbert's *The Gondoliers* 1889) Trimble sells aristocratic privileges, helps people 'get on', attends dinners and capitalises on his social standing.

The Times established Pinero as a master of skilful irony and a dramatist of consummate skill.

The Princess and the Butterfly or The Fantastics was produced at the St. James' Theatre in March 1897. The Princess Pannonia and Sir George Lamorant are old friends and are now going to marry because it 'would make both — safe.'

Sir George : At our age I suppose there is no love but in folly (she makes a movement). Forgive me, the expression 'our time of life' was your own. (She assents by a nod). I speak of course of passionate love. Otherwise, am I quite outside the reach of your tender regard! As for passion let us make ourselves believe that we would not be five-and twenty if

> we could! Passion! My dear Laura, has it ever happened to you to stroll through a garden on the morning following a great letting off of fire-works? Oh! the hollow, blackened shells of the spent cartridges trodden into the turf. We should at least be spared the contemplation of that. But you and I are already fast linked by many associations, and sympathy is affection. Certainly, in that spirit, I love you most sincerely.

Within a month their destiny is changed. She falls desperately in love with Oriel, a youth of five-and-twenty, and Sir George is under an equally violent infatuation for Pay Zulliani, the Princess's adopted child. Both find their happiness in their young mates and the happy couples learn that 'love is ever young.'

The Princess and the Butterfly is a comedy of manners. The passionate love which gave to the Princess and Sir George their new happiness could be modified to present a saner view of life in which passion is a greater tranquilliser than a violence. The former friends, above forty, were so obsessed with age-consciousness that they are concerned about each other's position. Shaw[1] was evidently surprised to find Pinero ending the play on a note of love winning over age. *The Princess and the Butterfly* ironically depicted the haunting vexation of middle-age, the search for passionate love and security, an attempt to recapture youth.

Pinero's plays show a curious mixture of the serious and the sentimental in keeping with the contemporary taste. Also his concern for stage values led him to write comedies with a happy blending of these two elements. The Comedies discussed above form a separate group in themselves. But Pinero's mind and art showed their real stature when he wrote plays with a dominant social note—plays that ruthlessly bared social wounds. Sentimen-

---

[1] "Upto the last moment, I confess, I had sufficient confidence in Mr, Pinero's saving sense of humour to believe that he would give the verdict against himself, and admit that the meteoric girl was too young for the hero (twenty-seven years' discrepancy) and the heroine too old for the fiery youth (thirteen years' discrepancy). But no, he gravely decided that the heart that loves never ages". Shaw : *Plays and Players*, p. 207.

tality, of course, was a part of his art and never left him; it is here subordinated to higher aims. The new note appeared intermittently but forms part of a different phase in the development of his art which began with *The Weaker Sex*.

The Weaker Sex (1889) deals with the movement for women's rights. Emancipation of women, socially and morally, from the control of men was a disputed issue with the Victorian audience. Numerous articles appeared in newspapers and magazines on this question. Some held "that intellect in a woman should conduce to her being loved, that it should even be compatible with it, it must be thus subordinated to her womanhood".[1] Others thought that women should have full freedom to take up occupations for which only men were considered. On the question of political rights to women, opinions varied. While there were keen enthusiasts for Female Suffrage, Louise Creighton felt that a woman "will be a greater power, if she is not struggling for her rights, but is trying to live her own life nobly and unselfishly".[2] Pinero in *The Weaker Sex* deftly handles the question of women's emancipation and realising his limitations as a 'thinker' and difficulties of the taste of the audience, offers no solution to the issue. The love interest in the play gets more importance clearly showing what held Pinero from leading a new movement.

Philip Lyster, one time lover of Lady Vivash, left England after her rejection of his marriage proposal. He, now a poet, returns as the lover of her eighteen-year-old daughter, Sylvia. The mother has preserved the memory of her lover, admitting that she had been 'wilful, capricious, cruel'. The lover of Sylvia in the poet faces the mother Lady Vivash. He is in a fix, but solves the riddle in the manner of a sentimentalist:

Dudley : Oh! Philip, is there no way but this?
Philip : None. You know it Dudley. Once my shadow is taken from the lives of those two women there will be light again.

---

[1] A. Orr: 'The Future of Englishwoman'—*Nineteenth Century Opinion*, Ed. by Michael Godwin, p. 95

[2] *Ibid. The Appeal Against Female Suffrage*, p. 104

> I pray to time to do the rest. Time will bless some worthier man than I with Sylvia's sweet companionship, and then the first laugh from Sylvia's lips will wake Mary from her long dream.

For the London audiences Philip Lyster passed out of the lives of the two women. For the provincial audience Pinero made Philip marry Sylvia. The play suffers from Pinero's lack of courage displayed in his inability to take bold decisions. The old love-triangle could not be resolved.

The Weaker Sex which meant to satirize 'gentlemanly ladies and zoological gentlemen' ended on a very ineffective note. The women agitators are quietened by sentiment. In *The Weaker Sex* Pinero drew his female characters on well-defined lines and with an inward boldness: Lady Vivash and Mrs. Boylechewton. With this play Pinero began his studies in women characters which climaxed in *The Second Mrs. Tanqueray* and *The Notorious Mrs. Ebbsmith*. Besides this excellent characterization *The Weaker Sex* was a transitional piece leading to the production of more mature plays.

The Profligate (1889) was a mature attempt to tackle a social problem. Here is the story of a man who had 'lived a man's life' in his youth and whose past sins wreck his marital happiness. The play-bill presenting the play had these lines:

> It is a good and sooth-fast saw,
> Half-roasted never shall be raw;
> No dough is dried once more to meal,
> No coach new-shapen by the wheel.
> You can't turn curds to milk again,
> Nor Now by wishing back to Then;
> And, having tasted stolen honey,
> You can't buy innocence for money.

It was an indication that *The Profligate* was going to be a story of the past overwhelming the present. Fate of the hero is already decided. For a man of his character there is no happiness in society. When he is honeymooning with his wife, the timely appearance of Janet, his earlier victim, shatters his conjugal felicity. Renshaw's snivelling plea for mercy is turned down by the shocked wife. Their love disappears and the wrong done to Janet stands between them. Renshaw, deeply penitent, soliloquizes for a long time in a maudlin way:

> "Supposing there is some chance of my regaining her. Regaining her! How dull sleeplessness makes me! How much could I regain of what I've lost! Why, she knows me—nothing can ever undo that — she knows me. Every day would be a dreary, hideous masquerade; every night a wakeful, torturing retrospect. If she smiled, I should whisper to myself, 'Yes, yes, that's a very pretty pretence, but she knows you.'......

Renshaw takes poison.

His suicide kills off all chances of a brave tussle with circumstances. The struggle is avoided and his character is weakened. It was a tragedy and the audience liked to see comedies only.

Pinero supplied the manager with an alternative end. Dunstan Renshaw was reconciled to his wife. Once again considerations of a stage success weighed heavy with Pinero. But he retained the original ending for the published edition. In *The Profligate* Pinero had a firm grip on the plot. The denouement was in complete harmony with the previous developments in the theme. With the victim of Dunstan's thoughtless flirtation living, a happy domestic life was out of the question and the play had to follow the tragic pattern or end in the "grim, opaque atmosphere of Ibsenian fatality, with the implication of a severe Nemesis."[1] The unrelieved seriousness showed Pinero's determination not to palter with truth to suit the popular taste. He was in his own way introducing grimness on the domestic level before Ibsen's plays could raise this to a tragic standard.

In order to be 'literary' Pinero gave long maudlin speeches to Dunstan but failed to capture the tragic grandeur of *Macbeth* or *Hamlet*. *The Profligate* dealt with a serious problem seriously and showed no weakness towards comic relief or a sub-plot. This showed his determination to carry the story to its logical

---

[1] Pellizzi, Camillo, *op. cit.* p. 50, *English Drama*.

end without pandering to the vulgar taste. It was a courageous attempt to infuse seriousness.

At this stage Ibsen arrived in England. Two months after the production of *The Profligate*, Charles Charrington produced *A Doll's House* at the Novelty Theatre (now called the Kingsway Theatre). Two years later J. T. Grein produced a series of plays by Ibsen at the Independent Theatre, and Shaw gave a series of lectures on the 'Quintessence of Ibsenism.' Ibsen was a sensation in England. Whereas some critics regarded him as disgusting, many hailed him as a symbol of the new spirit of drama.

The new drama, however, did not become instantly popular. It was limited to a coterie of intellectuals. Pinero laid no claims to advanced thinking. He was genuinely touched by the contemporary movements. He gave character its due importance and realised that plot could no longer be given supreme consideration. His new play startled John Hare who refused it as 'immoral'. After some hesitation it was produced at St. James' on May 23, 1893.

The Second Mrs. Tanqueray[1] opens on a scene laid in Aubrey Tanqueray's chambers where friends are talking together on a winter evening. Aubrey informs them of his marriage that is going to take place very soon. It is Aubrey's second marriage and Cayley Drummle, a friend, informs Aubrey about his first wife who "was one of your cold sort, you know—all marble arms and black velvet". (Act I, p. 22). The sort of woman who kept "a thermometer in her stays and always registered ten degrees below zero. However, in time a child came, a daughter" (Act I, p. 23). It was Ellean, and the first Mrs. Tanqueray sent her daughter to a Convent in France, then to Ireland. All the necessary information has been given and Aubrey returns to the scene, as during Cayley's speeches he was writing letters in another room. Aubrey then reveals the identity of his would-be wife! "Cayley, the lady I am going to marry is the lady who is known as—Mrs. Jarman".

---

[1] Published by William Heinemann, London, 1922.

And Cayley then recounts Mrs. Jarman's past associations as Mrs. Dartry and Mrs. Jarman. Aubrey strikes the keynote:

> She has never met a man who has treated her well. I intend to treat her well. I'll prove to you that it is possible to rear a life of happiness, of good repute, on a — miserable foundation.

Paula and Aubrey are married, and, ostracized by society, settle at 'Higher Combe'. Ellean is also with them. Their life is dull and Paula feels bored. "Oh! I've no patience with you! You'll kill me with this life!"

Paula's efforts to win the affection of Ellean fail and she (Ellean) is taken to Paris by Mrs. Cortelyon. To Aubrey it is a safe course to save the innocent Ellean from any ill-effects that the company of her stepmother may have. Paula is pained at this treatment. She feels insulted in her own home. In the third act when Ellean returns home, she brings Hugh Ardale with her. Paula and Hugh Ardale face each other.

> Ellean : Paula, this is Captain Ardale — Mrs. Tanqueray. (Paula rises and turns, and she and Hugh stand staring blankly at each other for a moment or two; then Paula advances and gives him her hand).
>
> Paula : (In a strange voice, but calmly) How do you do?
> Hugh : How do you do?

Paula and Hugh are left together. They discuss matters. Hugh threatens, makes faces and leaves.

Hugh is gone. Paula tells Aubrey of her past relations with Hugh. Aubrey forbids Ellean to have any further connection with Hugh. A tense dramatic scene between Paula and Ellean follows:

> Ellean : What you know! Why, after all, what can you know! You can only speak from gossip, report, hearsay! How is it possible that you — I (she steps abruptly. The two women stand staring at each other for a moment, then Ellean backs away from Paula slowly). Paula!

English Drama 1860-1900

Paula : What — what's the matter?

Ellean : You — you knew Captain Ardale in London!

Paula : Why? What do you mean?

Ellean : Oh! (She makes for the door, but Paula catches her by the wrist).

Paula : You shall tell me what you mean!

Ellean : Ah! (Suddenly looking fixedly into Paula's face) You know what I mean.

Paula : You accuse me!

Ellean : It's in your face!

Paula (hoarsely): You — you think I'm — that sort of creature, do you?

Ellean : Let me go!

Paula : Answer me! You've always hated me (shaking her) Out with it!

Ellean : You hurt me!

Paula : You've always hated me! You shall answer me!

Ellean : Well, then, I have always — always —

Paula : What?

Ellean : I have always known what you were!

Paula : Ah! Who — who told you?

Ellean : Nobody but yourself. From the first moment I saw you I knew you were altogether unlike the good women I'd left, directly I saw you, I knew what my father had done. You've wondered why I've turned from you! There — that's the reason! Oh, but this is a horrible way for the truth to come home to every one! Oh!

Paula : It's a lie! It's a lie! (forcing Ellean down upon her knees) You shall beg my pardon for it. (Ellean utters a loud shriek of terror). Ellean, I'm a good woman! I swear I am! I've always been a good woman! You dare to say I've ever been anything else! It's a lie!

Paula is stunned and shocked. Ellean hits at her weakest point. Aubrey is willing to forget and think of a new future but Paula knows the truth: "I believe the future is only the past again entered through another gate."

Aubrey and Paula discuss whether or not it is possible for her to remain with the Tanquerays. Paula presents a classic picture of a pretty woman getting old, of a beautiful face defeated by age, and then "that horrid, irresistible truth that physical repulsion forces on men and women will come to you, and you'll sicken at me". She looks into his eyes and says:

> You'll see me, then, at last, with other people's eyes! You'll see me just as your daughter does now, as all wholesome folks see women like me. And I shall have no weapon to fight with—not one serviceable little bit of prettiness, left me to defend myself with! A worn-out creature—broken up, very likely sometime before I ought to be — my hair bright, my eyes dull, my body too thin or too stout, my cheeks raddled and ruddled — a ghost, a wreck, a caricature, a candle that gutters, call such an end what you like......And this is the future you talk about! I know it — I know it!

Paula takes poison.

Paula moves to her doom with the helplessness of a doomed character, struggling back to the wall against circumstances. She cannot fight the ghosts of her past. The past overtakes Paula as it did Renshaw.

Her sensitiveness, her frustration at her failure to gain Ellean's love, and the love of a true companion in life—for Aubrey remains at best a kind and sympathetic friend, the search of peace after a troubled past—all unite to crush Paula's brave effort.

Shaw misjudged Paula's tragedy and thought it was due to Pinero's want of "sympathy with character," of judging a character "from the point of view of others instead of merely describing or judging them from one's own point of view in terms of the conventional systems of morals."[1] Some critics thought it was Pinero's timidity which made Paula commit suicide. It was a general misunderstanding and a failure to grasp the real meaning of the play. Pinero meant to dramatise a fallen woman's fate and failure. He never wanted to show off as an 'advanced' playwright by going out of the way to change the course of events in

---

[1] Shaw, *op. cit.* p. 24.

the play. Paula is human and moving. She cannot suddenly turn bold and brazen in the end. Pinero was keen to show her inner-self. She is a helpless victim of circumstances, struggles within human limits and never adopts the 'advanced' outlook of the new woman.

Aubrey's cold sympathy towards Paula accounts partly for her end. The warm-hearted redeemer of Paula in the first act sinks into the role of a friend with imperfect sympathies. Aubrey is almost priggish. Ellean is a conventional middle-class Victorian girl steeped in prudery and Cayley is the good-natured and practical mediator between the audience, and Paula and Aubrey. None of these characters matches the tragic stature of Paula.

The Second Mrs. Tanqueray put English drama in line with European dramatic movements. A play on such a theme was long awaited, and but for the inveterate faults of the Victorian outlook, it was a great achievement for Pinero and a landmark in the development of English drama.

Ibsen had arrived and so had Pinero. *The Second Mrs. Tanqueray* aroused vehement critical notice, specially from the Ibsenite critics. The lovers of the orthodox Victorian morality and 'anti-Ibsen' drama blamed Pinero for taking his audience 'for a stroll in Regent Street by night', and for recommending itself to the 'lovers of the revolting in art.'[1] This was a clear misunderstanding of the play and read too much of Ibsen in the text. The orthodox groups of critics thought Pinero was 'advanced' and the 'advanced' critics thought he was still a backward, unprogressive dramatist who "used realistic detail as little more than a facade behind which to conceal the rigid dictates of Victorian moralism according to which a fallen woman must remain fallen."[2] Shaw observed that Pinero wrote nothing "from which it could be guessed that he is a contemporary of Ibsen."[3] Both the anti-Ibsenites and the Ibsenites were unjust to Pinero.

---

[1] J. P. Nisbet in *The Times*, quoted by Fyfe, *op. cit.* p. 146
[2] John Gassner: *Form and Idea in Modern Theatre*, p. 89
[3] *Plays and Players*, p. 21

Arthur Wing Pinero

It would be a misreading of Ibsen's characters to think that only successful rebels were truly 'Ibsenites' and those who failed were not. The spirit of Ibsen lay in the revolt and lack of compromise with certain useless human and social institutions like marriage and property. In *The Second Mrs Tanqueray* this is a secondary question. The major and better part of the play centres on the conflict in Paula's mind whether to accept Aubrey's promise of a future on her present beauty which failed to get her real warm human love. She is haunted by a cruel past and scared of a bleak future. Beauty is her defence. That, she knows, will leave her. There is no love. There is only a friendly husband who fails to restore her faith in life and keeps making promises to save his appearance before his friend Cayle Drummle. The suffering of such a soul is truly tragic. It should not matter whether it is Ibsenite or not.

Despite adverse criticism and enthusiastic appreciation, there is no denying the fact that *The Second Mrs. Tanqueray* inangurated a new form of drama in England. Unknowingly, Pinero infused new life and boldness in contemporary drama.

Finding himself leader of a new *avant garde* theatre, Pinero made one more attempt at writing about another type of modern woman, a woman agitator. This time John Hare made no mistake and *The Notorious Mrs. Ebbsmith*[1] appeared at the Garrick Theatre on 13th March, 1895.

The story can be presented from two points of view: first, as an intellectual drama, a problem play; secondly, as a tragedy of human feelings and relationships. Let us study it as a play based on serious and advanced thinking. Agnes is the daughter of a secular agitator. After eight years of married life, one year of youthful indulgence and the seven as his mistress, her husband dies and gives her freedom. She takes up her father's ways, lecturing, "spouting perhaps you'd call it, standing on the identical little platforms he used to speak from, lashing abuses with my tongue as he had done". Lecturing brings starvation which in

---

[1] Published by William Heinemann, London, 1914

English Drama 1860-1900

turn, liads to hospital nursing, where she comes into contact with Lucas Cleeve who is "dying for a miserable marriage". They decide to work together and their relations are to be completely free from physical passions. Social reforms, free thinking and socialistic jargon are their means of communication. But Lucas Cleeve fails to hold to his promise. The man in him betrays itself. He presents her with a beautiful gown.

Lucas	:	My dear Agnes, I can't understand your reason for trying to make yourself a plain-looking woman when nature intended you for a pretty one.
Agnes	:	Pretty!
Lucas	:	(Looking hard at her) You are pretty.
Agnes	:	......And when would you have me hang this on my bones?
Lucas	:	Oh, when we are dining, or —
Agnes	:	Dining in a public place?
Lucas	:	Why not look your best in a public place?
Agnes	:	Look my best! You know, I don't think of this sort of garment in connection with our companionship, Lucas.

The Duke of St. Olpherts, uncle by marriage to Lucas, interviews Agnes to discover whether "matters could not be arranged". When the Duke speaks about that small, unruly section to which she has attached herself, Agnes with changed manners, flashing eyes, harsh voice and violent gesture harangues him about the "sufferers, the toilers, that great crowd of old and young—old and young stamped by excessive labour and privation all of one pattern".

The Duke reveals to Agnes another side of Lucas' character.

The Duke	:	......You have looked upon my nephew as a talented young gentleman whose future was seriously threatened by domestic disorder; ......with a share of the brain and spirit of those terrible human pests called 'reformers'.
Agnes	:	I don't deny it.
The Duke	:	Ah! But what is the real, the actual Lucas Cleeve?

×   ×   ×   ×   ×

Arthur Wing Pinero

> Poor dear fellow, I'll tell you. The real Lucas Cleeve. An egoist. An egoist.

Agnes has a meeting with Lucas, wears the gown and sacrifices her ideal because she has, what she calls "only one hour in a woman's life". Lucas goes gaily to see his relations who have come to 'rescue' him. Agnes is left to face the attacks of the parson's sister and the parson himself. They leave a copy of the Bible with her. Agnes thrusts the Bible into the stove, since to her it is the source of all her misfortunes, watches it consumed, then suddenly with a cry, snatches it out.

The disillusion takes place and Agnes realises the wrong she had done to Mrs. Lucas. She leaves with the parson and his sister, leaving a card for Lucas: 'My-hour-is-over'.

The new critical theorists at once found faults with the play. As a woman-agitator Agnes is unconvincing. Her character seems to be drawn from newspaper reports of such women. Pinero had no idea of a woman platform speaker and fails to infuse a true intellectual spirit in the Agnes-Lucas relationship. The critics were right in their opinion.

Yet it offered more to think and talk about than any other of Pinero's dramas, and in it we have a drama consisting simply of the interaction of two characters, their conflicts and trials. Here we have the sexless, intellectual relationship between Agnes and Lucas, as in *The Weaker Sex* and *The Second Mrs. Tanqueray*. It is women's emancipation and marriage, with reformation at the core of it. How far do Agnes and Lucas succeed in keeping up the facade of an advanced and intellectual relationship?

Agnes' sacrifice of her ideals to follow the dictates of her new self is psychologically convincing. This is a tragedy in itself, this surrender of the higher nature to the lower, the failure of the mind to escape from the common bondage of sex. Her head resents forces of the flesh and blood whereas her heart holds her back from any attempt at renunciation. The ineffectuality of her sacrifice gives her greater pains than the actual deed.

The Notorious Mrs. Ebbsmith is a tragedy of human relationship. Agnes is really a woman of flesh and blood in every sense of the word. Despite her experience of an ill-matched marriage in her father's house, she agrees to live with Lucas. She has suffered in her married life the over-indulgence of her husband for one year and then physical servitude to him for seven years, after which he dies. Lucas also is fleeing from a marriage with a shrew who has nothing of sympathy and love for him. These qualities he finds in Agnes. How to get Agnes? He flatters her by pretending to share her faith in sociology and in her aspiration for a "closer, more temperate, more impassive companionship". To him it is a cloak hiding his real physical attraction for her. To her it is her defence against any other marriage and enslavement. Agnes and Lucas live together under these misconceptions. These are uncovered and when he presents her with a gown she discovers the passion underneath. The vagary of her intellectual companionship is discovered and her deep love for him survives this insight into his character given by the Duke. She clings to the only one hour in a woman's life when she can get to the truth of human relationship through love and not intellectual socialistic discussion.

For this one hour she sacrifices her intellectual pretensions. Then Mrs. Lucas comes between them. After all, Agnes is not married to Lucas. The 'hour' soon is over and she leaves the household of her dream for ever.

In the earlier parts the conflict between sex and intellect is well worked out but towards the end it degenerates into an intrigue play on marriage. Pinero is a master of situations, but beyond that he is a slave to Victorian ideals much to the detriment of the play. This established the view that Pinero did not care for a 'philosophy'. What mattered to him was a well constructed play on a fairly good theme. He wrote these plays to keep abreast of the new movements with no inner calling to lead or begin any movement. During this period of serious playwriting he also busied himself with comedy and farce. Between *The Second Mrs. Tanqueray* and *The Notorious Mrs. Ebbsmith* Pinero wrote a farcical comedy *The Amazons*. While this prove the versatility of his genius, it also shows his limitations as a dramatist. He never thought his plays would make history or that he could bring in a revolution in drama. He lacked 'vision' and had no idea of the future drama or even his plays in the national context. This was his greatest failing and it never left him. His only merit was that 'he kept the theatre open'.[1]

The theme of marital relations was continued in the next play *The Benefit of the Doubt*[2] which was produced only seven months after *The Notorious Mrs. Ebbsmith*, Here the characters are human beings with no philosophic pretensions. The opening is more interesting than that of *The Second Mrs. Tanqueray*. Conversation in the drawing room of the Emptages prepares the ground for the main characters who are involved in the 'Allingham vs. Allingham Fraser Intervening' case. Alexander Fraser and Theophilla are one couple and John Allingham and Olive another. John and Olive are greatly dissatisfied with each other as the jealous Olive has made it unbearable for John to continue. One night John is so tortured and upset that he seeks relief in the house of Theophilla in the absence of Fraser. On suspicion, Olive sues for separation. Theophilla is also involved but gets the benefit of the doubt. Theophilla, whose character has been careless, indiscreet, "hardly characteristic of a woman who is properly watchful of her own and her husband's reputation", shows that the events have a sobering effect on her. Sir Fletcher, the uncle, and Mrs. Cloys have planned a future for Theo in case there is any trouble. Theophilla and Fraser are left alone:

Theophilla : I say! I want to tell you — I am — truly sorry.

Fraser : (raising his head) Sorry!

Theophilla : (with an effort) and I humbly beg your pardon.

Fraser : (rising and facing her) For what?

Theophilla : Why, for all the bother I've caused.

---

[1] P. P. Howe: Fyfe. *op. cit.* p. 192
[2] Published by William Heinemann, London, 1922

Fraser only says 'oh'. Theophilla wants to move out together to show that it has caused no breach between the husband and the wife, but Fraser has already decided:

> Theophilla, there will be no season for us in London, and no Lochean even for me, for two or three years at least. We're going abroad.

Fraser wants no play acting and before he goes out to convince people he has to convince himself.

Theophilla : You — think there's some — some truth in it then? (He makes no answer). It's true, you believe?
Fraser   : I want time — I want time —

To Theophilla this is the final blow. She leaves a note and puts the wedding ring in it, and leaves the house. All are worried. Mrs. Cloys guesses. The note has a line 'Jack Allingham would not treat a woman so like dirt'. Theophilla has gone to Jack. They all go to Jack Allingham and reach earlier. They are as shocked to see Olive there as she is to see them. Theophilla sends a note asking whether she can see Jack. He refuses. Olive insists on his admitting her as this is a test of his position. Olive hides herself in the library and the relatives of Theophilla in another room. Theophilla is brought in. She speaks about the way Fraser has treated her and is greatly shocked.

> You know, there's always a moment in the lives of a man and woman who are tied to each other when the man has a chance of making the woman really, really, his own property.........If he had just put his hand on my shoulder this afternoon and said, "You fool, you don't deserve it, for your stupidity, but I'll try to save you—" If he had said something, anything of that kind to me, I think I could have gone down on my knees to him and......But he stared at the carpet and held on to his head and moaned out that he must have time, time! time!

So far Olive's experiment in admitting her has justified itself. Jack offers Theophilla a glass of champagne because she has had a bad day. The drink makes Theophilla more confidential and she proposes to elope with Jack. The relatives can bear this no longer. They knock loudly for admittance. Theo is bewildered to see them, and before she has recovered, receives another shock— Olive reveals herself. Theo falls at the feet of Jack in a swoon. Thus brilliantly the second act reaches its climax on a note of intense suspense. The play, highly serious so far, ends on a note of reconciliation in the third act.

In *The Benefit of the Doubt* Pinero was unhampered by any philosophy. Here was a deftly made out picture of marital suspicion and conflict. The two couples well bring out this tension which keeps mounting till the climax. It was a genuine comedy of manners, a veritable picture of the age. Even Shaw acknowledged it as containing "humour, observation, genuine comedy and literary workmanship".[1] Portrayal of the world of fashionable and aristocratic people was Pinero's forte. He said, "I must start my theme in a city. I must have life around me—eager, strenuous, pulsating life."[2] Pinero's craft appeared at its best when working on familiar ground.

Pinero gave up the serious note in his next play, *The Princess and the Butterfly*, a comedy. The play that followed it was a historical piece, although it had no relation with the previous plays. *Trelawny of the 'Wells'* is about a very solemn magistrate whose nephew and heir falls in love with an actress. Sir William Gower's household is a veritable prison for the gay young heroine, Rose Trelawny. In contrast to the heavy atmosphere of the Vice-Chancellor's establishment is the bohemian atmosphere in the lodgings of the old repertory company. In the character of Tom Wrench, Pinero presents an artist with ideals for the development and reformation of drama. His likeness to the character of Tom Robertson, writer of *Society* and *Caste*, appeared in his eagerness for reform. The language is also of the sixties.

Trelawny of the 'Wells' was a sentimental comedy. Pinero presented theatrical folk and non-theatrical folk with great skill.

---

[1] Shaw: *op. cit.* p. 232
[2] Fyfe, *op. cit.* p. 253

His experience of the stage helped him in drawing the theatre-folk. The most important point about *Trelawny of the 'Wells'* was that Pinero very successfully captured the atmosphere of the sixties. The reforms which Robertson introduced on the stage were transferred to the person of Tom Wrench. It was for this that Dickinson called it "a beautiful specimen of a difficult form, the historical comedy".[1] J. T. Grein also praised the play by crediting it with "far more depth......than in many volumes of bulky proportions".[2]

In his next play Pinero reappeared in his true colours as once again the people he was dealing with were the fashionable elite, the aristocrats. In *The Gay Lord Quex* (April, 1899), Sophy, the New Bond Street manicurist, is the sister of Muriel Eden. The real interest of the play lies in the Marquess of Quex, an old rake now determined to reform himself. He is accepted by the Edens as a match for Muriel but Sophy who knows about the past of the Gay Lord does not approve of the match. She tries to catch Quex in some unguarded moment. The opportunity comes in the form of an invitation from the Duchess of Strood to spend an evening. Sophy, already in search of a clue, finds a ready answer. Eavesdropping over the hedge, she hears Quex and the Duchess part with a promise for 'to night'. It is enough for Sophy to decide her action. Attending upon the Duchess, she comes nearer to her.

Quex, really, has gone to return the presents and documents of the Duchess so that he may be freed. The Duchess who wanted a farewell 'in keeping with their attachment' is dolefully sentimental. During their meeting, Sophy is discovered at the keyhole. The following scene, equal to the screen scene in *The School for Scandal*, is the best, most adroitly contrived and conceived in the finest traditions of the comedy of manners. Quex is now determined to save the reputation of the Duchess. She is sent to a friend's

---

[1] *op. cit.* p. 110.

[2] In *Dramatic Criticism* 1899 *on Trelawny of the 'Wells'* Jan. 1898 in A. C. Ward's *Specimens of English Dramatic Criticism, XVII-XX Centuries*, pp. 218-221.

apartment and in the bedroom of the Duchess all the doors are locked except that which brings Sophy in, only to be locked up as soon as she has entered. Quex and Sophy are together. Quex offers money. Sophy refuses. Quex's next move is more practical; he maintains that if Sophy refuses his bidding, she denounces herself too. She will be found with Quex in a room closed from all sides at midnight. The rest can be imagined. Sophy is bewildered by the scheme. She appeals for pity. Quex refuses. In her dread of exposure, Sophy consents to sign a letter which puts her in Quex's power. Should she say anything against him she is doomed. But suddenly Sophy realises her mission, and in a moment of self-sacrifice decides to save Muriel from Quex. "Why, it's like selling Muriel!" She cries "just to get myself out of this. I'm simply handing her over to you! I won't do it! I won't!" She pulls the call bell violently.

Sophy's remarkable change of heart is accompanied by an equally remarkable transformation in Quex's. Admiring Sophy's character Quex returns the letter and with some changes in the scene, the servants are dismissed on the pretence of a message about the Duchess's letters. Quex is all admiration for Sophy. "Be off", he says kindly "go to bed, serve me how you please. Miss Fullgarney, upon my soul I — I humbly beg your pardon". And the curtain falls on Sophy's, "God bless you. You're a gentleman! I'll do what I can for you!"

The story of *The Gay Lord Quex* should end here. But after this bedroom scene, there is one more act in which nothing happens except that Muriel, abandoning her flirtation with Captain Bastling, accepts Quex, and Sophy returns to her man, the Bond Street Palmist.

The success of *The Gay Lord Quex* was in a large measure due to the scene in the Second Act and not to any other feature of the play. Expressing no view in particular, except the opposite of that in *The Profligate*, *The Gay Lord Quex* sketched a picture of the decadent society. Pinero drew a picture of the respectable and fashionable people and held it to ridicule for its follies. The sneer and irony matches well with the much advertised satire of his later contemporaries. This play studied marriage from a new point of view. There was little romance in the play, as it objectively dealt with the question of marriage in every-day life. *The Gay Lord Quex* was the only play of Pinero's in which he "rose once to the full possibilities of the comedy of manners", in which "the vivacious dialogue has the audacious savour of the eighteenth century. Like Congreve and Sheridan he is content to present a picture with a deft, ironic touch and without social or moral commentary".[1] Technically *The Gay Lord Quex* was perfect. It was produced in 1899 and Pinero did not write any other play till 1901.

Pinero's plays written after 1900 include a few good ones: *Iris, His House in Order, The Thunderbolt* and *Mid-Channel*. These plays establish Pinero's strong predilection for domestic themes, themes on the relation of husband and wife. They bore the unmistakable colour of Victorian outlook. *Iris* was about a weak woman, her indecision between a poor lover and a wealthy suitor. *His House in Order* was about the worries of Mrs. Jesson in her husband's household. It was wonderful for its craftsmanship and could hardly be improved upon. *The Thunderbolt* dealt with a man's will and the question of his property. *Mid-Channel* centred on the boredom in married life caused by age. Pinero continued writing even much farther. His last play was *The Enchanted Cottage* written in 1922.

Pinero's greatest merit was his excellent characterisation. His skill lay in the portrayal of men belonging to the upper-classes of society. His social comedies have reflected the life and manners of the upper-classes. In a conversation with William Archer, Pinero justified his predilection for the aristocracy: "I think you would find, if you tried to write drama, not only that wealth and leisure are more productive of dramatic complications than poverty and hard work, but that if you want to get a certain order of ideas expressed or questions discussed, you must go pretty well up in

---

[1] Sawyer: *op. cit.* p. 167

the social scale".[1] It was for his excellent portrayal of the aristocracy that his plays received favour from Sir John Hare who played the disreputable Lord Dangers, the wicked Duke of St. Olpherts and the Gay Lord Quex.

Besides the aristocracy and the upper-class people, Pinero introduced 'raissoneur', a character who advocated the conventional views: Cayley Drummle in *The Second Mrs. Tanqueray*, the Duke of St. Olpherts in *The Notorious Mrs. Ebbsmith*, Peter Mottram in *Mid-Channel*. These 'raissoneurs' acted as representatives of wisdom and the saner view of life.

A notable feature of Pinero's characterisation is the galaxy of women characters. His versatility in this respect is admirable. Agatha and Charlotte (*The Magistrate*) Georgiana Tidd (*Dandy Dick*) and Lady Castle Jordan (*The Amazons*) are all excellently drawn lively comical characters. Beryl, Paula, Agnes and Sophy established his superiority over his contemporaries in the wonderful felicity with which he drew feminine characters.

In the late nineteenth century dramas few female characters are so magnificently drawn as Paula and Agnes, despite the author's regard for Victorian traditions. Archer suspected Pinero of "holding views on to feminine nature in general."[2] It is true that but for his lack of courage to break the shackles of traditions, Pinero's would have been a bigger name than Shaw's. A point which shows a similarity with Ibsen's technique, unknowingly though, is Pinero's greater attention to women than to men. The oppressed soul appears in full tragic grandeur only in a female form. Renshaw, Aubrey, Lucas, Fraser and Quex look rather anaemic compared to the verve of their female counterparts. Ibsen also used female characters as vehicles for his new ideas.

One can hardly fail to notice the striking similarity which plays of Pinero bear to Restoration comedies in general. The same hankering after social status and the same lust of fashion which

---

[1] Archer: *Real Conversations*, p. 21, quoted by Sawyer, *op. cit.* pp. 160-61
[2] On *The Notorious Mrs. Ebbsmith*, p. 231 in James Agate — 'The English Dramatic Critics'

characterises people in the comedies of Congreve, Wycherley and Etherege reappear in Pinero. Of course the Restoration encouragement to fashion and foppery is unimaginable in the Victorian rule, and there is no unpunished flirtation. The ways are the same and the faults also, only they don't go unnoticed and uncriticised.

Victorian England had its own codes of conduct. In *The Times* Pinero showed the Egerton Bompass family on the lookout for an opportunity for stepping into the aristocracy. In *The Princess and the Butterfly* he reflected on the boredom of life, the monotony of middle age and sought escape in romance. Fashionable people taking to 'slumming' out of their ennui with luxurious life, women at cards, and fashionable upper-class women taking part in the women's emancipation movement with mock seriousness'— formed the themes of *The Hobby Horse, The Money Spinner* and *The Weaker Sex* respectively. Pinero's pictures of fashionable life were realistic in *The Times, The Benefit of the Doubt* and *The Gay Lord Quex*.

Pinero's picture of fashionable life as contrasted with that portrayed in Restoration comedies is a little severe and hence dull, because he never forgot the high place of virtue in both men and women. In Pinero's drama people even on suspicion of being reproachable are ostracized. Fraser prepares to go abroad for fear of the fuss his wife's conduct has created (*The Benefit of the Doubt*). Aubery and Paula settle at Higher Combe away from fashionable life as Paula is a woman with a questionable past (*The Second Mrs. Tanqueray*). The strictness with which Mrs. Grundy governed the morals of the people was great and it has an immense influence on dramatists. No such restriction existed in the Restoration period. In *The Times* when the Bompass couple discover that their son has married the landlady's daughter, their higher aspirations for his marriage end suddenly. Even then they plan to 'educate' the girl and plan the deceptive remarriage to achieve the semblence of a high-class wedding. In such a society where, "one's life seems to be made of parade and pretension, life is stifled."

Pinero published his plays. He had to think both of his readers as well as his spectators. For this he gave his dialogues, what he thought was, a literary flavour in *The Profligate*, *The Second Mrs. Tanqueray*, *The Notorious Mrs. Ebbsmith* and *The Gay Lord Quex*. His conscious effort to create such an effect resulted only in an artificial and stylized speech-making. Platitudes were uttered in the most maudlin way. Here is Renshaw in *The Profligate:*

> Supposing there is some chance of my regaining her. Regaining her! How dull sleeplessness makes me! How much could I regain of what I've lost! Why, 'she knows me'—nothing can ever undo that — 'she knows me'. Every day would be a dreary, hideous masquerade; every night a wakeful, torturing retrospect......

Paula Tanqueray replies to her husband in *The Second Mrs. Tanqueray*:

> You'll see me then, at last, with other people's eyes; you'll see me just as your daughter does now, as all wholesome folks see women like me. And I shall have no weapon to fight with — not one serviceable little bit of prettiness left me to defend myself with! A worn-out creature—broken up, very likely, sometime before I ought to be—my hair bright, my eyes dull, my body too thin or too short, my cheeks raddled and ruddled — a ghost or wreck, a caricature, a candle that gutters, call such an end what you like......

Even Agnes's reply to the Duke of St. Olpherts in *The Notorious Mrs. Ebbsmith* gives sufficient proof of the so-called literary quality of Pinero's plays. She says:

> The sufferers, the toilers; that great crowd of old and young—old and young stamped by excessive labour and privation all of one pattern— whose backs bend under burdens, whose bones ache and grow awry, whose skins, in youth and in age, are wrinkled and yellow, those from whom a fair share of the earth's space and of the light is withheld.........

On the stage Pinero was greatly applauded for these speeches which were delivered by the great actors of the day, John Hare, the actor of aristocratic roles, Forbes Robertson in *The Profligate* and Mrs. Patrick Campbell in *The Second Mrs. Tanqueray* and *The Notorious Mrs. Ebbsmith*. The published texts, particularly those cited above, do not create that impression of simplicity and ease which is the real pleasure of literature. Instead, they appear to be steeped in the traditions of the stage and are, at best, theatrical. This strained effort to be literary earned for it scornful comments such as "spurious literary quality",[1] "an attempt to reproduce that peculiar stage effect of intellectual dramas"[2] and "nothing but the lowest and most piteous kind of journalese."[3] It is a fact that in his endeavour to produce literary effect Pinero, on many occasions, over-exercised his pen. This is in no way a hindrance to the enjoyment of his plays as books. They are very original and interesting.

For brilliant characterisation and skilful play-construction Pinero was superb. He lacked 'vision' but he perfected the art of play-writing and touched upon themes which later were called 'advanced' and new. In his own way he pioneered a revolution that made "the revival of English drama—the work of Arthur Pinero."[4]

---

[1] Nicoll: *Late Nineteenth Century Drama* Vol.. I, p. 181
[2] *Shaw's Dramatic Criticism* p. 24
[3] *Around Theatres*, p. 289
[4] St. John Ervine: *The Theatre in My Time*, p. 203

Chapter V

Henry Arthur Jones

> "The first rule is not to write like Henry A. Jones, the second and third rules are the same."
>
> Oscar Wilde

> "Mr. Jones' technical skill is taken as a matter of course..."
>
> G. B. Shaw

Jones earned fame with the production of *A Clerical Error* on 16th October 1879. Earlier, his efforts to establish himself on the London stage had met with little success but, undeterred by failure, he put in all his experience of the theatre and literary talent into a comedy which made critics look at him with admiration.

A Clerical Error was only a humorous one-act play with a country vicar as the hero. Rev. Richard Capel, the guardian of religion and public morals develops a romantic fancy for his wardress Minnie and actually proposes to her. The pretty girl is in love with the Vicar's nephew. The embarrassment of the Vicar ends as he accepts the situation with humour. Jones did not attack the Vicar's profession. He only mixed irony and satire in the character of the Vicar. There was no touch of spirituality or severity in Jones' handling of a religious character on the stage.

A Clerical Error became an important play for bringing religion on to the stage. The seventies had in Cardinal Newman a leader of Church reforms. *Tracts of the Time* inaugurated a good deal of religious writing. John Hale White's *Autobiography* and the *Revolution in Tanners' Lane* brought out the corruption of the clergy. It was around this time that the Oxford Movement was gaining force and then there was Matthew Arnold so critical of the 'Philistinism' in people. Jones was aware of all these religious sentiments but was chained by his limitations as a dramatist, hence the comedy on clerical *amour d'affair* with the pretty war-dress.

Jones was aware of the varying demands of audiences and realised that the romantic playwright's lack of interest in the theatre-goer's needs must give way to a compromise between the necessity of a higher drama and popular taste. In the *News Review* of July 1891 he wrote that "a wise statesman does not attempt to make laws so far in advance of the moral and intellectual condition of the peoples—the playwright must not disclaim to be popular."

The Silver King (1882) showed well what Jones meant by this term 'popular'. In this play he exploits the dramatic possibilities of a guilty conscience. Wilfred Denver, a gambler, runs away believing he has murdered his wife's former suitor, Ware. The train carrying him is involved in an accident and destroyed, but his prayer, "O God, put back Thy Universe and give me yesterday", is answered. He is safe but his sense of self-accusation relentlessly persecutes him. He returns home to find his wife and children hard-pressed by Spider, the landlord. He learns the truth about the murder and his conscience is finally freed from the guilt that had been haunting him.

The Silver King was appreciated for its psychological and dramatic features. Wilfred Denver's mental torture was well brought out by Jones and despite his leaning towards enlarging the picture of villainy, too obvious contrasting of the good and bad, and the pervading sentimentality, *The Silver King* was a very unusual play. London stage in the eighties was catered to by playwrights who made capital of the public taste for 'sensational' themes. Jones exploited this general weakness for the 'sensational' and produced a play which earned Matthew Arnold's appreciation as "something new and highly praiseworthy."

Jones understood his responsibilities as a dramatist during a period of general decline in the drama. He showed a keen interest in the social significance of his profession and he was perhaps the first English dramatist among his contemporaries to have consciously made efforts to reconcile amusement with purpose. The English theatre was poor in original dramatic talent and the dearth of originality in writers was greatly felt. The visits of foreign troupes to London made the realisation of this want all the more acute. A touring company of the Comedie Francaise visited England for the first time in 1871 and was warmly welcomed. The company paid a second visit in 1879. The result of the visit of the touring company of the Comedie Francaise in 1879 was to reawaken the sense of responsibility of the country towards its theatre. The man who felt acutely about the poverty of English theatre was Matthew Arnold. In an article on 'The French Play in London', published in *The Nineteenth Century* Arnold observed the conditions and concluded: "The theatre is irresistible; organise the theatre."[1] Jones felt that it was high time for him to make his own plan. In his article 'The Theatre and the Mob' written for *The Nineteenth Century*, (September, 1883) Jones observed the conditions of drama and the enormous difference

---

[1] "......We are at the end of a period", he wrote "and have to deal with the facts and symptoms of a new period on which we are entering;...... what is certain is that a signal change is coming over us and that it has already made great progress......The attraction of the theatre begins to be felt again, after a long interval of insensibility, by the middle class also ......And in this condition of affairs I see the middle class beginning to arrive at the theatre again after its abstention of two centuries and more; arriving eager and curious, but a little bewildered. What are we to learn from the marvellous success and attractiveness of the performances at the Gaiety Theatre; and what is the consequence which it is right and rational for us to draw? Surely it is this: the theatre is irresistible; organise the theatre".

Quoted by Dickinson, *op. cit.* pp. 62-63

between the drama of art and purpose and that of popular amusement:

> It is a hybrid, and unwieldy Siamese twin, with two bodies. two heads, two minds, two dispositions, all of them, for the present, vitally connected. And of these two bodies, dramatic art is lean and pinched and starving, and has to drag about with it wherever it goes, its fat, puffy unwholesome, dropsical brother, popular amusement.[1]

Later in his lecture on 'The Renascence of English Drama' Jones claimed for the dramatist's freedom "to deal with every aspect of human life, religion and morals not excluded". By way of self-assertion Jones claimed to "have fought for the sanity and wholesomeness, for largeness and breadth of view......against the cramping and deadening influence of modern pessimistic realism, its narrowness, its littleness, its ugliness, its parochial aims". Jones realised that: "our great need is, then, for a school of plays of serious intention, plays that implicitly assert the value and dignity of human life, that it has great passions and great aims, and is full of meaning and importance"[2]. Thus while responding to Arnold's call for organizing the theatre, Jones took his first step to educate the mind of the public. He lectured, exercised the arts of persuasion and advertisement learned in the world of commerce. In his first two important plays *A Clerical Error* and *The Silver King*, Jones clearly showed the two most striking features of his future work. His plays can be classed in two groups: first, plays religious in theme and moral in tone; secondly, plays with melodramatic elements and of the comedy of the manners 'genre' with a distinct note of social criticism. Throughout his career. Jones alternated between these two forms but he could never entirely free his art from melodramatic proclivities. In the same year, 1884, Jones wrote *Saints and Sinners*, a play on the theme he wished to substitute for popular amusement.

The saint among the sinners is Fletcher, a non-conformist

---

[1] D. A. Jones: *The Life and Letters of Henry Arthur Jones*, pp. 78-79

[2] 'The Renascence of the English Drama'—a lecture delivered in 1884, published in 1894

minister, good and simple, who gives his all to the poor. His life is given to sermons, service and charity. He is at loggerheads with certain members of the dissenting congregation. Fletcher is a trustee for the property of some poor orphans and Hoggard, a speculator who is also one of the most devout attendants at the chapel, wishes to get Fletcher's signature on a contract which would ruin the latter completely. The minister refuses to sign. Hoggard, the speculator, and Prabble, the local chemist, vow vengeance on him. Letty, the daughter of the minister, has been seduced by a rascally captain, and has eloped with him to London. Fletcher brings her back to the holy precincts of the church. Nobody in the congregation knows of her sin except Hoggard. The defunct speculator and the bogus chemist are embodiments of the hypocrisy in the Victorian religion. Their purpose in attending the church is to secure victims for their trade. The church, to them, is like a fair where they meet people for business. As Prabble says to Fletcher "If I support your chapel, I expect you to get the congregation to support my shop".

The story ends here but the play does not. To achieve the happy ending in the last act, Letty's betrayer, the captain, gets killed in India, the rascally financier Hoggard goes bankrupt and is wanted by the police, Letty's character is completely redeemed and the good minister, after a few years of poverty is about to return to his fold at the express request of the old dissenting flock.

Saints and Sinners poses two important points for consideration: Jones' view on religion; and, the melodramatic leanings of his art. Jones' picture of the middle-class people in their concern for religion was based on his own observations. In a letter to Mr. James Waldo in 1924, Jones wrote: "The setting in my play (*Saints and Sinners*) was mainly that of my own early life in a small English dissenting community, and the view that I took of the English middle class life was that of Matthew Arnold. If you read his prose writings, you will note their influence on *Saints and Sinners*".[1]

---

[1] D. A. Jones, *op. cit.* pp. 26-27

A few years that he spent with his uncle at Gravesend gave him a good understanding of their ways. His uncle was the deacon of a Baptist chapel. Also, the picture of the middle class dissenting community, with Hoggard and Prabble as their representatives, tallies with the impressions of Elie Haevy, who writes of "the pastor of a non-conformist congregation, the walls of whose humble chapel confronted the Anglican church on the parcel of ground, which the tolerance of the great land-owner had permitted him to purchase, had no contact with the latter or with any of his circle......Too frequently he had no other resources save the generosity of his congregation on whom he was financially and morally dependent. He was confined to the narrow circle of small farmers and small shopkeepers who were members of his sect. Everyone else despised or disliked him, or at best regarded him with complete indifference".[1] In a society where the shopkeeper expected the minister to support his bogus shop because he supported the minister, there could be only hypocrisy, deceit and corruption. Mark Rutherford pictured the same society in *The Revolution in Tanners' Lane* where the clergy is corrupt and further corruptible by the pressure of the wealthy middle class.

Saints and Sinners is a mordant and effective criticism of the meannesses hiding under the facade of religious fervour. In sheer protest against this bogus devotion, Jones stayed away from the church and like Shaw, early in his life, harboured an antagonistic attitude towards such a religion. The picture of the congregation in *Saints and Sinners* offended the people and he was charged with blasphemy. He immediately explained his point of view. Jones wrote "...I should like it to be known that in *Saints and Sinners* I intended no offence to religious succeptibilities. At the same time I can see no reason why large fields of modern life should be closed to treatment on the stage merely because the truthful portraiture of them is unpalatable to the unco guid".[2]

---

[1] *A History of the English People in the Nineteenth Century*, vol. IV p. 387.

[2] Letter to the dramatic critics of *Daily News* on 29th September 1884- quoted by D. A. Jones, *op. cit.* p. 90

So, as Archer claimed, the originality of *Saints and Sinners* lay in "the picture of a poor dissenting minister tyrannised by the grasping and hypocritical tradesmen of his congregation."[1]

In its theme *Saints and Sinners* revealed some influence of Ibsen's *Pillars of Society*. Jones disclaimed any debt to Ibsen. He had, possibly, seen the solitary matinee performance of *Pillars of Society* in 1880, but recollected nothing of it when he came to write *Saints and Sinners*. Ibsen was the subject of many heated discussions in literary circles and Jones might have heard about him. The similarity of approach of Jones and Ibsen is significant as it is greatly to the former's credit that he thought and wrote as he did in 1884 when Ibsen was not as controversial as he later became after *A Doll's House* and *Ghosts* were performed in 1889.

Jones' candour in the portraiture of religious personages was part of his aim to enlarge the province of drama. He gave full expression to his ideas on the question of including the clergy in the *dramatis personnae* in his article, 'Religion and the Stage' in *The Nineteenth Century* (January, 1885).[2] *Saints and Sinners* illustrates well the dilemma in which Jones found himself, as a dramatist struggling helplessly against "the cheaper and coarser art of melodrama" and finding it indispensable for success on the stage. The play has a pure heroine, dark villain, sentimental pathos and a general division of characters on the basis of vice and virtue. Despite its apparent weaknesses, *Saints and Sinners* pleased Arnold and he wrote to Jones: "You have remarkably the art—so valuable in drama—of exalting interest and sustaining it."

---

[1] *Old Drama and the New*, p. 294.

[2] "It is for those who would deny to the dramatist the right to depict religious life on the stage, to show either that religion has become a quite unessential and useless portion of human life, and is effete and defunct and has no bearing upon character in England today, in which case the playwright can afford to treat it as the naturalist does an organ that has lapsed into a rudimentary state, or it is for them to show why religion should not occupy the same part in dramatist's scheme and view of human life as it is supposed to do in the outer world around him — shall we say a seventh......"

—'Religion and the Stage' in *Saints and Sinners*, p. 128.

Critics, impressed by his 'earnestness of purpose', were disappointed to find Jones writing pot-boilers. Jones' collaboration with Barrett produced three plays immediately after *Saints and Sinners*: *Hoodman Blind* (1885), *The Lord Harry* (1886), and *A Noble Vagabond* (1886). Two other worthless plays followed: *Heart of Hearts* (1887) and *Wealth* (1889).

In *The Middleman* (1889) Jones resuscitated some of his social awareness. It dealt with the struggles of Cyrus Blenkarn, a pottery maker, to discover the old method of glazing. His daughter has been ruined by Julian Chandler, son of his employer. Chandler crushes Blenkarn into dire misery and suffering. Blenkarn breaks his furniture to feed the furnace but all goes against him. The last act of the play finds him rich and happy, living in Chandler's old home with his daughter happily married to Julian.

In the character of Blenkarn Jones has to a great extent exploited the theatrical element in a human being's suffering under social and economic injustice. Characterisation lacks the subtlety of a psychological insight into the nature of things. Blenkarn is all—suffering and nobility. Chandler is cruelty, greed and injustice. But this basic black-and-white distinction is too fascile. Jones, in an effort to make Blenkarn psychologically more convicing, gives him, the fire of revenge damaging his erstwhile 'virtuous' appearance: "Show me some way to bring him to the dust! Give him and his dearest into my keeping! Make them clay in my hands so that I may shape and mould them as I choose and melt them like wax in the fire of my revenge!" This incongruity in the character and speech leaves Blenkarn a less powerful and impressive person than intended. Despite this weak characterisation *The Middleman* was appreciated by *The Times* of 28th August, 1889, as "by far the most original......and literary play of the year" and declared that the public had seen a psychological play without knowing it![1]

---

[1] Morjorie Northend: *Henry Arthur Jones and The Development of the Modern English Drama*, Review of English Studies, vol. 18, 1942, No. 72, pp. 454-55

The Middleman was a significant step towards plays like *Strife*. Jones' contribution to the development of the English problem play lay in having presaged the work of Shaw and Galsworthy. Jones tested the theatrical possibilities of such themes and later Shaw and Galsworthy found their path cleared of preliminary obstacles.

After writing a melodrama with a dash of social criticism in *The Middleman*, Jones returned to his favourite theme of religious hollowness. He agreed with William Hale White on the question of spiritual suffering and loneliness, expressed with telling effect by the latter in an account of his own life.

In his plays Jones dramatised these struggles. Earlier in *Saints and Sinners* he pictured the tragedy of a dissenting minister, now again found himself attracted by a similar theme. Jones' new play was *Judah* (1890). It was the story of a minister, Judah, who is ready to sacrifice his faith, his ecclesiastical disguise for the sake of love. The Earl of Asgarby is in trouble because his only daughter, Eve, is ill and may not be saved. Miss Dethic, a girl famous for curing patients by miracle, is called in. She actually fasts for a few days and then by some spiritual power cures patients. She has already cured some. Soon it is revealed that her fast is only a hoax and that she is secretly given food by her father. Professor Jopp, writer of *The Scientific Conception of Truth*, does not believy in this and arranges for a close guard on the girl to see that nobode gives her food. The minister, Judah Llewellyn, is in love with the girl. He also secretly keeps a vigil on the girl, and comes to know how her father gave her food. But his love for Miss Dethic closes his lips and he tells a lie on oath.

Judah : My oath — I have not brought Miss Dethic any food.
Jopp : Your oath — You have not seen her take any.
Judah : My oath — I have not seen her take any.

All this is due to Judah's love for Miss Dethic:

"......You have been the secret spring of all my power. When I speak to the people, it is your voice that speaks through me. Your love is a flame on my tongue. All the world is transfigured because you are in it......I love you, I love you!"

Lady Eve is cured of her illness. But the secret of Miss Dethic's power is discovered and she faces ruin. But Judah cannot leave her a sinner. Together they make a confession of their sin.

Vasthi:......I have deceived all who believed in me. I have no supernatural powers. It has been all a pretence — a falsehood from beginning to end......

Judah: "Stay! I have my share of the burden to bear". He makes the confession ...... "Then hear me, hear me, all of you! I lied! Take back my false oath! Let the truth return to my lips". He refuses to accept money for building a church and leaves saying, "We will build our new church with our lives, and its foundation shall be the truth."

Judah was a new thing for the Victorians. But for Jones it was only a matter-of-fact picture of the people. The opposition Judah has to face is not so much to his spiritual standpoints as it is for Popworthy's complaint that he was deeply infatuated with the ordinary Miss Dethic, whereas his own daughter, who did knit a pair of slippers for Judah was neglected as were other girls of the congregation. Popworthy's reason for removing Judah betrays the greed of the people for winning husbands for their daughters. Cases, where clergymen were removed for their unorthodox opinions, were not rare.[1] In having expressed the religious conditions of the hypocritical and smugly complacent Victorians, Jones incurred the hostility of critics.

Mark Rutherford was much pleased with *Judah*, and he wrote to Jones: "I cannot resist a very inarticulate expression of delight. About the 'moral' and 'aim' and all that I will say nothing because it goes without saying. What I enjoyed was the artful contrast between the love making of those two scientific people and that of Llewellyn and Vasthi. Such is the attraction of love against

---

[1] In 1849, the pugnacious Bishop of Exeter charged a clergyman named Gorham of heresy and wanted him to be removed. Of course he was retained, the Government having allowed Gorham liberty of free thinking. Earlier than Gorham's case, Dr. Hampden's appointment by Lord Russell to the See of Hereford was questioned. Elie Halevy: *A History of the English People in the Nineteenth Century, vol. IV*, pp. 355-58

the Ten Commandments. The exhibition of such a passion as that is surely the noblest of morals."[1] *Judah*, certainly, had a novelty: the infusion of human sentiments in religion. Whereas throughout the play no character talks of 'spirituality', religion forms a part and a way of living.

But in spite of his 'ideas', Jones never quite forgot the importance of commercial success. It was proved by the play following *Judah*. *The Dancing Girl* (1891) contained many popular ingredients of successful plays. Druisilla, a quakeress, comes to London, becomes mistress of the Duke of Guisebury and achieves popularity as a dancer. She is the source of his downfall. The Duke is the landlord of an island. In order to reduce the sufferings of the islanders, he proposes to construct a breakwater and forgets. The men embarking on an Arctic expedition are lost.[2] Druisilla suffers poetic justice in death. His good angel, Midge, the lame girl, is the source of his regeneration as Druisilla was of destruction and disintegration. Even the Arctic explorers return in the end to form a happy tableau.

Almost of similar nature was *The Crusaders* (1891). The social and moral consciousness of Jones perceived the absurdity of the reform movements. Behind an inconsequential story Jones succeeded in touching upon the fads of the people for reform. Cynthia Green-Slade's Reform Committee consists of members most unsuited for the job they have undertaken. In order to escape ennui Cynthia has taken to this new amusement. It may be worthwhile here, to recall Pinero's satire on 'slumming' in *Hobby Horse*

---

[1] *The Life and Letters of Henry Arthur Jones*, p. 110

[2] The Duke is deserted by Druisilla at a moment when he needs her most.
Guisebury: Don't throw me over, Druisilla. If you do, I don't know what will become of me......let's save what we can from the wreck.

Druisilla: No, my dear Val — no, no, no!

Guisebury: You refuse me?

Druisilla: I refuse you......I must have my London, my Paris, my theatre, my dancing, my public to worship me.

(1886). As Sawyer justly observes: *The Crusaders* is "a bitterly chronic, almost fantastic arraignment of the empty, fruitless, quixotic efforts of the classes to uplift the masses".[1] The spirit of *The Crusaders* continues in *The Bauble Shop*, which exposes the moral decreptitude of a prime minister, who introduces a bill on public morality, being himself guilty of it in his own life. He marries the girl he had seduced to appease the people against any violation of the rigid moral code.

Jones' genius appeared only in flashes. Occasionally he wrote a good play like *The Silver King*, *Saints and Sinners* and *Judah*, and then returned to the usual staple fare of cheap values, of melodramatic exhibitionism. He disappointed his critics when he wrote *The Tempter* (1893), a verse play about the devil who drew a fourteenth century prince from Lady Aris to Isobel, a nun. Isobel sins in transgressing the holy pledge and then stabs the prince after a quarrel. She herself commits suicide. The Priest at last declares that the evil is evanescent and that 'the unfathomed ocean of God's love' will do justice to the prince and Isobel.

In *The Masqueraders*, the play following *The Tempter*, Jones returned to social satire. Dulcie Larondie, the heroine, serves as a barmaid. At the inn, a kiss from her is auctioned and Sir Brice Skene wins the kiss as well as her. Sir Brice runs through all his fortune. Dulcie's former lover, Remon, aids her and wins her when gambling with Sir Brice. But he leaves Dulcie unstained and 'pure', as he starts off on a scientific expedition. The story is rather undramatic, but it shows Jones' felicity in dealing with light themes, when he is working without the encumbrances of an 'idea' or a 'plan.' He observed society in its varied aspects; the parvenus and prigs, discontented wives, idealists and reforms. Jones' flair for satire was greatly helped by the splendid gift for story telling and incisive dialogue. It gave to some portions of *The Masqueraders* a brilliance. In scenes of light comedy, specially the kiss-auction scene, Jones showed dramatic skill.

The same ease with which Jones worked out his story in *The Masqueraders*, is in evidence in *The Case of Rebellious Susan*

---

[1] *Comedy of Manners from Sheridan to Maugham, op. cit.* p. 170

1894). Lady Susan revolts against her unfaithful husband. She sails too close to the wind in an unfortunate flirtation in Egypt, but is ultimately reconciled to him, if only he would not remind her of her mistake. On this main theme of the absurdity of a futile attempt of Susan's rebellion, is tagged a second theme of Elaine Shrimpton's plans to form a new morality. The 'new woman' in Elaine fails to accelerate the progress of the new epoch. Her plans are foiled to great comic effect. The aggressive individualism of Lady Susan and ridiculous radicality of Elaine's views prove fruitless. Pinero had written a play on an almost similar theme. Free thinking women only toyed with ideas of emancipation from family bonds for sometime and then returned to their circles. Pinero's *The Weaker Sex* (1888) and W. S. Gilbert's *Princess Ida* (1884) showed how women had to accept their defeat and revealed to them the meaninglessness of such movements. Jones in *The Case of Rebellious Susan* attempted a play on the same theme. Jones thought that there was an immense future for women as wives and mothers and a very limited future for them in any other capacity. The conclusion of *The Case of Rebellious Susan* was predetermined and to the writer of *Breaking a Butterfly* Mrs. Susan's rebellion was interesting only in so far as it reflected on her childish effort to free herself from marital bonds. As a comedy showing the futility of such women emancipation movements, *The Case of Rebellious Susan* was successful.

Jones felt bitterly the need of castigating the thoughtless people in his next play, *The Triumph of the Philistines, and how Mr. Jorgan preserved the Morals of Market Pewbury under very trying Circumstances* (1895). The smug Mr. Jorgan, leader of the self-righteous people in the Market Pewbury, demands 'in the interest of morality' that the painting of Bacchante be destroyed. Mr. Jorgan privately yields to the wiles of a French model Sally Lebrune. When Mr. Jorgan's scapegoat prepares himself to face public opinion, he is told: "You're fighting the strongest force in English life—that black, bitter, stubborn Puritanism that you'll never change, my dear boy, till you've changed the climate of the country and the very bone and marrow of the English race." *The Triumph of the Philistines* was a mordant satire on philistinism.

Jones was content with the delineation of follies without offering a solution for the evils he mentions. *Saturday Review* justly praised *The Triumph of the Philistines* as an "unusual attack on the stage moralist: it is courageous, uncompromising, made with sharp weapons and left without the slightest attempt to run away at the end".[1]

The small provincial surroundings, hypocritical philistines, dominating public opinion, respectability covering gross baseness and immorality, remind one of Ibsen's attack on the pillars of society. Jones denied any influence of Ibsen and his immediate reaction to Ibsen's plays appeared in *Breaking a Butterfly* (1884), an English stage adaptation of *A Doll's House*. The heroine in Jones' play, Flossie, returns to the arms of her husband, instead of banging the door on her husband as Ibsen's Nora did. In *Breaking a Butterfly* he was aided by Henry Herman. Later on Jones regretted having written it. Jones declared that he was not influenced by Ibsen in his work and that the apparent similarity of outlook on certain social questions was only incidental. Jones was the most voluminous advocate of the new drama. This fact has been amply borne out by the evidence which plays like *Saints and Sinners* and *Judah* furnish. He wrote plays on advanced ideas, and social satire, and lectured with gusto on the need of a new drama.

In his next play, *Michael and his Lost Angel* (1896), Jones appeared with his 'serious style at its best'.[2] The choice of theme was prompted by the success of *Saints and Sinners* and *Judah*. In its story *Michael and his Lost Angel* is much like the previous plays. It is a story of a soul's degradation in the eyes of a congregation. In *Saints and Sinners*, the priestly hero fights against hypocrisy, and in *Judah* the hero, in love with a phony miracle-maker, finds the real meaning of life, in *Michael and his Lost Angel* the hero hopelessly struggles against love and passion. Michael Feversham, a scholar and a priest, compels his secretary's daughter

---

[1] Quoted by D. A. Jones, *op. cit.* p. 169
[2] Nicoll, *op. cit.* p. 168

Rose to make a public confession of her sin. Soon Michael commits that sin himself. Audrie Lesden is the woman who has donated large sums for the construction of the church and falls in love with Michael who retires to an island alone to atone for his sin. Audrie follows him there and they pass the night together. Under the strain of his own transgression Michael is tortured. Activities in the newly completed church begin with Michael's confession of his sin before the congregation:

"I have sinned as David sinned. I have broken the sanctity of the marriage vow. It is my just sentence to go forth from you, not as your guide, your leader, your priest, but as a broken sinner, humbled in the dust before the Heaven he has offended".

Michael leaves the church but has kept with him the red rose placed by Audrie. In the last act Michael falls in the arms of his dead Juliet. Audrie:

"Take me! I give my life, my will, my soul to you! Do what you please with me! I'll believe all, do all, suffer all, only, only persuade me that I shall meet her again!"

The hero, a priest, contrary to the dignity becoming his position, yields to passions too easily, and is too obviously a weakling at heart. But the play was not a religious play as much as a play of character—a psychological study. The changes that Michael undergoes in his love for Audrie have been depicted with keen interest. In these lines: 'Oh! give me back only one moment of the past, one look, one word from her—and then take all that remains of me and do what you like with it" Jones wanted to reproduce the effect of "O God! put back Thy Universe and give me yesterday' of *The Silver King*. In the earlier play the hero's psychological crisis was natural, but in *Michael and his Lost Angel* this is unaccountable. He declares in private that he is not sorry, in the congregation he speaks of his humiliation. Jones here seems to be governed by his tendency to exploit to the maximum the theatrical propensities of the theme, overlooking its dramatic convincingness. Besides an unconvincing and a too easy transformation, the play accommodates much of the picture-poser sensationalism, typically melodramatic. Leslie and Michael provide a beautiful character contrast on the stage and the play establishes the victory of love and such finer sentiments over fake religious barriers. The 'life-force', as Shaw later called it, knew no bounds and was uncontrollable.

The ease and mastery over plot which Jones displayed in *Michael and his Lost Angel* continued in his next play *The Rogue's Comedy* (1896). Bailey Prothero, a cheat, pretends to possess occult powers. Aided by his wife, he hoodwinks many people by telling them of their past and professing to know their future. His own son Lambert, ignorant of his parentage, is the source of his father's downfall and the truth about Prothero is revealed. In *The Rogue's Comedy* Jones proved the efficacy of his technical felicity when uncramped by ideas or philosophic purposes.

The same gay spirit continued in his next play *The Physician* (1897). Dr. Carey has caught "the disease of our time, of our society, of our civilization. Middle age. Disillusionment. My youth's gone. My beliefs are gone. I enjoy nothing. I believe in nothing." The disillusioned doctor is cured of his infatuation for a *femme fatal* by falling in love with the simple daughter of a country parson. She comes to seek the doctor's help in bringing her beloved back to life. Magnanimously the doctor conceals from her the fact that he loves her and that the patient is a drunkard. She perceives the truth and before the last curtain is dropped the doctor and Edna, the girl, are in each other's arms. The patient conveniently dies.

The Physician offered nothing unusual in characterisation. A doctor, a drunkard, a parson and a simple village maiden were all characters of popular plays. But it showed Jones' good humour. This good humour and his talent for comedy are conspicuous in his next play which by common judgment is his best comedy.

The Liars (1897) is an excellent play in the comedy of manners genre. Lady Jessica is engaged in a trifling flirtation with Falkner. The husband, Gilbert, is informed of this by his brother George.

Henry Arthur Jones

Lady Jessica and Falkner's plan to have a luncheon is foiled by an interesting complication of circumstances in which George and Lady Rosamond upset the plan. Lady Jessica is afraid to tell Gilbert that Falkner was with her. The whole neighbourhood is shown honeycombed with the falsehood in a brilliant scene.

Dolly : (to Lady Jessica) Very well, dear. I quite understand. After George went away you were so upset at his suspicions that you came back to town without any dinner. Did I stay and have the dinner?

Sir Christopher: No, no, I wouldn't go so far as that.

Dolly : But what did I do? I must have dined somewhere, didn't I? Not that I mind if I didn't dine anywhere. But won't it seem funny if I didn't dine somewhere?

Lady Jessica: Very well, then, where did I dine? Do tell me. I know I shall get into an awful muddle if I don't know. Where did I dine?

Falkner confesses his love for Lady Jessica to Gilbert. Sir Christopher is persuading him to go to Africa and to give up the affair. "Marriage may be disagreeable, it may be unprofitable, it may be ridiculous, but it is not as bad as that!" and "Take any of the other dozen alternatives and find yourself stranded in some shady role or corner, with the one solitary hope and ambition of somehow wriggling back into respectability". Falkner prepares himself for Africa and Lady Jessica is reconciled to her husband at a supper at the Savoy.

The Liars laid fair claims to be regarded as the best comedy of manners written by Jones. In *The Liars* there were no fulminations against lying and Jones was content to show the dangers of indiscreet flirtation and household intrigues. The scene where all are engaged in inventing falsehood is managed with the skill of a dramatic genius.

The dialogue is the finest here and at times takes on the refinement of a Congreve comedy. Dolly addresses Mrs. Crespin: "Oh, my dear, you don't expect me to remember all the things that are inconvenient to you. Besides, other people don't wrap up. Jessica is out on the river with absolutely nothing on her shoulders" and Mrs. Crespin replies: "Is it not a psychological fact that when our hearts reach a certain temperature our shoulders may be and often are, safely left bare?"

It was the brilliancy of the dialogue which led people to doubt Oscar Wilde's share in it. A notice in California said, "After his seclusion, Oscar Wilde pulled himself together and wrote one supreme masterpiece, *The Liars*.[1] *The Liars* was so fine in its texture, in dialogue, and in its situations that it came "very close to the gay insouciance, the banter and moral holiday of Restoration Comedy".[2] This success of *The Liars* assured Jones of his strength in plays of light satire and comedy. Whether Jones' greatness was due to these comedies of manners and satire or to the unsuccessful plays of ideas—the religious plays—is a question to be decided in the perspective of other contemporary dramatists. Yet it is clear that with his comedies Jones did his best to elevate the tradition of broad farce to high comedy.

The gaiety of attitude and freshness of approach which appeared in *The Liars* were missing in *The Lackey's Carnival* (1900), a comedy about domestic servants. The play reveals no aspect of Jones', greatness and is an insignificant play. *The Manoeuvres of Jane* (1898) was about relationships between children and their parents, and young women and their lovers. Individuals shine. Lord Bapchild and his entourage at Chancy Court promise the beginning of another comedy of manners but soon the play is reduced to husband hunting and hoodwinking of parents. Jane and Constancia, girls of a petulant and unruly type, are representatives of the new society. This play is half farce, half intrigue, a play of a mediocre standard. It was only a temporary phase in Jones'

---

[1] *The Life and Letters of Henry Arthur Jones, op. cit.* p. 187
[2] Sawyer, *op. cit.* p. 176

career as in his next play he reappeared with all his powers. His interest in contemporary incidents was keen. Jones perceived great dramatic merits in a trial. A Mrs. Osborne was accused by her friend of stealing jewellry. Mrs. Osborne had sued her for defamation. Sir Charles Russell was the defence counsel. Everything was going in favour of the defendant, when a jeweller produced damaging evidence. Russell cross-examined Mrs. Osborne and one statement of hers shook the whole defence. Russell discovered the truth: "Woman, you are lying". Jones used this sentence as the climax of the cross-examination scene in *Mrs. Dane's Defence*.

Mrs. Dane's Defence (1900) was based on this trial of Mrs. Osborne. Mrs. Dane is engaged to Sir Daniel's foster son, Lionel. News about the similarity between Mrs. Dane and one Miss Hindemarsh who had a scandal in Viene, reached the Carteret household. Sir Daniel cross-examines Mrs. Dane. She defends herself well when a vital fact slips involuntarily from her mouth:

Mrs. Dane	:	We had governesses.
Sir Daniel	:	We? You said you were an only child. Who's we?
Mrs. Dane	:	My cousin and I.

This new relationship leads to the climax:

Sir Daniel	:	Does Risby know who you are?
Mrs. Dane	:	What do you mean?
Sir Daniel	:	Does Risby know who you are?
Mrs. Dane	:	Yes, he knows I am Mrs. Dane.
Sir Daniel	:	The cousin of Felicia Hindemarsh.
Mrs. Dane	:	(after a pause) Yes.
Sir Daniel	:	You told Risby a mere acquaintance, that Felicia Hindemarsh was your cousin, and you didn't tell Lionel, you didn't tell me?
Mrs. Dane		I — I (she looks at him) I oh — I'll answer you no more. Believe what you please of me! I want no more of your help! Let me go!
Sir Daniel	:	(Stopping her) How much does Risby know?
Mrs. Dane	:	Don't I tell you she knows I am Mrs. Dane?

English Drama 1860-1900

> Sir Daniel : Woman, you are lying!
>
> Mrs. Dane : (flashes out at him) How dare you? How dare you? (stands confronting him).
>
> Sir Daniel : (Looking straight at her) I say you are lying! You are Felicia Hindemarsh.

No more hiding of the facts is possible and Mrs. Dane's true identity is discovered. The scene is magnificent and "a consummate example of Mr. Jones' gift of wringing the last drop of drama out of a situation".[1]

In the last act, Mrs. Dane quits Lionel without any fuss because Sir Daniel can't see a woman of her repute live within his household. The ineffective end of the play continues the worst traditions of the Victorian domestic play. The autocracy of Mrs. Grundy demanded its sacrifice. A fallen woman has no place in a respectable household. Jones, inspite of his 'ideas', only sailed with the wind and this fact detracts much from his claim to be a leader of the new drama. His deep rooted love of Victorian morality never allowed him to show light in the dark corridors.

Mrs. Dane's Defence was Jones' last play in the nineteenth century. He wrote for well over fifteen more years. His last play *The Pacifists* was written in 1917. Among the notable plays of 1900-17 period are *White Washing Julia* (1903), *The Hypocrites* (1906), *Dolly Reforming Herself* (1908) and *Mary Goes First* (1913).

A word about the technique of Jones' plays may be well worth adding here. Jones began his stage career with a series of melodramas and farcical comedies. The *Silver King* brought him success for the first time and he became known to a large audience. He wrote melodrama under necessity, as he said later. The influence of this training was that he could well work out his plans till the crescendo of events reached the pinnacle. The Victorian stage traditions required him to justify virtue and defeat vice. The last act was usually devoted to this 'prize distribution'; the audience would not feel happy without it. All the good comedies and other serious plays suffer from this defect. In *The Dancing*

---

[1] Archer, *op. cit.* p. 302

Girl, The Case of Rebellious Susan, Michael and his Lost Angel, The Liars, and *Mrs. Dane's Defence,* the interest of the audience and the readers is kept up wonderfully till the climax, but the perfunctory endings are the bane of Jones' plays as of the whole contemporary playwriting scene. As Mario Borsa observed about *Saints and Sinners:*

> The last act is useless ......destroys the whole impression of the work and betrays the heavy hand of the earlier author of melodrama......the real study of life, with Henry Arthur Jones, is always thrown overboard in this very way. Jones seems always tempted to smooth it down or else to patch it up somehow—to take off the hard angles and bring it all down to the same comfortable level. And this treatment often amounts to a defect. Between Jones and a high level of art this patchwork asserts its unwelcome presence.[1]

Almost all the plays of Jones are, right till the climax, examples of superb craftsmanship. In an answer to Archibald Handerson's questionnaire[2] Jones revealed a few significant points.

Q. 4 : Do you begin with a group of clearly defined characters, and let the situation develop from the conflict to the characters?

A. : (by Jones) : Character and situation in a play should jump together and be inseparable.

Q. 5 : In writing a play, do you begin from one central or dominant or controlling idea.

A. : (by Jones) : I do not start from 'ideas' or 'opinions'. I take the keenest interest in social matters, and I think I may claim to have studied them. But the dramatist's main business, and his great delight, is to paint men and women faithfully as he sees them — not to air his 'ideas' and 'opinions' but by their actions the dramatist must frame his characters in a story. So far as he uses the stage to exploit his 'ideas' and 'opinions' he is not a dramatist but a propagandist.

Q. 15 : Have you at any period of your career, altered your dramatic technique? Explain fully, why.

A. : (by Jones) : ......To get a footing on the English stage I had to write melodramas. The technique of melodrama is different

---

[1] *The English Stage of Today, op. cit.* p. 59
[2] 'Dramatic Technique — Revealed by Dramatists' — in *The Life and Letters of Henry Arthur Jones,* pp. 433-37.

> to some extent from the technique of comedy. But though the technique of playwriting changes, the main principles of dramatic construction remain the same — perhaps it would be more correct to say that the conventions rather than the technique of playwriting, change from time to time. I have not deliberately changed my technique, but, as I studied and practised playwriting, my technique became firmer and more assured......

Nothing more needs be added to these answers by Jones himself. In characterisation Jones shows a little mechanisation of figures. They are wonderful stage creatures but rather stagey and lifeless. His most moving characters, Fletcher, Judah and Michael can move an audience well, but it is difficult to find the like of them in life. This defect is not so grave and it is in no way meant to deny Jones that glory which he rightly deserves as one of the pioneers of the new dramatic movement in English in the late nineteenth century.

For a writer whose dramatic career extended for over fifty years, Jones displayed great imagination. His first written play was *The Golden Calf* (1869), and the first acted play was *It's Only Round the Corner* (1878). He wrote eighty-seven plays in all, of which twenty-three plays were never produced and acted. Fifty-two plays were written before 1900 and thirty-three plays in the twentieth century. By virtue of the subject matter of his plays and his sincere concern he helped bring about the rejuvenation of drama in England.

He found English drama languishing amid the musicals, spectacular shows and melodrama. He left it as one of the most respected arts flourishing and mature. He installed drama as a significant social force and an institution for social education.

Chapter VI

Henrik Ibsen and the Development of the Problem Play

> "......high dramatic art does mean Ibsen"
>
> G. B. Shaw

> About Ibsen the fuss "made the scandal, and, in the way of scandals they made the success, they made Ibsen."
>
> Raymond Williams

> "......the theatre he came to conquer......was neither so lacking in ideas nor so poor in its stagecraft as they suggest. Ideas and social criticism were already coming into the theatre......"
>
> J. B. Priestley

English drama in the 'eighteen nineties' was dominated by the Norwegian dramatist Henrik Ibsen. Already playwrights had been showing signs of Ibsen's influence in dramatic technique, and, more than that, in their approach to various social problems. If there were any real innovators in the late nineteenth-century drama, they were William Robertson in England and Henrik Ibsen in Norway. Robertson's *Caste* and Ibsen's *A Doll's House* ushered in a new era in English and European drama. The new turn given to English drama by Robertson received a powerful support from Henrik Ibsen whose plays appeared before the London audience: *A Doll's House* in 1889 and *Ghosts* and *Hedda Gabler* in 1891. The huge uproar of denunciation with which these plays, particularly *Ghosts*, were received showed the interest they had been able to arouse by the shocking novelty of their themes.

The advent of Ibsen on the English stage posed a question before the British theatre-goers as to whether they should accept or reject this new dramatist. Critics grouped themselves into two parties, fiercely opposed to each other. Clement Scott in *The Daily Telegraph* thundered and roared over the gross and putrid indecorum of these plays. He had no better word for *Ghosts* than 'an open drain.' Opposed to Scott was Bernard Shaw among critics and J. T. Grein among producers. While Grein staged *Ghosts* at the Independent Theatre, Shaw lectured on 'the quintessence of Ibsenism', and used all his rhetoric in persuading people to accept Ibsen in 'his own right to canonical rank as one of the major prophets of the modern Bible.[1] Two keenly opposed opinions on Ibsen's work earned for him and not for him only but the drama in general, the much needed attention of the theatre-goers. The fuss that was created "made the scandal, and, in the way of scandals they made the success, they made Ibsen".[2] One could go on adding that they made way for drama to claim a share in the serious consideration of those who cared for literature.

Ibsen's plays can be divided into four categories as done by Shaw in view of their importance to English drama. Plays that influenced the new dramatic movement in the nineties were only a few. Ibsen's 'apprenticeship' plays include *Catiline*, *Lady Inger of Ostraat*, *The Vikings at Helgeland* and *The Pretenders*. The second group consists of 'autobiographical' *Anti-Idealist* extravaganzas: *Brand*, *Peer Gynt*, and *Emperor and Galilean*. The third group of 'visionary' plays or 'Down Among the Dead Men' as Shaw calls them, include *The Master Builder*, *Little Eyolf*, *John Gabriel Borkman* and *When We Dead Awaken*.

Ibsen's reputation as the greatest dramatist of the nineteenth century rests on the fourth group of 'objective anti-idealist plays'. *The League of Youth*, *Pillars of Society*, *A Doll's House*,

---

[1] *Major Critical Essays*, p. 148

[2] Raymond Williams: *Drama: From Ibsen to Eliot*, p. 42

Ghosts and *An Enemy of the People*, are the best known of this group and the most important in view of the influence they apparently exercised on English dramatists.

The 'objective anti-idealist plays' were Ibsen's main contribution towards the growth of the 'problem play' in England. Their subject-matter offered a very realistic criticism of society. In these plays Ibsen criticised the bogus commercial political ideals and sham respectability. His greater emphasis on the importance of 'individualism' as against the vast majority of society gave him the distinguishing note. His targets of attack were the decadent institutions of marriage, degenerated morals and putrid and effete codes of public conduct. In these plays Ibsen, who scourged any bond that crushed individuality, emerged as the champion of individuals' rights.

In Ibsen's plays the most striking feature was his criticism of society. In his prose plays Ibsen openly attacked the views and weaknesses of the people. *The League of Youth* has for its hero, a demagogue who is ready to lick the boots of the conservatives while he flatters the ears of the mob. Ibsen attacked politics and politicians against the background of the provincial local 'conditions' as he found at Grimstad or in his native Skien. The hero, Stensgaard is an upstart with a great lust for power. What is important about *The League of Youth* is the directness with which Ibsen attacked certain false political ideals. In Ibsen the satirist, the distinctive feature is his irony for false ideals which men have created to govern their conduct. He ruthlessly exposed the preposterousness of such ideals whenever occasion permitted him. In *The League of Youth*, Ibsen had false political ideals in mind and the play is a forceful study of corruption of men by the spirit of party politics.

The Pillars of Society attacks sham respectability in the case of business magnate Karsten Bernick who is steeped in the mire of corruption, deceit and guilt. He jilts his first love and makes a scapegoat of his own brother-in-law. Bernick's conscience suffers a terrible change when he finds his own son facing death as a victim of his deeds. When the townfolk come to honour him the burden of deception becomes too heavy for him to carry. He confesses his guilt courageously before the people, like the Russian sinners. *The Pillars of Society*, thus proclaimed, are Truth and Freedom. The play is an ironical satire on the bogus upholders of these ideals in society and establishes Ibsen's reputation as a dramatist and social critic.

Ibsen's influence on contemporary English drama was overwhelming. Directly and indirectly his ideas and techniques seeped through the minds of dramatists. Henry Arthur Jones did not openly acknowledge the influence of Ibsen on his works yet in many of his plays he showed a clear awareness of the new atmosphere. The hollowness of social ideals which Ibsen presented in *The Pillars of Society* was also dramatised by Jones in *Saints and Sinners*. The world of mean and selfish interests hiding itself behind the mask of religious fervour was uncovered by Jones. Even in plays like *The Middleman* (1889) and *The Triumph of the Philistines* (1895) Jones took up the theme of capitalist exploitation and bogus self-righteousness. In his first play about capitalist exploitation *Widower's House*, Shaw wrote directly under the influence of Ibsen. *Mrs. Warren's Profession* also showed the source of prostitution. To Shaw the significance of Ibsen's plays lay in the latters's ruthless exposition of social weaknesses and thus the creation in theatre-goers of an awareness of their share in the social ills.

Ibsen in his prose plays tried to lay bare crimes committed by respectable people. He tried to show how far every citizen was responsible for any crime. *An Enemy of the People* attacked the commercial and political ideals of society. Vested interests in the township oppose Dr. Stockman who has discovered disease germs in the baths. They appear as Society, People, Democracy and Solid Liberal Majority. Even the Press refuses to publish the doctor's report. His voice is drowned in the uproar of the majority. Dr. Stockman declares that the 'minority is always right.' In his attack upon democracy and other social political ideals Ibsen agreed with Dr. Stockman who remains in the town to fight the pestilential foundations of its material prosperity to the end. In a letter to Brandes on January 3, 1882, Ibsen wrote: "It will never in any case, be possible for me to join a party which has the majority on its side......I must of necessity say: 'The minority is always right'...the minority which leads the van, and pushes on to the points which the majority has not yet reached. I mean: that man is right who has allied himself most closely with the future".[1]

Forces of individualism joining hands to work against corruption found supporters among contemporary English dramatists. Shaw's *Mrs. Warren's Profession* best shows this conflict between individualism and social forces. Vivie Warren cuts herself off from her own mother when she discovers the source of her income. Vivie settles down to work out her destiny alone, unaided by her family friends like Dr. Stockman. Jones striving as before to snatch the last drop of comedy out of all situations presented the absurdity of reform movements in *The Crusaders* (1891). Earlier Pinero in *Hobby Horse* had depicted the same theme. Of course there is a big difference between Shaw on the one hand, and Pinero and Jones on the other. Whereas Shaw was very seriously concerned about social questions which were raised by Ibsen, Jones and Pinero were interested in such problems as productive of dramatic effect. Shaw actively participated in activities of social regeneration. Jones took only theoretical interest. Whatever be the degree of their interest both Shaw and Jones showed an awareness of Ibsen's influence.

Ibsen was genuinely concerned with social questions but he was more fascinated by individuals. *The League of Youth* and *An Enemy of the People* showed the individual in relation to society. In two of his most powerful plays, *A Doll's House* and *Ghosts*, Ibsen tried to show the relationships of individuals against a social perspective.

The story of *A Doll's House* is too well known to be discussed at length. The idealist in this play is Nora's husband Torvald Helmer, a lawyer by profession, who has in him all the qualities of an ideal husband—he is respectable, honest, hard working and

---

[1] Quoted by Janko Larvin: *Ibsen*, p. 86

loving. All the bourgeois virtues are possessed by him. His love for Nora is part of his showmanship in his role of an ideal citizen. With no real understanding of his wife, he does not prize human values and the sacredness of the ideals of marriage, although he uses these ideals in defence of his attitude. He shirks from saving his wife for fear of social degradation.

Nora is shocked by Torvald's callous response in the moment of crisis. The ideal husband talks like the ideal citizen that he is to the world outside. In response to her husband's "No man sacrifices his honour even for one he loves," she says 'Millions of women have done so". This exchange is very significant as it shows the difference between a man's and a woman's point of view. Finding stark reality staring at her Nora has no illusions left. She leaves the house where she had lived only as a doll.

The Ibsen-enthusiasts persisted in regarding the slammed door as a symbol of women's emancipation, although Ibsen categorically denounced any such motive in his speech to the Norwegian Women's Rights League on May 26, 1898. Ibsen said that he wrote *A Doll's House* "...without any conscious thought of making propaganda. I have been more poet and less social philosopher than people generally seem inclined to believe......must disclaim the honour of having consciously worked for the Women's Rights Movement. I am not quite clear as to just what the Women's Rights Movement really is......My task has been the description of humanity."[1]

English playwrights thought women's emancipation to be the message of the play. In Pinero's *Notorious Mrs. Ebbsmith*, the heroine tries to live on equal terms with a male friend without any sex motive. Her efforts fail because it is not possible in a society ridden by the conventional notion of women's inferiority. In *The Case of Rebellious Susan* (1894), Jones showed how Lady Susan leaves her husband only to return after a little flirtation in Egypt. Jones' immediate reaction to *A Doll's House* appeared in his travesty of this play entitled *Breaking a Butterfly* (1883). Flossie, the English version of Nora, returns to her husband's arms after

---

[1] *Ibid.* p. 25

a little storm in the teacup. The husband remarks complacently: "Flossie was a child yesterday: today she is a woman". Jones later in his life wished he had not written it. Even in America the Polish actress Helena Modjeska appeared in *Thora* (1883), an oddly titled version of *A Doll's House*. In this play Thora towards the end of the play, changes her dress, 'discusses', but instead of banging the door, stays in the house with her husband and children, all in the name of religion and morality. *Thora* shows a general misreading of Ibsen's play and Jones alone could not be blamed for this. Shaw, possibly, was unaware of *Thora* when he wrote his appreciation of *A Doll's House*[1]. But *Breaking a Butterfly* shows the English misreading of Ibsen's meaning. Even Shaw who claimed to have understood the quintessence of Ibsenism could not successfully explain it. In *The Philanderer* and *You Never Can Tell*, Shaw tried to present what he thought was new woman. In *The Philanderer*[2], a topical comedy, Shaw made fun of the new woman.

Charteris : ......Grace, I have a question to put you as an advanced woman. Mind! as an advanced woman. Does Julia belong to me? Am I her owner — her master?

Grace : Certainly not. No woman is the property of a man. A woman belongs to herself and to nobody else!

Charteris : Quite right. Ibsen for ever!

A little later Charteris tells another woman with whom he had philandered earlier: "Did I not find out, before our friendship was a fortnight old, that all your advanced views were merely a fashion picked up and followed like any other fashion, without understanding or meaning a word of them?" The same can be said about Ibsen's supposed meaning in *A Doll's House*. Even in *You Never Can Tell* Shaw made Gloria believe in the existence of a sexless womanhood, as Pinero had done in *The Notorious Mrs. Ebbsmith*. Both the plays illustrate a misrepresentation of

---

[1] John Gassner: *Soundings in World Theatre*, p. 100
[2] *Plays Unpleasant*, Penguin Books

Ibsen's basic 'idea'. In their dramas, playwrights of the nineties failed to capture Ibsen's real spirit. This misreading was also due to a misunderstanding of the concept of liberation of women by the society. The Married Women's Property Act of 1882, extended by that of 1893, gave the married and unmarried women equal share in property. Two years after *A Doll's House* was performed in 1889, the Court of Appeal in the case Reg. versus Jackson,[1] (1891), ruled that a husband cannot forcefully keep his wife in his house—thus giving women also a feeling of freedom from marriage laws.

To the Victorians the striking point about *A Doll's House* was the act of a married woman's leaving her husband and children and denouncing the ideals of marriage, religion and society—ideals so dear to the Victorians. The truth about it was the discovery of slavery to such false ideals. Ibsen's aim was to probe into the ethical factors behind the laws which unite two people in marriage and that understanding of each other's person, that self-sacrificing urge on which depends the success and happiness of marriage.

A Doll's House, except for being a positive statement in favour of the rights of women, does not go beyond the usual intrigue plays of France: "It merely provides the reversal within the romantic framework. It is not a new dramatic standard; it is simply unromantic"[2]. It has its value as a problem play as it deals with a problem which immediately concerned the people of the nineteenth-century England. The nearest English approach to the meaning of *A Doll's House* was made by Shaw in *Candida* where the ideal husband Morell, basking in the glory of his respectability and honour outside, finds himself pitted against a poet, Marchbanks, in his claim for the love of his own wife. Candida reveals the truth of his position to Morell: "I should care very little for your sermons: mere phrases that you cheat yourself and others with every day", She ultimately gives herself to the weaker of the two—her husband. Nora, similarly, discovers the truth about her husband

---

[1] R. C. K. Ensor: *England 1870-1941*, p. 339

[2] Raymond Williams: *op. cit.* p. 68

which disillusions her about all ideals of love: "that I had been living here for eight years with a stranger and that I'd borne him three children."

Nora gives up Torvald in a moment of self-realisation.

Helmer : To leave your home — to leave your husband and your children! What do you suppose people would say to that?

Nora : It makes no difference. There is something I must do.

Helmer : It's inconceivable! Don't you realize you'd be betraying your most sacred duty?

Nora : What do you consider that to be?

Helmer : Your duty towards your husband and your children — I surely don't have to tell you that!

Nora : I've another duty just as sacred.

Helmer : Nonsense! What duty do you mean?

Nora : My duty towards myself.[1]

The core of Ibsen's philosophy is reached in Nora's retort to Helmer's statement "You have no understanding of the society we live in". She says "No, I haven't. But I am going to try and learn. I want to find out which of us is right, society or I".

To discover and realise one's individuality beneath the crushing burden of society is the real meaning of *A Doll's House*. Present marriage conditions are only one of the many such restrictions imposed by society on the individual.

To those who had suggested that Nora should have stayed with her husband, Ibsen answered with his next play, *Ghosts*. Mrs. Alving married a reprobate and repented. She had loved Pastor Manders and, after marriage when once she deserted her husband

---

[1] *Six Plays of Henrik Ibsen*
Newly translated, and with an Introduction by Eva La Gallienne. The Modern Library, New York; *A Doll's House, Ghosts, An Enemy of the People, Rosmersholm, Hedda-Gabler* and *The Master Builder*.
Texts referred to in this chapter are from this volume.

for Manders, the clergyman sent her back having successfully appealed to her conscience and religion—words which had no meaning for Nora. Mrs. Alving is shocked to see her son Oswald flirting with his maid Regina who is his own half-sister. Bitter disappointment shatters the life of Mrs. Alving. She is convinced that "we're all haunted in this world—not only by things we inherit from our parents but by the ghosts of innumerable old prejudices and beliefs, half forgotten cruelties and betrayals...... The whole world is haunted by these ghosts of the dead past."

When the truth finally dawns upon her, she tells Pastor Manders: "...you forced me to obey what you called my conscience and my duty; when you hailed as right and noble what my soul rebelled against as false and ugly. And one day I saw quite clearly that all that you stand for—all that you preach is artificial and dead—there's no life or truth in it".

The woman who throughout her life was taught nothing other than her duty is left alone watching the remorseless hand of duty draining the last dregs of hope out of her life. As Oswald sits crying for the sun in an incurably imbecile fashion the question remains whether Mrs. Alving will poison her son or not.

The question of inherited sex disease in *Ghosts* offended critics and audiences alike. Ibsen believed that marriage for external reasons, religious or moral, brings a Nemesis upon the offspring. Unwillingly Mrs. Alving obeys the commands of religion and social ethics. Nora also suffered because she failed to distinguish between social and private responsibilities. She forged her father's signature without thinking of the consequences, because to her this hardly had any seriousness. Pastor Manders is responsible for this atmosphere of deceit and 'lie in the soul'. He is a satirical portrait of an idealist who brings disaster where he himself could have been the saviour.

Ghosts develops the theme of self-realisation through the individual's awareness of his position in society. In *A Doll's House* and *Ghosts* Ibsen presented his own view on marriage and heredity "from one extreme position and then opposite, toying with dogmas but always forced into an undogmatic dualism".[1]

The atmosphere in *Ghosts* is suffused with a helpless resignation to the forces of nature and inheritance in a deeply realistic and symbolic manner and Ibsen uses the properties of a sentimental melodrama combining the advantages of expressionism and naturaralism. It is an objective picture of life's disintegrating process, and the relentlessness of the natural order which crushes the human beings. Even Nora and Dr. Rank in *A Doll's House* are only what they inherit from their parents. There is hardly any struggle against natural forces. Mrs. Alving, 'seeking significance in life within a deterministic order', fails to find any and becomes only "an agent of circumstances, and whether she does something or does not do it is of no consequence. Her effectiveness as an individual has been completely destroyed by those very forces she herself sought to master."[2] *Ghosts* in this sense suggests the defeat of the individual when pitted against the forces of nature and hence the play, as it wants in struggle, is pessimistic in tone.

Among the English dramatists, only Shaw tried to say something about this deterministic order of things in *You Never Can Tell*. Gloria, heroine of the play, tries her best to live up to the ideals of a woman above the ordinary class of females who subordinate themselves to male dominance. When her instincts wake up she feels herself helplessly in the grip of the very forces she was trying to control. The theory that the forces of nature are predetermined was well-known in England during the later part of the nineteenth century, where Darwin's Theory of Natural Selection was common knowledge.

Ibsen not only introduced and developed certain new themes that caught general attention; he also effected certain technical innovations. He began under the influence of Scribe, the most prominent dramatist before him, but soon his own dramatic genius began to assert itself and he evolved new points of technique

---

[1] Robert Brunstein: *The Theatre of Revolt*, p. 47
[2] Sverre Arestad: *Ibsen's Concept of Tragedy*, *P.M.L.A.* LXXIV, 1959, p. 291

which comprise plot construction and development; dialogues and language; presentation of ideas and setting. It is his dramatic form which constitutes the nucleus of his contribution to English drama.

In plot-construction Ibsen remains the master of the later nineteenth-century English dramatists. Specially in the prose plays we have referred to, the beginning corresponds to the fifth act of a Shakespearian drama. In *A Doll's House* and *Ghosts*, the action begins only after events, whose origins lie far back in the past, have come to a climax. The forgery Nora committed in the past to save her husband's life succeeded but the play begins only when she is caught in her own net. Similarly in *Ghosts* the main question was of Mrs. Alving's marriage with the man she derided. She was advised by her lover to undergo that lifelong suffering against the dictates of her own conscience. The result is that the son, sent away before he could scent his father's clandestine debaucheries, inherits the same habits. The play begins at this moment when all that remains is only the carrying out of the punishment nature has inflicted. Coupled with this technique of beginning at the climax is the retrospective method of unveiling the past of characters. Whereas characters pay for their mistakes made in the past it lends to plays "this dim atmosphere of something hidden, that fills the air and the rooms and gives the words an undertone of unavoidable fatality".[1] While this teachnique is useful to demonstrate Ibsen's faith in guilt retribution in a predeterministic order, it is nothing new, being actually as old as *Oedipus* and *Oedipus Rex*. Ibsen's skill lies in his masterly control of events and the gradual unravelling of the past.

Dialogues in Ibsen's plays are simple and realistic. Verse form which he used for his earlier plays was discarded in favour of prose. Replying to an actress, Ibsen expressed his opinion on this aspect of dramatic art: "Prologues, epilogues and all such things ought to be unconditionally banished from the stage. Dramatic art alone belongs there; and declamation is not dramatic art!"

---

[1] Francis Bull: *Ibsen: The Man and the Dramatist*, p. 12

He further expressed his opinion on the harm verse has done to drama as it "will scarcely be of any significance in the drama of the near future".[1] A real innovation of Ibsen, according to Shaw, was his introduction of scenes of serious discussion. In *A Doll's House* the scene where Nora and Torvald sit down for a discussion of problems, Ibsen made an "addition of a new movement, as musicians would say, to the dramatic form", and it was in this "that *A Doll's House* conquered Europe and founded a new school of dramatic art".[2] It is with great precision and directness that the point is presented before the audience. In the boldness with which Nora and Mrs. Alving denounce religion and society and their domestic duties lies the source of this "terrible art of sharp-shooting at the audience, trapping them, fencing with them, aiming always at the sorest spot in their conscience".[3]

Another distinguishing feature of Ibsen's technique is his effort to make each scene in his plays dramatically effective and, indedependent of 'scenes' as Pinero's and Jones' were. In this he developed the need and shape of play as an artistic creation, laying greater emphasis on the total effect rather than on the parts. Among critics and dramatists Ibsen's greatness is taken for granted on account of wide propagation by Shaw, Archer, and other enthusiastic admirers more than it is deduced from a careful observation of plots in his plays. To take the most criticised and appreciated of plays *A Doll's House* for appraisal of its technical novelty a few significant points may be noted. In *A Doll's House* the heroine is simple, pure and beloved wife of Torvald Helmer who, in his love for his wife and children has created an idyllic atmosphere of family happiness. This sentimental woman does

---

[1] Quoted by P. F. D. Tennant: *Ibsen's Dramatic Technique*, p. 52

[2] *Major Critical Essays*, p. 130. Shaw further observes "......the play in which there is no argument and no case no longer counts as serious drama... In the new plays, the drama arises through a conflict of unsettled ideals rather than through vulgar attachments, rapacities, generosities......and so forth to which no moral question is raised......", p. 139

[3] *Ibid.* p. 145

not look at legal forgery with any seriousness and signs for her father to get money for her ailing husband. Her forgery is discovered when their family happiness is at its height. Revealing a past secret at a critical moment may be part of Ibsen's art but it is also a stock-in-trade trick of the intrigue plays. Exchange of letters, threats of a villain, a secret lover, a sentimental heroine, oscillating temper of the husband, love, anger, protest and repentance, all in turn, are the usual features of popular plays which Ibsen was supposed to have left far behind. From this point of view *A Doll's House* is a perfect pastiche of scenes and tricks from French plays in vogue. But as we shall see a little later the greatness of *A Doll's House* lay somewhere other than in the novelty of theme.

The two significant features of Ibsen's plays, retrospective technique and realistic setting greatly influenced contemporary British dramatists. Shaw of all dramatists came nearest to Ibsen. In *Mrs. Warren's Profession* Shaw intelligently unfolds the past of Vivie's mother while expressing his own opinion on her life. But Shaw is more given to proselytising on this occasion than he is artistic. This retrospective narration of the past is done better in *You Never Can Tell* where the story of Mrs. Clandon's life with her husband is unfolded bit by bit. The naturalness which Ibsen imparts to his scene on such occasions is inimitable. Jones and Pinero only used this retrospective method sparingly. Mrs. Tanqueray's past is discussed by Aubrey himself. The confession scenes in Jones' plays are but remotely influenced by Ibsen.

The realism of Ibsen's plays appeared in Shaw's plays. Pinero and Jones kept away because of the limitations of their approach. Discussion, which Shaw so much appreciated in Ibsen, was well incorporated in a few of his early plays. Discussion scenes on capitalism and slum-landlordism in *Widower's Houses* and on causes of prostitution in *Mrs. Warren's Profession* were carefully planned and placed by Shaw. Here, as in many other points, the Ibsenites failed to capture the real spirit of his art. Whereas in *A Doll's House* and *Ghosts* the discussion followed naturally in the course of events and was part of the theme; in Shaw's plays it was evidently prearranged as a 'scene' and became a part of the technique.

As we have seen in the analysis of a few important prose plays and discussion of a few points, Ibsen's real greatness lay in his strikingly fresh approach to his subjects and a felicity of style which, without much novelty, was yet greatly original and impressive.

We may now note two important features of his plays which distinguish him from other dramatists: characterisation and themes. In technique and message Ibsen's plays were greatly ahead of their time. His greatness lay in inventing characters who very appropriately delivered their message to the audience and readers. From this point of view his female characters are more impressive and his grasp of female psychology wonderful. The fearless individualism of women impressed Ibsen most. Nora Helmer, Mrs. Alving, Hedda Gabler and Hilda Wangel are unforgettable creations. Ibsen was not a feminist but he understood their problems. In the first draft of *A Doll's House* he wrote: "There are two kinds of spiritual love, two kinds of conscience, a man's and—a very different—a woman's. They do not understand one another, but woman is judged in actual life according to the laws of man, as if she were not a woman but a man."[1] In the light of these observations the conduct of Nora and Mrs. Alving is justified. "Like Mrs. Aliving, Ibsen felt the puritan cloak constricting his throat, and knew how difficult it was to escape from one's ghosts."[2]

Ibsen's female characters considerably influenced British dramatists' concept of female characterisation. Even dramatists who did not openly acknowledge allegiance to Ibsen showed how deeply they were impressed by him. Pinero's Paula Tanqueray and Agnes were apparently modelled on Ibsen's women, although in their conception, vitiated by strident Victorian thinking on the subject.

The dramatist who was most impressed by Ibsen's women, however, was Shaw. Vivie, Candida, Gloria and Grace were all

---

[1] Martin Lamn: pp. 119-20
[2] *Ibid.*, pp. 120-121

drawn on the Ibsen model. The individualistic tendencies in Ibsen's female characters were reflected in Shaw's. Before the advent of Ibsen, English drama like English life, showed the dominance of men over women. After his appearance on the stage women characters gradually seemed to realise their latent powers and set themselves free of all the bondages of which Ibsen's plays complain so loudly. Shaw in his long preface to the published edition of *Mrs. Warren's Profession*, echoed Ibsen's ideas on the question of dual morality.

Male characters in Ibsen's plays are comparatively weak. They represent in most cases the shortcomings of society. Bernick in *The Pillars of Society* represents the corrupt business executive enthused only with profiteering. Torvald Helmer has in him all the hollowness which external respectability of position in society produces in a man. Pastor Manders is one of the many who stifle the spirit of love for obligations to society. Dr. Stockman, alone among heroes of Ibsen's prose plays, tries to fight a battle against the evils of society. Ibsen's male characters are thus mere embodiments of types in society who act and speak not for their genuine impulses as human creatures but under the stress of social conventions of the times. Their passions, desires and ambitions are all guided by their desire to conform to the established social values. Their personalities do not evolve from within but are shaped by stress from outside. But his women are different. They are creatures of genuine and natural, human and particularly feminine passions. They think their feelings are shared and responded to bytheir male counterparts, which when the truth dawns upon them, is the source of their rebellion. It lends psychological depth and human interest to them. His men are devoid of any depth.

This characteristic contrast between male and female characters seems to have passed on as a legacy to Shaw and others. Pinero and Jones showed no change. Shaw alone in his *Plays Unpleasant* tried to write after the Ibsen fashion. *Widower's House* and *Mrs. Warren's Profession* had no dominant male character. In both these plays the role of social forces has been so overwhelming that characters act more like puppets than as individuals possessed of a will of their own. Sartorious and Trench in *Widower's Houses* are both involved in capitalist intrigue. *The Philanderer* also has no outstanding male figures. Conflict in *Mrs. Warren's Profession* is divided between the mother and the daughter. Following Ibsen, contemporary English dramatists improved on women characters and not on male ones.

A significant point about Ibsen's characters noted by Robert Brunstein is that : " Ibsen's drama is the product of this ambivalence, precariously balanced between the author's involvement and detachment...the rebellious and the controlled...a double level in which a drama of ideas coexists with a drama of action......."[1] The drama of ideas emanates from Ibsen's idealism and the drama of action from the objective framework of the plot. This sometimes leads to a conflict between the two. When the 'ideas' clash with 'action' there is a little ambiguity on the surface, as for example in *A Doll's House* and *Ghosts* Nora and Mrs. Alving lead a life in total contrast with the ideas they hold. Their intellectual existence comes into conflict with their existence on the stage and apparently it weakens the image Ibsen has been trying to forge throughout the play. This subtle distinction between the intellectual and objective existence works imperceptibly and even a critic like Shaw, who claimed to have comprehended the quintessence of Ibsenism, failed to grasp it. In *Mrs. Warren's Profession* and the earlier *Widower's Houses* Shaw tried to create a similar 'dual' personality by combining the oppressor and the oppressed into one.

To Shaw there was a sharp distinction between Ibsen's 'idealism' and 'realism'. He thought that the 'objective Anti-Idealist' plays of Ibsen were great. In fact the 'idealism' that Shaw derided in *The Master Builder*, *Little Eyolf* and *John Gabriel Borkman* never entirely left Ibsen and reappeared in the individual's quest for self-realisation in *A Doll's House* and *Ghosts*. Nora is not only seeking freedom from effete institutions like marriage and religion but she

---

[1]*Op. cit.* p. 48

is in search of a greater ideal—love of one's own ideals—marriage and religion are only external hindrances she must get over.

In the play she puts on this ambivalence because of Ibsen's lack of adjustment between idealism and objective realism.

The second important point about Ibsen is the greatness of his themes. He showed considerable boldness in expressing the basic revolt by an individual's inner-self against society. He endeavoured to scrutinize old decadent ideas, dead values which haunt us like ghosts. But he never sought to accomplish this by forcing his thoughts and ideas through his characters. Ideas are not imposed upon characters; instead they are embodied in the very texture of their being and when they issue from them they sound temperamentally natural and psychologically true. Two recurring themes in his plays are: the supreme importance of the individual personality; and, love as the redeeming and atoning power in the world.

Of these two themes, the one which contributed to the development of drama in England is his insistence on individual freedom, freedom from false ideals which society imposes on men in the name of religion, marriage, duty and respectability. On compromise between individuality and these ideals depended success in life. Victorian drama adopted the same pattern. This was the guiding factor in Pinero and Jones. Mrs. Grundy was the ubiquitous and all powerful deity presiding over affairs of mankind. Ibsen knew no compromise. Dr. Stockman in *An Enemy of the People* maintains: "The strongest man in the world is he who stands alone". Regeneration of individuals is Ibsen's fundamental creed without which all attempts to regenerate society must fail. It was the realisation of their slavery to others that lead Nora and Mrs. Alving to rebel against their state. False ideals of marriage ruin both Nora and Mrs. Alving.

The second dominant theme in Ibsen's drama, love, is according to him the connecting link among individuals. The tragedies of Nora and Mrs. Alving happen because of the absence of this factor in their relations with their respective husbands and physical relationship is no supplement for love. *Ghosts* repudiates ideals of marriage and love. Another aspect of this theme is the supremacy of women in Ibsen. The reason probably is that love is a more imperious passion in women than in men. It pervades and permeates their whole being and so they cannot surrender their individual self to social conventions as easily as men can. Men first surrender to women and then exploit them to keep themselves in conformity with social conventions. Naturally when a woman realises that she is the victim of exploitation, she revolts both against her exploiters and against the conventions which demand exploitation. Women embody nearly all the redeeming virtues: decency, truth, love, reason and energy. Actually Ibsen saw women as a great redeeming force in society in which men were too busy with the world to think of any redemption. To Victorians this assertion of superiority of women over men was startling. With the advent of Ibsen the status and psychology of women changed and men also realised their position. Ibsen's ideas came at the right moment. The social and economic emancipation transformed the entire pattern of old established traditions. Shaw echoed Ibsen in *Major Critical Essays* when he said that "our society, being dominated by men, came to regard women not as an end in herself like Man, but solely as a means of ministering to his appetite".[1] Shaw suggested that unless "woman repudiates her womanliness, her duty to her husband, to her children, to society, to the law, and every one but herself, she cannot emancipate herself."[2] This meant that even love should be stripped of its romantic halo and be recognised and represented as the creative urge in woman, a view which Shaw fully developed in *Man and Superman*: "Vitality in woman is a blind fury of creation. She sacrifices herself to it; do you think she will hesitate to sacrifice you?"

The influence of Ibsen penetrated deep into the texture of English drama and was to a considerable extent responsible for the change in theme, characterisation and technique. Besides Ibsen's

---

[1] *op. cit.* pp. 36-37

[2] *Ibid.* p. 40

influence there started a new movement which came to be known as Naturalism. It freed the convention-ridden stage from old tricks and aimed at a clearer and more photographic representation of life on the stage. Naturalism was a reaction against the intrigue play.

Naturalism was "an increasing closeness to objective facts; special techniques for their reproduction; an empirical outlook...... a candid account of the world about us......to present a slice of life instead of a carefully constructed plot—a technique, that is, which keeps us close to the raw flesh of life itself; and it adopts a particular form of empiricism—a philosophy of scientific determinism based on facts of heredity and environment".[1] Zola was the most successful exponent of this sort of Naturalism. He proposed, in literature, to enfranchise the masses, the toilers—all those sufferers and sinners hitherto deemed unworthy of notice. Recoiling from the dreamy idealisations of romance, Zola offered painful spectacles of wretchedness and crime, of brutish love and bestial lives. The main emphasis was on truth and a candid presentation of life. Naturalism as Eric Bentley observes, laid great stress on environment, and on crime and disease as the result of social and pathological conditions. Influence of Darwin's theory of evolution was seen in the new conception of society as full of struggle and competition. Biological equality of sexes was the new feature.

Naturalism must be distinguished from realism as during the eighties and the nineties these two tendencies combined to give birth to a new trend in dramatic literature. Naturalism is a dramatic convention which demands an exact portrayal of life on the stage, without the interference of the author who might give events a different interpretation. Naturalism does not mean realism. Realism is concerned with the technique of presentation. It demands correctness of stage properties and does not depend on theme which may be fantastic, hence the realism of Charles Kean's Shakespearian productions. Naturalism brought changes

---

[1] Eric Bentley: *The Modern Theatre*, p. 4

Henrik Ibsen and the Development of the Problem Play

in the concept of characterisation and dialogue which now had to convey the various 'inner' changes in the minds of people in the play. It gave a fresh intensity to the whole approach to dramatic writing. Naturalistic drama grew more subjective, in that it dealt with the individual's response to various social and ethical issues. In the nineties realism as it emanated from Robertson and naturalism as derived from the French dramatists combined to make 'realistic naturalism'. Ibsen, while emphasising the ordinary details of life in the naturalistic fashion, insisted on realism on the stage.

A detailed account of the naturalist writers may be beyond our scope, yet a brief mention must be made of a few representative writers from the European countries to show their points of view. Important names in this context are of Hauptmann, Sundermann and Strindberg.

Gerhart Hauptmann presented in *Before Sunrise* a very realistic and revolting picture of the bestial atmosphere in the family of Krause, a debauchee, who has two daughters. Hauptmann portrays Helene as a psychologically tortured girl, who suffers for her father and is deserted by her lover, to end in a tragic suicide. Sundermann shows greater concern for the conflicts between the old and the new ideals, bourgeois interests and the narrow outlook of provincial society. Hauptmann and Sundermann contributed a grimness to the dramatic portrayal of family life and the suffering people. They gave a psychological depth and convincingness to such pictures without which they would be but melodramas of a sentimental kind.

August Strindberg, in his preface to *Lady Julie* (1880), complained of the existing dramatic conditions where "we have not got the new form for the new contents, and the new wine has burst the old bottles". Strindberg was against the creation of 'type' characters. He felt that this "should be challenged by naturalists who know the richness of the soul-complex and recognize that 'vice' has a reverse side very much like virtue." He proclaimed that his characters, 'souls' as he called them, were "conglomerations from past and present stages of civilization".[1] Strindberg distinguished naturalism from realism as an art concerned with the sensational. "The true, the great naturalism seeks out those points in life where the greatest conflicts occur. It loves to see what is not to be seen every day......let us have a theatre where we can be shocked by what is horrible, where we can laugh at what is laughable, where we can use life without shrinking back in horror if what has hitherto lain veiled behind theological or esthetic preconceptions be revealed to us".[2]

In *Lady Julie* Strindberg demonstrated his new conception of the complex character and the biological warfare between the sexes irrespectve of class and creed. The 'aristocratic' and haughty heroine, Julie, proves herself to be a real 'slave' to physical passions. Her suicide in the end proves the great power of sexual instincts over temporary considerations of honour, pride and class.

Heredity and determinism were attacked by the naturalists. Ibsen's *A Doll's House* and *Ghosts* in this sense, were his nearest approach to naturalistic ideals. Nora inherits her father's carelessness, whereas Dr. Rank is suffering from a hereditary disease. Oswald's tragedy also emanates from the legacy his father has left him. *A Doll's House* and *Ghosts* are both tragedies of the naturalist order and show the destructive effect of heredity and environment. Naturalism and social realism combined to give shape to an entirely new form in playwriting which was to a great extent picked up by Shaw alone in England. Yet any search for an example of a naturalist play from the English playwrights of this time is futile as they were very slow in responding even to Ibsen. Naturalism influenced the contemporary English drama as a trend which was more talked about than practised.

Ibsen and Strindberg created the new drama. It was difficult to understand at first what Ibsen meant to convey. Only Shaw made a little effort to break through the barriers set by the Victo-

---

[1] *Preface to Lady Julie* translated by C. D. Locock: in *International Modern Plays*, pp. 8-9

[2] Quoted in Chandler: *Aspects of Modern Drama*, p. 33

rian morality and ethics. Gilbert, Pinero and Jones could never revolt openly and courageously against social conventions. Individuals, in Ibsen and Strindberg hate and break bonds of mediocrity, complacency, cowardice, hypocrisy and like obstacles. Characters in Pinero and Jones run away from the filth in society and make no efforts to rid the people of it. Ibsen directed all his energies and attention towards it. In Strindberg there is a constant search for the new as the old values are attacked vehemently by the new searching spirit. Ibsen and Strindberg put all their ideals to test in their play and tried to forge a new future.

The new drama in England, thus, came to be fashioned out of such attitudes. Ibsen led a new movement of revolt against worn-out traditions. Strindberg opened out new dimensions in a 'soul'. This quest of the 'new' was tested as a 'problem' in a play, a question that was to be settled in a way not attempted earlier by Pinero and Jones. The new influences worked together to formulate the kind of drama generally known as the 'Problem Play'. The term was coined by Sydney Grundy for satirising the intellectual drama of the nineties which, he believed, was 'marching to its doom' in the hands of 'a coterie of enthusiastic eccentrics'.[1] The term 'Problem Play' was used for "the new realistic and intellectual drama that developed in Europe in the later half of the nineteenth century especially for the English variety".[2] The term was used for dramas which deal "with certain conditions in society which cause trouble" and analyses "the opposition between social custom and the law, or between custom and justice".[3] Its main aim was to differentiate the new drama written under the influence of Ibsen and the naturalists from melodramas, farces and other French adaptations.

The problem play was an experiment in the art of drama and it derived its force from its contempt of false romantic ideals and

---

[1] S. Grundy: 'Marching to Our Doom' in *The Theatre* (1896), pp. 196-200

[2] Martin Ellehauge: *The Initial Stages in the Development of the English Problem Play*, Englische Studien, vol. 66, p. 373

[3] Donald Stuart Clive: *The Development of Dramatic Art*, p. 530

mere commercial ventures. Supporters of this new genre claimed that they sought to rescue drama from the highly degraded condition to which it had sunk under the weight of the popular conception which regarded theatre as a source of entertainment alone. According to Scribe, the inventor of the '*piece bien faite*', people go to the theatre not for instruction or correction but relaxation and amusement. In this new form of play people were generally disappointed. Even plays which do not strictly belong to this group and which hardly touched upon a 'problem' like *The Second Mrs. Tanqueray* had aroused an uproar. John Hare declined to stage it and Alexander was also doubtful of its success and whether 'the public would stand it'. Charles Wyndham doubted if *The Case of Rebellious Susan* could ever be staged. In these circumstances Ibsen and Shaw joined hands to alter conditions of drama in England. Writers directed their efforts to showing the public the real face of social diseases and weaknesses. No sugar coating of the pills was required and the Problem Play came into existence amid cries of general denunciation.

The main opposition to the problem play came from the seekers of entertainment in the theatre. Even great dramatists like Yeats and Synge opposed the idea of theatre ushering in reform of any kind. Synge held: "Drama, like the symphony, does not teach or prove anything" (Preface to *The Tinker's Wedding*). All opposition to the problem play was crushed by Shaw who sincerely believed in the new role of the theatre as an instrument of social reform. Of course the fear of Synge and others that "analysts with their problems and teachers with their systems are soon as old-fashioned as the pharmacopeia" proved true, for any problem was likely to become outdated. In days when women were struggling for social position, Ibsen's *A Doll's House* appeared great. It loses half its importance today when no such problem faces women. But the Problem Play was only a reaction to the popular forms of drama then in vogue. The play that was written to wake people from idle day-dreaming and extravagant complacency had to show them the hard realities of the world around them. The Problem Play was sometimes identified with frank propaganda due mainly to Shaw who favoured free serious discussion over social questions in plays and who himself spared no occasion for advocating the problem play. In the extraordinary social and intellectual ferment of the *fin du siecle* the problem play emerged as an offshoot of that new energy which sought expression in all quarters.

The Problem Play dealt with some important social problems seriously. It come to advocate the rights of individuals against overwhelming social forces. It also gave equality to women and aimed at ending the dual code of morality for men and women. Questions of economic and social importance were taken up. Shaw's plays were the first full length Problem Plays, evidently dedicated to the task of removing certain evils from society. Dramatists came to realize the potentiality of drama as a great social regenerating force. At first it met with great, and in some cases violent, opposition from critics but gradually members of the audience and critics alike began to accept the fact that they could no longer look upon drama as a means of entertainment alone and that to give drama its deserved importance it was necessary to uplift it from the doldrums of melodramtic and farcical writings.

The dramatist who propagated the cause of the Problem Play at the risk of his own career was Bernard Shaw. The eighteen nineties were very significant in the development of English drama as two great factors worked together simultaneously: the growing importance of serious drama, the problem play; and, Bernard Shaw, as he was no less than any other foreign influence.

Chapter VII

George Bernard Shaw

"I only wanted to share with Ibsen the triumphant amusement of startling all but the strongest headed of the London theatre critics......"

G. B. S.

"My stage tricks and suspenses and thrills and jests are the ones in vogue when I was a boy."

G B. S.

"*Widowers' Houses* marked the 'beginning of a new epoch' in drama"

Allardyce Nicoll

With the advent of Ibsen on the English stage a great change appeared in English drama. The man who best understood the new changes and most effectively expressed them through his creative and critical works was George Benard Shaw, the well-known dramatic critic of *The Saturday Review*. The devastating wrath with which Shaw assailed his contemporary dramatists and the enthusiastic appreciation with which he recommended Ibsen had made him a noted figure. These were preambles to his first play *Widower's Houses* which marked a significant break from the English drama of the eighties.

From the biographical side we need recall to our minds only his Irish birth in a period of national struggle, the drunkenness of his father producing misery at home from which his mother sought refuge in music, and the boy George Bernard's experience of poverty which nurtured his fighting spirit, a crusader's zeal against social inequality and injustice.

At an age when the young Gilbert and Pinero regularly visited the theatre, Shaw was struggling hard to free himself of the falsehoods of life, and developing that diff dence and roughness which later became his chief defence. Here his dissastisfaction with the existing organisation of life received further impetus from his complete failure as a novelist intensifying his poverty, his listening to Henry George and his reading of Karl Marx, introduction to the Fabian Society, and finally the miserable and ignominious failure of the Trafalgar square demonstration on 13th November 1887, which disillusioned him in the efficacy of Fabian tactics.

In London Shaw studied economic problems and literature together. Along with *Das Capital*, he studied the orchestral score of Wagner's 'Tristan and Isolde'. In the British museum he met William Archer who got him the job of reviewing plays for the *Pall Mall Gazette*, then edited by W. T. Stead. In the following years he served on various journals and wrote criticism for *The World* and *The Star*. His music criticism appeared under the name of Carno de Bassetto. In 1891 Shaw lectured on the 'Quintessence of Ibsenism', his first step toward ushering in a new era in contemporary drama. Shaw did not merely recommend Ibsen's views on religion, on idealism, on emancipation of women and the new dramatic technique to his contemporary dramatists but he also imbibed all these Ibsenite features for use in his plays. In fact Shaw's exegisis of Ibsenism was indirectly a statement of his own views on various social issues and drama in general.

In 1892 when J.T. Grein needed a play to continue his programme at the Independent Theatre, he sought Shaw's help. The latter soon completed a fragment of an earlier play and offered it for production . *Widower's Houses* met with a very cold reception at the hands of critics who unanimously denounced it as a mere pamphlet. Shaw's frankness about the evils of capitalism and his impassioned concern for the poverty-stricken people were thought outrageous. His enthusiasm for socialism increased his bitterness. He failed to realise that what is good for the pulpit or the platform is not necessarily good for the stage. Shaw dealt with the capitalists not as a dramatist but as a socialist and this was the cause of opposition from the critics.

Blanche, daughter of Sartorious, is first engaged to Trench. Cokane, the latter's friend, has something to say about it: "Moral, but not a moralist. If you are going to get money with your wife, doesn't it concern your family to know how that money was made?" Cokane is the author's mouthpiece. Human interest now gives way to discussion of economics. *The Star* called *Widower's Houses* "an exposition in dialogue of New Economics". And another journal *Black and White* thought it was "a discussion with open doors, of the pros and cons of slum landlordism". The audience entirely unprepared for such an attack. was shocked.

Characters in *Widower's Houses* share the author's point of view and have their importance in the play only as part of the general background of slums and poverty. Sartorious, Trench, Blanche and Lickcheese have their share in the general unhappy conditions. The callous indifference to the sufferings of the poor in the rich class and their greed for more money are responsible for the degradation of the poor, the whole system has now become so gigantic that Trench, realising his helplessness against it, compromises with it. It was the hypocrisy of the whole social system which provoked Shaw to unveil it and show vice its own face under the pleasant appearance of generous scheme and construction which aimed at exploitation rather than general welfare.

In the Preface to the play he attributed it to his observation of poverty which defaced his sense of beauty and, as in the case of Dickens, the stamp of misery, squalor and corruption never left his mind entirely. Shaw succeeded in ventilating the problem but proved his lack of playcraft. The play is an exposition of the evils of capitalism without any dramatic event. It has no conflict in it and no human interest at all. Trench accepts the system without any effort to free himself of it and reacts in a lifeless, mechanical fashion which makes the mere realisation of corruption an aim in itself rather than finding ways out of it. The reason for this seems to be the lesson the Fabians had learnt from the Bloody Sunday demonstrations. It was enough at this stage that people be brought to a realisation of their share in the injustice and wrong prevailing in society. The self-glorification of Trench suffers a setback at the realisation of his own share in the capitalist system and he is disillusioned of his righteousness and idealism.

For the general condemnation of its ruthless exposure of false idealism and pretensions, *Widower's Houses* matched *Ghosts* which two years earlier had aroused a similar reaction. In a theatre which still throve on Pinero and Jones, *Widower's Houses* in 1892 clearly marked the beginning of a new kind of drama in England.

Widower's Houses was followed by *The Philanderer* which aimed at dramatizing "the grotesque sexual compacts made between men and women under marriage laws which represented to some of us a political necessity (especially for other people), to some a divine ordinance, to some a romantic ideal, to some a domestic profession for women, and to some that worst of blundering abominations, an institution which society has outgrown but not modified, and which 'advanced' individuals are therefore forced to evade".[1]

The 'advanced' individuals in the play are Grace Tranfield, Leonard Charteris and Julia. Charteris exhibits his advanced thinking by philandering with both the ladies. *The Philanderer* is a satire on the outmoded character of marriage as an institution and a farce on the prevalent Ibsenite women and other similar 'advanced' notions. Marriage may be an outmoded institution but the answer to it is not philandering as 'advanced' individuals in the play seem to think. Despite an occasional mention of Ibsen's name, *The Philanderer* offers only a well-worn love triangle. Grace shows some knowledge of Shavian principles, of the economic slavery involved in marriage. She loves Charteris but refuses to marry as it will give him too much advantage over her: "No woman is the property of a man. A woman belongs to herself and to nobody else". *The Philanderer* shows Shaw's failure to capture the essence of plays like *A Doll's House*. The force of personality

---

[1] Prefaces, p. 694

which is the essence of characters in Ibsen is wanting in Shaw. The three main characters, Julia, Grace and Charteris, are lifeless. At best, Shaw shows the conflict between a few Ibsen-mongers and those too old for a change. *The Philanderer*, thus, shows Shaw's essential error, of dramatising a false sense of womens' emancipation and ridicule of marriage as a hopless institution and an attempt to show that he was the first in England at grasping the contemporary trends in drama of which Ibsen was the new master.

The Philanderer shows his progress over *Widower's Houses* in technique. While the Ibsentites clash among themselves, there is a well-knit subplot from which, as in Shakespearian comedies, emanates the best humour of the play. The frustration of Dr. Paramore at finding that the disease he discovered really did not exist is a fling at the imaginary entities and too subtle schemes and projects in the scientific world, the prototype of which is to be found in Swift.

In his Preface to *Three Plays for Puritans* Shaw declared his intention to write serious drama on the lines of a 'genuinely scientific natural history'. The way he does it in *The Philanderer* is by depicting the conflict between passion and reason which lends the story a little dramatic interest. Charteris rejects Julia as 'intellectually incompatible', but eventually makes a genuine acknowledgement of the emotional debt he owes her, thus forsaking fake intellectual superiority over her. Another moment of dramatic tension follows when Grace asks Charteris: "Oh Leonard, does your happiness really depend on me?" Charteris: (tenderly) "Absolutely". (She beams with delight. A sudden convulsion comes to him at the slight: he records, dropping her hands enjoining) "Ah no; why should I lie to you? My happiness depends upon nobody but myself. I can do without you; the struggle between the Philosopher and the Man is fearful, Grace." This conflict between passion and reason figured prominently in a later play *You Never Can Tell*.

While in *Widower's Houses* Shaw used to advantage his knowledge of the socialist system gathered at the Fabian Society, in

The Philanderer he uses his own personal experiences. The scene of the quarrel between Grace and Julia is based on a similar quarrel between Mrs. Patterson, Shaw's first seducer, and Florence Farr, his second love. Shaw's extreme physical communion with women produced in him a 'celestial flood of emotion and exaltation of existence'. as a prestate of "what may one day be the normal state of being for mankind in intellectual ecstasy".[1] This experience of the overwhelming passion Shaw tried hard to subdue and in so doing "revealed in his own dissociated sensibility the philosophic dissociation caused by the ideological break-up of the world."[2]

The Philanderer was a tentative satire on people's fake intellectual fads. Characters in the play are lifeless and at best, stagey. Shaw's attempt to dramatize his own personal experiences was too crude and a clear failure as it lacked interest and art.

In matters of art and technique *Mrs. Warren's Profession* was a much more mature play and shows at best some of Shaw's powers as a dramatist. In this as in *Widower's Houses* the people are held responsible for evils in society. Shaw's chief concern is to show that "prostitution is caused, not by female depravity and moral licentiousness, but simply by underpaying, undervaluing and overworking women so shamefully that the poorest of them are forced to resort to prostitution to keep body and soul together."[3]

Mrs. Warren's Profession is a play about a woman with a past, but she is not a candidate for the high society like Mrs. Tanqueray. She at present owns a chain of brothels on the Continent. The person pitted against Mrs. Warren is her own daughter, who appreciates her mother's heroic struggle with circumstances and, for a moment, is overwhelmed by the story of Mrs. Warren's suffering. But she soon realizes her folly and decides to live alone. Technically, *Mrs. Warren's Profession* achieves dramatic conflict through the complexity of its theme and the economic and the

---

[1] Hesketh Pearson: *Bernard Shaw*: *His Life and Personality*, p. 121

[2] John G. Demaray, : *Bernard Shaw and C. E. M. Joad*: *The Adventures of two Puritans in their search for God*, PMLA, June, 1963

[3] Prefaces, p. 219

emotional aspects of its plot. Instead of being a direct hit at prostitution in the manner of a Fabian socialist, the play gathers dramatic interest through a domestic scene between mother and daughter. Also, the question of emancipation of women and capitalistic exhibition has been dealt with without overburdening the plot.

Shaw's portrait of the capitalist exploiter shows a little confusion as Mrs. Warren the capitalist, is no less a victim of the same system. Vivie, the force in opposition, belongs to neither of the two classes. The opposition does not come from the individualist or the sufferer but from a different source. Vivie as a pure virgin is set against 'the impurity of capitalism in general'. This results in the reversion to, as Alick West observes, "the bourgeois ideology of individual on the one hand and society on the other from which he was trying to free himself".[1] In the emptiness of Vivie's concept of self-possession, the impracticability of her ideals, Shaw has projected himself, renouncing his faith in intellectual life as opposed to middle-class respectability. The weakened reality of her character is an index of Shaw's lack of faith in bourgeois ideology of individualism and rationalism. Shaw's ideological convictions had not quite settled down.

Dramatic conflict in *Mrs. Warren's Profession* depends on the net of tense emotional quandry in which the mother and daughter are temporarily caught together. In the key scene in Act II which recalls a similar situation in Pinero's *The Second Mrs. Tanequeray*, Mrs. Warren and Vivie discuss their position and points of view. Paula Tanqueray was defeated by circumstances. Mrs. Warren does not yield to hard times and finds a way out: "The only way for a women to provide for herself decently is for her to be good to some man that can afford to be good to her." This is the basic difference between Pinero and Shaw that, whereas the essentially Victorian nature of the former checked any progressive move of his characters, the latter realised the power of independent judgement. Naturally whereas Pinero failed by a narrow margin in leading

---

[1] *A Good Man Fallen Among Fabians*, p. 64

a new dramatic movement, Shaw grabbed the opportunity and made capital of it.

In *Ghosts* Mrs. Alving's suffering resulted from her staying with a husband she did not love. Nora in *A Doll's House* meets unhappiness because of her conformity to the ideals of domestic life. In a moment of self-realisation she quits the household. A similar realisation comes to Mrs. Warren also and she does what she thinks proper. Instead of wearying herself out by 'scrubbing the floor for one and six pence a day and nothing to Look forward to but the workhouse infirmary', she takes up the profession of her sister Lizzy.

Shaw for the first time shows confidence in the forces of individualism but his tentativeness weakens the character of Vivie She at one stage (Act II) is converted to her mother's point of view but, when being accused of 'attitudnizing sentimentally' by Frank she shifts her ground and returns to her former self. This makes her character unconvincing as an individualist. Shaw sketched Vivie's character in a manner which departs from the conventional one of young heroines motivated by ideals of love instead of logic.

Vivie as an advanced and intellectual character lacks the power of psychological conviction. Ellean, in Pinero's play, conforms to her prudishness throughout the play but Vivie's mind is undecided, unsure of the next step. She has really more of a Victorian prudish attitude than Shaw suspected. Whether or not Pinero is an 'advanced' dramatist, his characters are psychologically convincing. The lack of "the higher dramatic gift of sympathy with character of the power of seeing the world from the point of view of others instead of merely describing or judging them from one's own point of view in terms of the conventional systems of morals,"[1] which Shaw pointed out in Pinero, is his own defect upto this stage of playwriting.

Apart from Vivie, Mrs. Warren, herself a self-willed woman, is nerveless in conception. In the Acts II and III of the play Shaw

---
[1] *Shaw's Dramatic Criticism* Selected by John F. Matthews, p. 23

has assigned to her long, sententious and highly stylized speeches with which she harangues Vivie on questions of her suffering. It betrays Shaw's penchant for writing 'parts' for star actresses. Mrs. Warren resorts to the stock-in-trade gimmick of appealing to the audience by talking of the mother-and-daughter relationship. When she fails to use reason she falls back on sentiment. It is to be recalled that in 1893 when Shaw wrote *Mrs. Warren's Profession*, Pinero's *The Second Mrs. Tanqueray* was running to full houses. Shaw's conception of the Mrs. Warren and Vivie relationship in Act III is indebted to Paula and Ellen in Pinero's play. Pinero's *The Weaker Sex* (1888) also placed mother and daughter in a tense dramatic situation in the last Act. In bringing Crofts as a possible candidate for Vivie's hand, refused by both mother and daughter, Shaw has shown his weakness in the construction of tense dramatic scenes. It betrays his indebtedness to Pinero, and his lack of dramatic skill.

Placing the mother and daughter opposite each other is only one part of the dramatic conflict. In the other we find an auction of the daughter. Frank offers his love for Vivie as his claim and is dismissed by the mother. "Your love's a pretty cheap commodity, my lad. If you have no means of keeping a wife, that settles it. You can't have Vivie". The other claimant is Crofts—Capitalist: "......a baronet isn't to be picked up every day. No other man in my position would put up with you for a mother-in-law. Why shouldn't she marry me?" He is refused by Vivie. A similar scene of auction of a lady for love and position was developed to a greater effect in *Candida*. Pinero in *Lady Bountiful* has the hero, Denis, refused by the heroine as mere love was not enough for a lady's hand. Here it must be noted how well Shaw recognized the best features of other playwrights' and boldly used them as his own. In his attempt to put in tenseness and suspense in the conflict between the captialist and the individualist as proposed in Act I, Shaw, soon turns it as one revolving around domestic conflict of sentiment between mother and daughter. He even suggested incest in the Frank and Vivie relationship. Frank is supposedly the son of Rev. Samuel Gardner, Mrs. Warren's former lover, and thus a half-brother to Vivie. These tricks of the popular stage hardly do honour to the 'advanced' and intellectual playwright and the devotee of Ibsen that Shaw professed to be.

Thus in the building up of dramatic tension in the play Shaw shows no originality. *Mrs. Warren's Profession* even as a study of contrasting characters is unconvincing. Samuel Gardner, drawn apparently in imitation of Paster Manders (*Ghosts*), is the most impressive. He collapses helplessly into his chair when Mrs. Warren defiantly asks him to give his reasons for being unwilling to marry off Frank to Vivie and is only able to mutter: "you know very well that I could not tell anyone the reason." This is a characteristically Shavian indictment of the real character of the clergy. When George Crofts describes his principles to Vivie: "Honour between man and man; fidelity between man and woman; and no cant about this religion or that religion, but an honest belief that things are making for good on the whole." Vivie interrupts him, "A power, not ourselves, that makes for righteousness, eh?"[1] Vivie here agrees with Shaw in denouncing religion with a sneer. She believes in the force of individuality and her mind does not accept an 'all controlling power' of God.

Widower's Houses, *The Philanderer* and *Mrs. Warren's Profession* were published as *Plays Unpleasant* taking into consideration the reaction they had on the audience. *Plays Unpleasant* were followed by *Pleasant Plays*, as the serious and sardonic outlook changed into a comic vision of life. This change was much needed to avoid a repetition of the dismal commercial failure of *Plays Unpleasant*. Only *Widower's Houses* was staged for a few performances at the Independent Theatre in 1892. The other two plays were thought indecent for public performances by the Lord Chamberlain. Also, the vogue of Ibsen had subsided by 1893 and Shaw only wanted to share "with Ibsen the triumphant amusement of startling, all but the strongest headed of the London

---

[1] The phrase, 'A power, not ourselves, that makes for righteousness,' has been borrowed from Matthew Arnold's *Literature and Dogma* (p. 32) where he speaks of God in similar terms.

theatre critics clean out of the practice of their profession".[1] Surely Shaw imitated Ibsen so far as his plays brought around discussion among critics. Now onward he realised that Ibsen was redundant hence he decided to change his way. *Pleasant Plays* first showed the 'romantic side' and then the light of realism revealed the absurdity of idealism, bringing disillusionment in its wake. The first of these *Pleasant Plays*, *Arms and the Man* illustrates the new changes effected in the technique of playwriting. The first of these was the replacement of direct experience by indirect narration. In *Arms and the Man* Shaw strips war of its heroism and romantic glamour: "idealism, which is only a flattering name for romance in politics and morals, is as obvious to me as romance in ethics or religion".[2] The title of the play was taken from Dryden's translation of Virgil's *Aeneid* with an unmistakable ironic twist.[3]

From the very beginning Shaw mingles irony and satire in order to sweep off romance, as 'the great heresy'[4] from art and life. The romantic heroine is shocked to learn from a refugee in her room that "nine soldiers out of ten are born fools". In his creation of a 'chocolate cream soldier' Shaw has shattered the glory of a warrior. Another war hero believes: "Soldiering is the coward's art of attacking mercilessly when you are strong and keeping out of harm's way when you are weak." What to Beerbohm appears as a 'rich fantastic streak'[5] in Shaw's new outlook on romantic hero-worship owes much to Gilbert's heavy dragoons (*Patience*).

The satire on romantic idealism had a mixed reception. A. W. Walkley in *The Speaker* praised the witty dialogues and the whimsicality of incidents and the "ironic humour to get out of the spectacle of a number of people hypocritically pretending or naively failing to act upto ideals which Mr. Gilbert and his people

---

[1] Prefaces, 'The Author's Apology to Mrs. Warren's Profession', p. 220

[2] Prefaces, p. 702

[3] Virgil's *arma Virumque cand* rendered as 'Arms and the Man I Sing.' Unlike Virgil Shaw does not praise the soldier and his arms.

[4] Prefaces, p. 700

[5] Beerbohm: *Around Theatres*, p. 493

hold to be valid".[1] There were a few critics who thought it to be an attack on Britain's "bravery; an apparent satire upon a nation (Britain) chiefly known to the world for her gallant struggle against tyranny and opposition," (*The News* 23rd April 1894). *Arms and the Man* was not an attack on England, just as *The Mikado* was no attack on Japan. In it Shaw wanted to show the absurdity of popular romantic notions. He made it "a serious play—a play to cry over if you could only have helped laughing",[2] but the audience did not take it seriously and thought it was an extravaganza. Shaw was himself responsible for this as he filled the play with light hearted banter, whimsicality and humour.

Realism appears in the character of Louka, the maid-servant, who refused to marry Nicola in a vein of irony: "Sell your manhood for 30 levas and buy me for 10". This is in reply to his offer of 10 levas if she was nice to him. Sergius marries Louka despite all opposition.

In *Arms and the Man*, as in *The Philanderer*, Shaw has modelled his characters on living human beings known to him. Sidney Webb and Cunningham Graham served as models for Bluntchli and Sergius respectively. This dependance on life was both an advantage and a hurdle to Shaw's work.

The theme of *Plays Pleasant* is one of conflict between romanticism and realism but also appears to be a conflict between passion and reason. In *You Never Can Tell*, Shaw tells the story of a mother belonging to a group of Radical Progressives and her daughter opposed to her mother in the violence of her emotions. Earlier in *The Philanderer*, Shaw depicted internal conflict between reason and passion resulting in the ultimate victory of Life-force. Valentine, the dentist, in no time at all, completely demolishes Gloria's intellectual attitudinzing and she curiously and helplessly surrenders herself to her real nature:

Valentine : Ah. I wonder! It's a curiously helpless sensation, isn't it?

---

[1] PMLA, 1959, p. 472
[2] *Bernard Shaw and Ellen Terry: Correspondence*, p. 66

English Drama 1860-1900

> Gloria   : (Rebelling against the word) Helpless ?
>
> Valentine: : Yes, helpless. As if Nature, after letting us belong to ourselves and do what we judged right and reasonable for all these years, were suddenly lifting her great hand to take us — her two little children — by the scruffs of our little necks, and use us, inspite of ourselves, for her own purposes, in her own way.

Thus the intellectual rationalism fades away in the face of the life-force of realism.

Life-force wins one more battle, both mother and father are reconciled to each other after a long forced separation. Mrs. Clandon is "a veteran of the old Guard of the Women's Rights Movement which had for its Bible, John Stuart Mill's treatise on the Subjection of women...passion in her is humanitarian rather than human." Crompton the father, is an authoritarian, and claims the love of his children as a matter of right. Both realise the meaninglessness of their 'ideals', renounce their pretensions and accept what they need—love.

Shaw's picture of conversion from intellectual pretensions to the realisation of the biological needs of love and passion, owes much to Pinero's *The Weaker Sex* (1889). Pinero's women agitators realise their folly and limitations. Lady Vivash also realises her mistake in having rejected her lover in her capriciousness. Mrs. Boyle Chewton, leader of women agitators and Lady Vivash give up their intellectual and cynical views about family life. Shaw makes Mrs. Clandon realise that the 'anti-love' lesson of Women's Rights Movement is useless. Her daughter discovers that her education has been incomplete as she was taught to ignore the needs of the body. In *The Notorious Mrs. Ebbsmith* Pinero again attempts a similar theme. Agnes realises the preposterousness of her intellectual socialist doctrines and the secret of Lucas' seeking her company. It is her companionship and love rather than her ideas that draw Lucas to her. The 'gown' she puts on showed how well it suited her; in fact better than her 'attitudinizings'. Pinero uses the gown as a symbol and on stage depicts this coversion better than Shaw who shows it through valentine's laughter as he breaks through

Gloria's defence. In Shaw there is little of the sentimentality which pervaded Pinero's plays; Shaw is repeating many good features of Pinero's plays in trying to establish his superiority over his contemporary.

In *The Man of Destiny* Shaw dramatised a fictitious episode in the life of Napoleon. The dramatic interest centres on the two principal characters, Napoleon and the unnamed lady, who are engaged in a duel of wits over a private letter which the latter has managed to steal from Napoleon's dispatches. Napoleon is shown in a realistic light shorn of the glamour of war. The letter in which his wife compromises brings the two characters together. Napoleon's harangue on the English Character is a famous purple patch: "There is nothing so bad or so good that you will not find an Englishman doing it; but you will never find an Englishman in the wrong. He does everything on principle." The voice of Shaw is unmistakable in these words of Napoleon: "When he wants a thing, he never tells himself that he wants it. He waits patiently, until there comes into his mind, no one knows how, a burning conviction that it is his moral and religious duty to conquer those who have got the thing he wants. Then he becomes irresistible ..and takes the market as a reward from heaven." *The Man of Destiny* only shows Shaw's struggle to find a place on the popular stage. It was written for Sir Henry Irving and Ellen Terry who refused it. It had not even the novelty of technique as Walter Lislie's *The Love Test* (1873) and Gilbert's *Comedy and Tragedy* which were two earlier attempts at presenting two important characters on the stage and limiting dramatic conflict only to them.

The play in which Shaw shows considerable maturity in technique and characterisation is *Candida*. In the theme of the traditional triangle of love, Shaw has infused a new spirit. The complacent and self-satisfied husband, Morell, has his self-esteem shaken to the roots by his wife's lover, the poet Eugene, "a shy youth of eighteen, slight, effiminate", with a "haunted, tormented expression". *Candida* is a marvellous combination of dramatic situation, suspense, sympathetic and truly human characterisation, with dialogue and social criticism that is driven home to various sections of the audience. In selecting a domestic theme Shaw betrayed his realisation of the fact that mere propaganda is not art. *Candida* is a landmark in the development of his dramatic art unhampered by criticism of moral and social ethics. His penchant for social satire is here artfully combined with the story of a careless husband and an impetuous lover.

As a domestic story *Candida* dramatizes the failure of a husband to understand his own wife. Morell, the preacher of sermons, takes for granted his wife's affection. His complacency in this sphere is shattered to find a young man of nineteen as a possible rival. He weakly surrenders himself to the mercy of his wife: "You are my wife, my mother, my sister: you are the sum of all loving care to me". To Eugene she is only a beautiful lady belonging to "the world where the marble floors are washed by the rain and dried by the sun". The realism of the husband is too strong for the poetic fancy of Eugene. To Morell, a happy married life is "a foretaste of Heaven" on earth and, "in a happy marriage like ours, there is something very sacred in the return of the wife to her home". Morell, who has such ideal conceptions of marriage, is in fact a parasite on his wife's work and has unwittingly reduced Candida's life to drudgery. Shaw thus shocked his playgoers by showing the reality of such external family happiness. *Candida* in its theme owes an apparent debt to Sundermann's *Dass Gluck un Winkel* played in England as *The Vale of Content* (1895). In this play the heroine Elizabeth, when given a choice between her husband and lover, prefers to live with the former. This is also the theme of many a Victorian play.

Shaw believed that the wife's decision to live with the husband was the real solution to the problem. It may be recalled here that *Candida* is anti-Ibsen in the sense that the wife knowing well the weakness and hollowness of Morell's love prefers to stay back. This is a significant point as it shows Shaw's striving to find his own way out of *A Doll's House* and *Ghosts*.

Shaw never completely abandoned his 'ideas' and this is clear when we look at another aspect of *Candida*. Candida shows an awareness of the duplicity of Morell's preaching when she says to him: "......how little you understand me to talk of your confidence in my goodness and purity...James: for if that went, I should care very little for your sermons; mere phrases that you cheat yourself and others with everyday." The spirit of *Saints and Sinners* and *Widower's Houses* reappears here. Burgess, the capitalist father of Candida, is pitted against Morell who has, earlier, let him down in the contract for the clothing manufacturing factory. Morell knows Burgess' motives in offering the lowest tender. "......because you paid worse wages than any other employer —stravation wages—to the women who made the clothing". Burgess now pays better wages to earn higher dividends. He dislikes raising the wages as it leads to "drink and uppishness in working men". Burgess's opinion agrees with that of Sartorious who thought the slum people unworthy of any improved conditions. Like the shopkeepers, Hoggard and Prabble (*Saints and Sinners*), Burgess seeks the clergyman's help because "you and your crew are getting influential." Morell is hesitant to accept Burgess' point when Candida persuades him, "Say, yes, James", which is incidentally her first dialogue in the play. Thus she opens her attack on the socialist. To her the capitalist and the socialist must join hands. Here in Candida's character Shaw shows a little inconsistency. She is not an advanced woman. She only uses Morell's susceptibility to her charms in her father's interests. Her "Say, yes, James" is very significant in this connection and there seems truth in Beatrice Webb's dubbing Candida a 'sentimental prostitute'. Later on she uses her charms to bring her husband back to her by feigning affection for the young poet. Between these capitalists and the pretending social preacher is Eugene who represents "Christian socialism in its striving to transcend itself, but he has not yet gone beyond the old attitude which finds social questions aesthetically distasteful."[1] This poetic character, modelled on Shelley, finds the world too distasteful and selfish and walks out with the realisation of the hard fact that winning the heart and love of a married woman was impossible despite the advanced and emancipated outlook

---

[1] Alick West: *op. cit.* p. 112

of a few. The Queen that governed England during Pinero's time continued to wield the sceptre.

The dramatic technique in *Candida* owes much to Shaw's experience as a novelist. The greatly expanded stage directions helped the reader in picturing in his mind the whole action of the play. Thus in words Shaw gave an equivalent for the arts of the stage designer and the actor. *Candida* may be called the first play in which Shaw combined theme and technique without overemphasising either, a fault which destroyed the artistic effect of his earlier plays. In *Widower's Houses* the problem was imposed upon a plot which failed to carry it to the satisfaction of his readers and audience. In *Candida* a similar theme is worked out with great effect. Despite a few similarities between Sartorious and Burgess on the one hand and Dr. Trench and Morell on the other, *Candida* has considerable artistic merit.

One feature common in *Plays Unpleasant* and *Pleasant Plays* is the dominance of feminine character, following the lines suggested by the successful plays of Pinero and Ibsen and the memorable roles played during the early nineties by Ellen Terry and Mrs. Patrick Campbell. Shaw had studied with minuteness the characters of Sartorious and Blanche, Julia and Grace, Mrs. Warren and Vivie, Raina and Louka, Gloria, the strange lady (*The Man of Destiny*) and Candida.

In the third collection of plays published as *Three Plays for Puritans*, Shaw gave more attention to the male characters. These plays for Puritans were written with the motive of bringing back to the theatre the highbrowed section of the audience.

The first of the *Three Plays for Puritans* is a melodrama, in which Shaw depends "for variety of human character, not on the high comedy idiosyncrasies which individualize people in spite of the closest similarity of age, sex, and circumstances but on broad contrasts between types of youth and age, sympathy and selfishness, the masculine and the feminine, the serious and the frivolous, the sublime and the ridiculous and so on."[1] Richard Dudgeon,

---

[1] 'Two Bad Plays', in *Our Theatres in the Nineties*, *vol. I*, p. 93

the hero in *The Devil's Disciple*, appears as the champion of the oppressed. He defends his cousin Essie, against his own family and creates a sensation when he says that the "Devil was my natural master and captain and friend."

Richard lets the soldiers arrest him when they mistake him for Anderson. The novelty of the scene lies in the 'devil's disciple' following an instinctively generous human impulse, "the law of his own nature, and no interest nor lust whatever".[1] Often Richard's action is mistaken as accruing out of his love for Mrs. Anderson but the anti-romantic, diabolic hero is interested only in himself, the vigour of his action is matched by Anderson's individuality. At a crucial moment in the play he realises that now preaching is not to be his job. It is action in which he discovers his mettle. Both the important characters undergo significant changes at critical moments in the play.

Apart from this interest in characters, which is psychologically convincing and dramatically interesting, *The Devil's Disciple* is a melodrama of the most common variety based on the stage gimmicks of suspense and thrills then in vogue. In this play, as in *Candida*, Shaw appears in a transitional stage between thinker and dramatist. *The Devil's Disciple* laid no claims to originality and this was most apparent in the scene in which Richard faces court-martial. The whole scene unmistakably borrows the design and dialogue of Boucicault's *Arrah-na-Pogue*. Bernard Shaw acknowledged:

......my stage tricks and suspenses and thrills and jests are the ones in vogue when I was a boy; by which time my grandfather was tired of them.[2]

In the court martial scenes in *Arrah-na-Pogue* and *The Devil's Disciple* of Bernard Shaw, there is a similarity to the point of imitation in the later play. Shuan has allowed himself to be arrested for another person. A severe Major and a kind Colonel are in the seat in *Arrah-na-Pogue*:

---

[1] Prefaces, p. 715
[2] 'Preface to Three Plays for Puritans' in *Prefaces by Bernard Shaw*, p. 720

English Drama 1860-1900

Major : Your name?

Shuan : Is it my name, Sir, Ah, you're jokin'! Sure there's his honour beside ye can answer for me, long life to him!

Major : Will you give the court your name, fellow?

Shuan : Well I'm not ashamed of it.

O' Grandy: Come, Shuan, my man.

Shuan : There, didn't I tell ye! he knows me well enough.

Major : Shuan (writing)......what is your other name?

Shuan : My mother's name?

Major : Your other name.

Shuan : My other name? D'ye think I've taken anybody else's name? Did ye ever know me, boys, only as Shuan?......

O'Grandy: He's called Shuan the Post.

Shuan : In regard of my carrying the letter-bag by the car, yer honour

Major : Now prisoner, are you guilty or not guilty?

Shuan : Sure, Major, I thought that was what we'd all come here to find out.

In *The Devil's Disciple*, Shaw had shown a severe Major (Swindon) and a gentle General (Burgoyne). The prisoner is Richard courting arrest instead of the intended person, Anthony Anderson.

Swindon : Your name, Sir?

Richard : Come: You don't mean to say that you've brought me here without knowing who I am?

Swindon : As a matter of form Sir, give me your name.

Richard : As a matter of form, then, my name is Anthony Anderson. Presbyterian Minister in this town...

Burgoyne : Any political views Mr. Anderson?

Richard : I understand that that is just what we are here to find out.

Shaw was ignorant of Burgoyne's character and the nature of his campaign. In Shaw's play, Burgoyne is in Hampshire. Historically he was never in New Hampshire. Shaw used historical details only as an aid to dramatic effect. *The Devil's Disciple* shows the author's desperate bid to try his hand at all kinds of plays. His success in *The Devil's Disciple* is limited to a study of characters. This infusion of human interest failed to revive the audience's interest in melodrama.

Then onwards Shaw learnt a new technique, keeping away from declared indoctrination. With *Captain Brassbound's Conversion*, Shaw left socialist and Fabian controversies far behind and started to gauge the depth of the human heart. Earlier entitled *The Witch of Atlas*, it is based on a Shelleyan theme; on faith in restraining oneself from the impulse to seek revenge. There is something of Arnold's philosophy as well. To Arnold, genuine repentance over a wrong should be the "setting up of an immense new movement for obtaining the rule of life...a change of the inner man". Lady Cicely, like the witch of Atlas brings about a new spirit of confidence, faith and service in a world suffering from selfishness, fear and revenge. Captain Brassbound seeking revenge on his uncle for the loss of property and injustice done to his mother, is a completely changed man under the spell of Lady Cicely who works with cool assurance. Under her influence he abandons his life's tragic purpose. *Captain Brassbound's Conversion* shows Shaw's excellent handling of a psychologically convincing change, brought about by the spirit of faith and peace over a mind fired with the passion for revenge, a feature symbolic of Shaw's development as a dramatist.[1]

Shaw's greatest study in characterisation is the portrait of the Roman General, Caesar in a play which dramatizes "the folly and wickedness of glorifying human vindictiveness by romantic codes of honour and institution in systems of jurisprudence".[2] In *Caesar and Cleopatra*, Shaw thus, appears to have attacked the traditions of legal and permissible ways of revenge in society. His Caesar is not the Caesar of history who would do anything to achieve his ambition but the embodiment of reason. His unruffled temper is the source of his greatness.

---

[1] Shaw was greatly disappointed to hear Ellen Terry's refusal to play it: "You suggest it is a one part play: I loathe that sort of thing" *Ellen Terry and Bernard Shaw: Correspondence* Ed. Christopher St. John, p. 302. Shaw firmly believed: "Ellen's skin does not fit her more closely than Lady Cicely Brassbound fits her; for I am a first class ladies tailor" *Bernard Shaw and Mrs. Patrick Campbell: Their Correspondence.*, Ed. Alan Dent, p. 21. Later on Ellen realised her mistake and played the part.

[2] *Bernard Shaw and the Nineteenth Century Tradition*, J. B. Kaye, p. 129

Shaw based his play on Mommsen's version of the story. Caesar's conquest of reason over passion appealed to Shaw most. At last he had found a character who embodied in himself the beauty of the mind. The extremely logical temperament of Caesar appears in the play in his concern for the taxes, for to him "taxes are the chief business of a conqueror of the world." He also understands the value of books but knows well that "the Egyptians should live their lives than dream them away with the help of books". This conqueror of the world hates murder, and at a significant moment tells Cleopatra: "And so on, to the end of history, murder shall breed murder always in the name of right and honour and peace, until the gods are tired of blood and create a race that can understand". In the life of Shaw's Caesar romance has no place. His relationship with Cleopatra is only that of an old man toying with a little girl.

This Caesar is not the Caesar of history. The historical Caesar felt relieved at the murder of Pothinus, who he suspected was plotting against him and might have kidnapped Ptolemy. Caesar was also set at ease at the murder of Pompey. The gay part of Caesar's life has been ignored by Shaw. "Caesar also appeared among all his victories to value most those won over beautiful women".[1] But in order to uphold his Caesar as an ideal of reason Shaw had him forget Cleopatra in the last scene[2] as if she was a plaything. In history Caesar had a son by her, Caesarian, and her age was twenty one and not sixteen when she met Caesar as Shaw says. Shaw's Caesar is an embodiment of all those virtues which, according to him, must go with an ideal hero. Shaw's Caesar is, thus, an idealised portrait of a historical hero.

In his portrait of Caesar, Shaw thus presented "a historically

---

[1] Mommsen: *The History of Rome*, trans. by William P. Dickinson revised Ed. V, p. 307

[2] Desmond McCarthy regards this scene in Shaw's plays as, 'stark fiction without a rag of probability to cover it.' Bernard Shaw's *Julius Caesar*, New Statesman (26th April, 1913), p. 83

one-sided but dramatically delightful hero"[1] As the sworn enemy of the romantic stage, Bernard Shaw's only complaint against Shakespeare's Caesar was based on the former's "technical objection to making sexual infatuation a tragic theme." Shaw's Caesar thus appears as far more credible and humanized. He has presented the greatness of a war-hero when he is in the palace and in this sense it is "the most antiheroic play in existence that manages at the same time to be heroic".[2]

In technique, thus, *Caesar and Clepotra* is essentially limited to focussing the limelight on Caesar alone. The play abounds in splendid and striking scenes which show his glory and greatness in different aspects. Together they serve to illustrate the shavian virtues of a hero. After the opening scene, in which he addresses the Sphinx, Caesar becomes the cynosure of dramatic interest as representative of the 'race that can understand'. Shaw's portrait of Caesar thus matches that of Napoleon, (*The Man of Destiny*) as an embodiment of reason.

In the Preface to *Three Plays for Puritans*, one section is entitled 'Better than Shakespeare'. It is a deliberate challenge to Shakespeare-worship, but shaw does not claim to write better plays. Shaw rightly observes: "It is the philosophy, the outlook on life, that changes— not the craft of the playwright." But he is fully conscious of his own limitations when he says: "It does not follow, however, that the right to criticize Shakespeare involves the power of writing better plays......I do not profess to write better plays."

Caesar and Cleopatra shows well the change in the outlook on life. Shaw's conception of a life governed by reason not impulse finds its first perfect expression in this play. In all his previous plays he had tried to show the power of the Life-force, reason and economic forces. In *Caesar and Cleopatra* Shaw has freed himself from these considerations which hamper the growth of true dramatic genius. This play alone shows Shaw at full command of his powers as a dramatist.

---

[1] Gordon, W. Couchman: *Here Was A Caesar*: *Shaw's Comedy Today* PMLA, 1957, p. 280

[2] John Gassner: *Masters of the Drama*, p. 605

Three Plays for Puritans was the last volume of plays to be written before 1900. Of course, Shaw's genius flourished in the twentieth century but *Unpleasant Plays, Plays Pleasant* and *Three Plays for Puritans* show his powers in the earlier stages of development. It will be of great value to find out his originality in themes on which is based his greatness as a dramatist. *Unpleasant Plays* were written driectly under the influence of Ibsen. Archer helped him with the plot in *The Widower's Houses.* The study of Ibsenism as a fashion was not new. Earlier, Gilbert had dramatised 'aestheticism' with greater effect. *The Philanderer*, in this sense, is based on a technique borrowed from Gilbert. In *Mrs. Warren's Profession* Shaw presents with greater effect situations earlier drawn by Pinero in *The Second Mrs. Tanequeray* and *The Weaker Sex.*

In *Arms and the Man* Shaw has studied the preposterousness of romantic ideals in an apparently Gilbertian manner. *Candida* recalls Sundermann's *The Vale of Content* and Jones' *Saints and Sinners. The Man of Destiny* is written after the fashion of Gilbert's *Tragedy and Comedy* and Walter Lisle's *The Love Test.* The influence of *The Weaker sex* and *The Notorious Mrs. Ebbsmith* is unmistakably suggested in *You Never Can Tell.*

The Devil's Disciple borrows a scene from Dion Boucicault's *Arrah-na-Pogue. Captain Brasshound's Conversion* and *Caesar and Clepotra* are the only two original plays in technique and ideas. The similarities between Shaw's plays and others' plays cited above do not suggest a complete lack of originality in Shaw. It is only meant to show that he was greatly influenced by contemporary dramatists, like Gilbert and Pinero, whom he criticized so much in his *Saturday Review* articles for their Victorianism. He even tried to write like Ibsen but he could only produce the rancour caused by economic problems. Shaw failed to grasp the poetic touch of the Norwegian dramatist.

What, then, is new and great in Shaw? Surely it is the Shavian outlook. Like Gilbert, Shaw gave to his dramas a typical personal touch. 'Shavian' is as expressive an adjective as 'Gilbertian'. Shaw unlike his predecessors and contemporaries, was clear in his thinking and dogmatic in his opinions. His ideas changed with the contemporary philosophy. The compromising attitude of Pinero and Jones was abandoned by Shaw in favour of a frank and fearless acceptance of facts. In this freedom from conventionality lies the source of Shaw's advanced opinions. In England Shaw completed the movement begun by Ibsen.

But Shaw's greatest contribution as a playwright lies in his writing of plays which showed the triumph of art for artists' sake. He did not write merely for art nor for the sake of the audience. He acknowledged the claims of the artist to hold his own views on certain matters. In *Caesar and Cleopatra* particularly, he shows the triumph of his own opinions on greatness in men. Caesar thus expresses the Shavian view of greatness. Shaw is the only dramatist in the nineteenth century whose ideas develop with contemporary philosophy and as such they are the best examples of drama in a process of development.

Chapter VIII

Oscar Wilde

> Wilde was "important as the representative of a mood......
> ...extraordinarily prevalent in the later years of the nineteenth Century. Of this mood he was in letters the only English representative..."
>
> Raymond, E. T.

> ..."Mr Wilde is to me our only thorough playwright. He plays with every thing: with wit, with philosophy, with drama, with actors and with audience..."
>
> G. B. S.

> *The Importance of Being Earnest* : "a sublime piece of nonsense."
>
> Graham Hough.

> "...Oscar has the courage of the opinions...of others !"
>
> Whistler.

Oscar Wilde was the most controversial figure of the eighteen nineties and was, in literature, the perfect symbol of the aesthetic tendencies of the period. Throughout his life he lived under the fear of being misunderstood and at the same time went on creating new startling impressions about himself. At Dublin and Oxford Wilde had a brilliant academic record. Professor John Mahaffay and Walter Pater shaped his intellect: the former with his wonderful conversation and art of winning popularity and the latter with his new aesthetics. Pater's observation impressed Wilde most:"...a counted number of pulses is given us of a navigated dramatic life. How can we see all that is to be seen in them by the finest senses? How can we pass most quickly from point to point and be present always at the focus where the greatest number of vital forces unite at their purest energy? To burn always with this hard gem-like flame, to maintain this ecstasy is success, in life...What we have to do is to be for ever curiously testing new opinions and courting new impressions..." At the same time Ruskin's humanitarian service fascinated Wilde and created in his mind two life long interests.

Pater's suggestion that he should write prose caught Wilde's fancy. He practised to extremes, Pater's opinions and suggestions in his life. Wilde's lust for the 'gem-like flame' led him to the scandalous pursuit of it in the male body, creating a derision for the female which decayed earlier than the other. Aestheticism, of course, never attained the dimensions of a movement. It centred around Pater, Morris, Swinburne and Whistler. Wilde translated it into his daily life and posed many a time as a flower-loving ethereal being, which gave to Gilbert occasion for satire in *Patience*:

> Though the Philistines may jostle, you will rank as an apostle in the high aesthetic band,
> If you walk down Piccadily with a poppy or lily in your medieval hand.

Wilde earned an invitation to tour America for his aesthetic attitudinizing but there he shocked them by his down-to-earth attitude. He was a living paradox. Even when he was at Dublin he gave tremendous displays of his physical virility when he beat single-handed a band of hooligans trying to humiliate him while he was engaged in poetry recitation. His 'effeminate' nature vanished in a moment. He beat all members at a drinking bout at San Francisco. This was the man who appeared delicate yet possessed great strength; apparently lost in a fancy yet writing of a freedom movement.

In his first play, *Vera, or the Nihilists*, Wilde wrote about the political and social problems of Russia. The romantic notions of individual's rights and liberty came to him from the French Revolution. His attempt "to express within the limits of art that Titan cry of the peoples for liberty..." was limited but he wisely declared *Vera* to be "a play not of politics but of passions". Wilde was too deeply steeped in Elizabethan playcraft to get rid of disguises, intrigue, romance, deceit and blood; hence Alexis, the heir to the throne, goes out in disguise to join the Nihilists against his own father, and retains the crown promising humanitarian reforms. The play abounds in sentimental outcries on liberty; "O liberty, do I dedicate myself to thy service? Do with me as thou wilt. The end has come now and by the sacred wounds, O crucified mother, O liberty, I swear that Russia shall be saved." This was Wilde's idea of nihilists in Russia as expressed earlier in *The Soul of Man under Socialism*. "No one who lived in modern Russia could possibly realise his perfection except by pain. A nihilist who rejects all authority because he knows authority to be evil and welcomes all pain because through that he realises his personality, is a real Christian!"

The ambiguity in characterisation marred the play. Alexis, the oppressor, falls in love with Vera, the leader of the nihilists. The passion of love and the passion of liberty get mixed up. She forgets her mission to kill him and, instead, kills herself. The play on the whole showed Wilde's feeble grasp of political sentiments, love of passions and a cultivated delight in epigrammatic conversation:

Baron Raff : A cook and a diplomatist! an excellent parallel. If I had a son who was a fool I'd make him one or the other.

Prince Paul : I see your father did not hold the same opinion Baron... For myself, the only immortality I desire is to invent a new sauce.

Many people recalled Sidney Smith, parson and wit, who was told by a Squire: "If I had a son who was an idiot, by Jove I'd make him a parson." Smith retorted: "Very probably but I see that your father was of a different mind". For a man of such wide reading as Wilde's such instances came handy and he was not hesitant to pass on any such remark as his own.

Politics was not enough. A revenge play, *The Duchess of Padua* (1883) followed. The Duchess falls in love with Guido who has come there to avenge his father's murder. In her love for Guido, the Duchess murders the Duke, but finding Guido unresponsive, lays the guilt at his door. Guido confesses guilt. In sheer exasperation the Duchess takes poison and Guido, torn between passion and duty, kills himself. As Wilde said of the play, it 'consisted solely of style', and the style comprises a good reading and assimilation of the Elizabethan revenge tradition. Henry Chettle's *Hoffman* seems to have lent Wilde the skeleton of the drama. In *Hoffman* the son's revenge for his father's murder is delayed by his passion for the mother of one of his victims. In Wilde's play the simple revenge is supplemented by lust and passion and melancholy. The Duchess in white recalls the Duchess of Malfi. The Duchess of Padua moves around in white, loves passionately and ultimately takes poison to end the torture of unrequited love. In revenge she follows Lady Macbeth's example—she decides to kill the Duke:

> Well, well, I know my business: I will change
>
> The torch of love into a funeral torch
>
> ×   ×   ×
>
> and yet tonight He may die also, he is very old

and her repentance after the act:

> ×   ×   ×
>
> ......put back the sun
> And make me what I was an hour ago

shows her the horror of her crime. Despite the apparent similarity between the Duchess of Padua and Duchess of Malfi there is a great difference in their reaction to death. Webster's Duchess faces death with a self-conscious dignity as well as a consciousness of something superior:

> ......heaven's gates are not so highly arched.
> As Princes' palaces — they that enter there
> Must go upon their knees.

But Wilde's Duchess is writhing with the fire of poison: " I did not know it was such pain to die." At the last moment Wilde robs her of tragic grandeur which makes the death of Duchess of Malfi so dignified.

The Duchess of Padua shows Wilde's groping for a form of drama which would suit his talents, and the political and revenge plays he tried assured him that sustained action and tragedy were not his forte espite his excellence at 'scene" construction.

Salome, written after *Lady Windermere's Fan*, was in blank verse and derived from the story in the Bible. It was originally written in French and was translated into English by Lord Alfred Douglas, Wilde's friend. What linked *Salome* with decadence was the use of a rich poetic language and a wide range of aesthetic symbols and images. When Wilde was in the French capital, in the vicinity of Verlain, Mallarme and Baudelaire, his mind was fascinated by the theme of *Salome* which opened to him an eldorado of sensuousness and sensations. The idea of " a woman dancing with her bare feet in the blood of a man she has craved for and slain,"[1] fascinated him. At a time when Naturalists were held in great esteem in England and Europe, Wilde selected this highly sensational theme for his play.

In Wilde's play, Salome, the daughter of Herodias loses her heart to Jokanaan, the prophet. Jokanaan has no love for her and meets Salome's passion with coldness. Herod insists on Salome dancing and, in return, Salome asks for the head of the prophet. She dances and gets the reward. Ultimately she is slain by the soldiers of Herod. *Salome* does not adhere to the Biblical story with any fidelity. Both St. Mathew and St. Mark state that Herodias instructed her daughter to ask for the head of the prophet. But in *Salome* the heroine does it of her own accord because she has been repelled by John who is 'ice to her sexual flame' and is still lusting for him. Jokanaan is surprised to see Salome. Without looking at her he talks of Herodias who "hath given herself to the young men of Egypt......whose bodies are mighty?......Though

---
[1] Pearson: *The Life of Oscar Wilde*, p. 226

she will never repent, but will stick fast in her abominations......"
He forbids Salome: "Come not near the chosen of the Lord. Thy mother hath filled the earth with the wine of her iniquities". Wilde makes the daughter infatuated with the physical beauty of Jokanaan, beauty which earlier had fascinated the mother. Wilde's own fascination for the 'precious youth' led him to make Salome enraptured of Jokanaan's body. Salome says: "I am athirst for thy beauty, I am hungry for thy body......"

Wilde derived much from the earlier versions of the Salome tale, Flaubert's *Tentation*, Heinrich Heine's *Atta Troll* and Laforgue's *Salome*. Herodias was the original source of Salome's demand for Jokanaan's head. In Flaubert's tale *Herodias*, Salome even forgets the name of the person whose head she obstinately demands. Above all it was Strindberg whose *Princess Maleine* (1889), and *Les Sept Princesses* (1891) provided Wilde with inspiration to explore further the tragic possibilities of the Salome theme. The vampire passion with which she fastens her lips on the head of Jokanaan "finally fixed the legend of Salome."[1]

Wilde's predilection for a decadent atmosphere appeared in the choice of colour and splendour, craving for sexual gratification, obsession with sensations and pain. Salome symbolised as the strange full moon, "a mad woman who is seeking everywhere for lovers", is an embodiment of all the decadent tendencies of the age.

Salome was severely critcised for the sexual infatuation of the heroine despite the Naturalistic expressionism with which Wilde depicted passion and lust. Only Strindberg had done it so beautifully. The atmospheric sensuousness, the "sterility of excessive civilization"[2] which, following Pater's suggestion, Wilde had portrayed in the *Picture of Dorian Gray* lends *Salome* a strange poetic beauty. The shadow of evil looms large over Salome's hankering after Jokanaan's body. Her insatiable lust has the grandeur of a decadent society.

---

[1] Mario Praz: *The Romantic Agony*, p. 332

[2] Holbrook Jackson: *The Eighteen Nineties*, p. 77

Salome was the first play in Engand which exploited all the possibilities of a Naturalistic setting. Wilde, however, did not give much importance to *Salome*, and wrote comedies which brought him success on the stage. *Lady Windermere's Fan* written before *Salome* was the first play that assured him of a dramatic career. In his comedies, Wilde had for his models the Restoration comedies of manners.

Earlier Pinero and Jones effected comedy of manners through plot and situation. Wilde achieved this with the refinement of dialogue. But like Shaw who denounced Pinero, Wilde also had only contempt for his two contemporaries. Of a certain play of Pinero's, Wilde said, "It is the best play I ever slept through" and of Jones he said, "There are three rules for writing plays. The first rule is not to write like Henry Arthur Jones; the second and the third rules are the same." Wilde who had written *Vera* and *Duchess of Padua* earlier, realised that such themes did not move the audience in the nineties. The year in which he wrote *Lady Windermere's Fan* (1892), a comedy of manners, was important as about the same time Shaw changed over from *Unpleasant Plays* to *Plays Pleasant* and Jones and Pinero were at the height of their popularity.

In his first comedy Wilde showed what he expected from contemporary dramatists. In *Lady Windermere's Fan* a secret is well kept around the central figure of Mrs. Erlynne. Lady Windermere is to celebrate her birthday and her husband insists on inviting a woman, Mrs. Erlynne, to the party. It is reported that Lord Windermere visited her frequently and even paid her bills. What sort of woman is this? This question is left undecided and the first act is closed with Lady Windermere and her husband on the brink of a quarrel.

Lady Windermere:	......If that woman crosses my threshold, I shal strike her across the face with it.
Lord Windermere:	Margaret, you couldn't do such a thing.
Lady Windermere:	You don't know me!

The second act presents the people at the party at which Mrs Erlynne at once attracts all the men present. Lord Darlington exploiting the situation, proposes to Lady Windermere but she refuses. On second thoughts she decides to abandon her husband leaving a letter behind. Mrs. Erlynne, knowing the suspicion in her mind and having read the letter, decides what she has to do:

> I feel a passion awakening within me that I never felt before. What can it mean? The daughter must not be like the mother—that would be terrible. How can I save her? How can I save my child?......

The third act repeats the technique of Sheridan's famous curtain scene. Mrs. Erlynne and Lady Windermere are face to face. The former pleads and persuades the latter to go back to her husband but suspecting a secret alliance between Mrs. Erlynne and Lord Windermere, she refuses to go. Almost pathetically Mrs. Erlynne speaks to Lady Windermere:

> You don't know what it is to fall into the pit, to be despised, mocked, abandoned, sneered at — to be an outcast! to find the door shut against one, to have to creep in by hideous byways, afraid every moment lest the mask should be stripped from one's face......One pays for one's sins, and then one pays again, and all one's life and pay......

Before Lady Windermere can escape, Lord Darlington and his friends arrive. Both the ladies hide themselves behind curtains. Friends talk about scandals, and Mrs. Erlynne. Then all of a sudden the worst happens.

Lord Windermere:	(walking over) Well, what is it?
Cecil Graham :	Darlington has got a woman here in his rooms. Here is her fan. Amusing, isn't it? (A pause).
Lord Windermere:	Good God! (Seizes the fan — Dumbly rises).
Cecil Graham :	What is the matter?
Lord Windermere:	Lord Darlington!
Lord Darlington :	(turning around) Yes!
Lord Windermere:	What is my wife's fan doing here in your room? Hands off, Cecil. Don't touch me.
Lord Darlington :	Your wife's fan?
Lord Windermere:	Yes, here it is!
Lord Darlington :	(walking towards him): I don't know!

English Drama 1860-1900

Lord Windermere:	You must know. I demand an explanation. Don't hold me, you fool (to Cecil Graham).
Lord Darlington:	(aside) She is here after all!
Lord Windermere:	Speak, Sir! Why is my wife's fan here? Answer me! By God! I'll search your rooms and if my wife's here, I'll—(moves).
Lord Darlington:	You shall not search my rooms. You have no right to do so. I forbid you!
Lord Windermere:	You scoundrel! I'll not leave your room till I have searched every corner of it! What moves behind that curtain? (Rushes towards the curtain C)
Mrs. Erlynne:	(enters behind R) Lord Windermere!
Lord Windermere:	Mrs. Erlynne!

(Everyone starts and turns around. Lady Windermere slips out from behind the curtain and glides from the room L)

Mrs. Erlynee : I am afraid I took your wife's fan in mistake for my own, when I was leaving your house tonight. I am so sorry.

The fourth act shows a complete reversal in Mrs. Erlynne's position. Lord Windermere realises that he was "mistaken in her. She is bad—as bad as a woman can be." But Lady Windermere has her recent experience in mind when she says: "And I don't think, Mrs. Erlynne a bad woman—I know she's not." Mrs. Erlynne comes to take leave of Lord and Lady Windermere and leaves after they have promised, separately, never to mention the last night's incident to each other. She herself accepts Lord Augustus' hand in marriage.

Lady Windermere's Fan was Wilde's first comedy and won instant success. This play reveals a few significant features of the Wildean drama. First, it is noteworthy as a realistic comedy of manners. Characters in this play live in a thoroughly artificial world. At Lady Windermere's birthday party some curious specimens of aristocratic society gather, a typical representative of which is a Lady Berwick seeking a rich husband for her daughter Agatha. Mr. Hopper is the bird in the net.

Duchess of Berwick	:	......Mr. Hopper, I am very very angry with you. You have taken Agatha out on the terrace, and she is so delicate.
Hopper	:	Awfully sorry, Duchess. We went out for a moment and then got chatting together.
Duchess of Berwick	:	Ah, about dear Australia, I suppose?
Hopper	:	Yes!
Duchess of Berwick	:	Agatha, darling!
Lady Agatha	:	Yes, Mamma!
Duchess of Berwick	:	(aside) Did Mr. Hopper definitely......
Lady Agatha	:	Yes, Mamma!
Duchess of Berwick	:	And what answer did you give him, dear child?
Lady Agatha	:	Yes, Mamma.
Duchess of Berwick	:	(affectionately) My dear one! You always say the right thing.

This is nothing new in a society where material prosperity overwhelms morality. The 'eighteen nineties' saw socialistic movements of reform and the dawn of Ibsen in England but the aristocracy looks impervious to all such happenings outside. It is a world of its own. Wilde portrayed what he observed and in this sense "he is neither satirizing, nor, very seriously, moralizing."[1]

The people at the party are smart and expert in the language of badinage and quips and apothegems. In the above excerpt from the conversation between mother and daughter, Wilde shows the deep practical sense in the latter although hidden beautifully under the naivete of the dialogue. The 'Yes Mamma' of Lady Agatha is thus a double-edged weapon—a technique of artful conversation well in vogue among the elite. Lord Darlington at one place in the play says: "It is absurd to divide people into good and bad. People are either charming or tedious." And what is the criterion of charm and tediousness in this world? The tedious people are those who have puritanical ideas on virtue and charming people are those who have cast off all puritanical touch from their outlook on life. Wilde's characters in this sense are charming.

---

[1] Alan S. Downer: *The British Drama*, p. 291

Lady Windermere in this play is first shown as extremely puritanical: "Well, I have something of the Puritan in me. I was brought up like that. I am glad of it!" and, "nowadays people seem to look on life as a speculation. It is not a speculation. It is a sacrament. Its ideal is love. Its purification is sacrifice." Towards the close of the play she appears to hold different views on people: "I don't think now that people can be divided into the good and the bad as though they were two separate races or creations."

Mrs. Erlynne represents erring women. But in the play, from the very beginning, she appears to be blackmailing Lord Windermere for some family secret; the audience is kept on tenterhooks waiting for enlightenment on this point—why should a man like Lord Windermere be in the grips of a woman like Mrs. Erlynne? The secret is very well kept up till the last Act. Wilde thought this suspense a merit of the play. He wrote to George Alexander about it in a long letter: " ......and the chief merit of my last Act is to me the fact that it does not contain, as most plays do, the explanation of what the audience knows already, but that it is the sudden explanation of what the audience desires to know, followed immediately by the revelation of character as yet untouched by literature."[1] This showed an excellent knowledge of dramatic suspense, construction as well as characterisation. Wilde's masterly handling of the plot should not make us overlook the unnaturalness of the scene at Lord Darlington's where both Lady Windermere and Mrs. Erlynne find themselves together and the men return at two at night to talk in the same vein. In *The School for Scandal*, Lady Teazle's appearance in the rooms of Charles Surface, is arranged following naturally the course of the plot and not with deliberate wire pulling as in *Lady Windermere's Fan*. Despite this technical weakness Wilde's play compares well with the best in the 'manners' genre.

A Woman of No Importance is also about a woman with a past. In this play people are divided into two groups: the puritans and the intellectual adventurers. Mrs. Arbuthnot is the mother of

---

[1] Letters: p. 309

Gerald who is now employed as secretary by Lord Illingworth. Mrs. Arbuthnot does not allow the enthusiastic Gerald to take up this position. To Mrs. Arbuthnot "the secret of life is never to have an emotion that is unbecoming" and, to Lord Illingworth "nothing is serious except passion. The intellect is not a serious thing, and never has been." Lord Illingworth is a pale copy of Lord Henry Wotton. He opens up the hidden secrets of Life to Gerald: "Remember that you've got on your side the most wonderful thing in the world—youth! There is nothing like youth. The middle-aged are mortgaged to Life. The old are in life's lumber-room. But youth is the Lord of Life." Lord Illingworth praises youth and modernity inordinately. He initiates Gerald into a new life as Lord Henry Wotton had initiated Dorian Gray before him: "The true mystery of the world is the visible not the invisible... a new Hedonism—that is what our century wants. You might be its visible symbol ...Youth! Youth! there is absolutely nothing in the world but youth."

Lord Illingworth puts forward his philosophy of life: "A man who can dominate a London dinner-table can dominate the world. The future belongs to the dandy. It is the exquisites who are going to rule." Gerald loves Hester Worsley, the American visitor. Lord Illingworth tries to kiss her. She, feeling offended, comes to Gerald for rescue. He is ready to kill Lord Illingworth for this act of his. In the meanwhile Mrs. Arbuthnot had told Gerald how Lord Illingworth had deceived a girl after a son was born to her and refused to marry her. This has changed Gerald's feelings for Lord Illingworth. When he is rushing at Lord Illingworth, Mrs. Arbuthnot tells him that the latter is his own father.

Lord Illingworth comes to attempt a reconciliation but Mrs. Arbuthnot will have nothing to do with him.

Mrs. Arbuthnot	:	I decline to marry you, Lord Illingworth.
Lord Illingworth	:	Are you serious?
Mrs. Arbuthnot	:	Yes.

Gerald and Hester return from the garden. He asks: "Halloy, mother, whose glove is this? You have had a visitor. Who was it?"

and the mother answers: ".....A man of no importance." The play ends here.

Mrs. Arbuthnot's "child of my shame, be still the child of my shame" is a rather sentimental excuse for keeping her son away from his own father.

A Woman of No Importance is the most autobiographical of Wilde's plays. Wilde, who moulded his own life on the precepts of Lord Henry Wotton, realised that "one could never pay too high a price for any sensations". The truth of the opinion that "the experimental method was the only method by which one could arrive at any scientific analysis of the passions..." dawned upon him too late to make amends. The dramatic irony of Lord Illingworth's epigram is almost prophetic: "It is perfectly monstrous the way people go about, now a days, saying things against one behind one's back that are absolutely and entirely true."

But *A Woman of No Importance* does not glorify this outlook. In ultimately defeating the cynical Lord Illingworth — Wilde appears to have offered criticism on his own life. How Constance Wilde kept her two sons away from Oscar Wilde and the pain he suffered in consequence, was the original experience on which he based the play. But the way he concluded shows Wilde's consciousness of the guilt and hypocrisy he practised on his family. *A Woman of No Importance* does not wholly approve of aristocratic depravity. In the person of Hester Worsley, Wilde presented a critic of fashionable English society. She says: "You shut out of your society the gentle and the good. You laugh at the simple and the pure....You have lost life's secret. Oh! your English society seems to me shallow, selfish, foolish. It has blinded its eyes and stopped its ears. It lies like a leper in purple. It sits like a dead thing smeared with gold." Rather self-righteous, yet it is quite true. Those who regard Wilde as a mere poseur will find in many such passages an abrasive censure on contemporary society. The trap that Wilde set for his audience is tightened through strings of shocking epigrams. The pose he strikes is not the reality. It is the image he keeps striking at throughout the play, and it solves his purpose in that the 'new look' is always defeated at the end of the play.

The year 1893 which saw the production of *A Woman of No Importance* also witnessed Pinero's greatest play *The Second Mrs. Tanqueray*. Jones' important play *The Case of Rebellious Susan* was produced in the following year. There is a marked similarity in their criticism of society as they do not approve of the growing lack of morals and disregard for traditions. Pinero and Jones held the strings too tightly, whereas Wilde was a little indulgent towards such follies. Wilde aimed at presenting a picture of the fashionable aristocratic world to which he had an easy access. His obligations and temptations conditioned his observations.

Wilde's growing awareness of a purpose in drama fed on the pseudo-problem plays of Pinero and Jones, whom he hated. His next play *An Ideal Husband* shows how poorly Wilde managed the reverse side within the same sphere. Sir Robert Chiltern, when young, sold a cabinet secret to a stock exchange speculator. The letter he wrote then was now used against him by Mrs. Cheveley who wanted Sir Robert to support publicly the Argentine Scheme. He cannot do it but he is caught in the net. If he refuses he is ruined. Lady Chiltern, a strait-laced puritan, dislikes Mrs. Cheveley. She believes: "One's past is what one is. It is the only way by which people should be judged." Not knowing the real source of Sir Robert's prosperity, she compels him to change the assurance he has given to Mrs. Cheveley.

Sir Robert is a dual personality, as he tells Lady Chiltern: "public and private life are different things. They have different laws and move on different lines." He tells Lord Goring how Baron Arnheim had opened the gate of fortune before him: "with that wonderfully fascinating quiet voice of his he expounded to us the most terrible of all philosophies, the philosophy of power." Lord Henry Wotton and Lord Illingworth held similar opinions on material prosperity.

The secret of Sir Robert's past is revealed to Lady Chiltern who shudders at the truth of her husband involved in a scandal.

The letter is taken away from Mrs. Cheveley by Lord Goring who knows that she is also a thief. Without the secret of Sir Robert's one weak point being made public the play ends, reuniting Sir Robert to his wife Lady Chiltern.

In *An Ideal Husband* characters are more life-like and despite their queer and cynical notions on life, Sir Robert and Lord Goring are representatives of the Wildean creed. Wilde depicts the working of a dual personality with a confidence that is based on experience. The comic situations in the play, although governed by Lord Henry Wotton's philosophy, manage to be interesting. Here is Lord Goring talking to his father:

Lord Caversham	:	......want to have a serious conversation with you, Sir.
Lord Goring	:	My dear father! At this hour?
Lord Caversham	:	Well, Sir, it is only ten o'clock. What is your objection to the hour? I think the hour is an admirable hour!
Lord Goring	:	Well, the fact is, father, this is not my day for talking seriously. I am very sorry but it is not my day.
Lord Caversham	:	What do you mean, Sir?
Lord Goring	:	During the season, father, I only talk seriously on the first Tuesday in every month, from four to seven.
Lord Caversham	:	Well, make it Tuesday, Sir, make it Tuesday.
Lord Goring	:	But it is after seven, father, and my doctor says I must not have any serious conversation after seven. It makes me talk in my sleep.

An Ideal Husband also shows a Gilbertian trifling with sentiments. Here are the lovers talking :

Lord Goring	:	You went away with the child-diplomatist.
Mabel Chiltern	:	You might have followed us. Pursuit would have been only polite. I don't think I like you at all this evening.
Lord Goring	:	I like you immensely.
Mabel Chiltern	:	Well, I wish you'd show it in a more marked way!

An Ideal Husband, like the previous plays, follows the technique of self-projection. In this play Lord Goring presents Wilde's views on various matters. He misrepresents his age, he is really thirty-four, but admits only thirty-two: "thirty one and a half when I have a really good button-hole." An early example of such a tailor-made gentleman occurs in Bulwer Lytton's *Money* (1840).

Patent :	Yes, Sir, this is the Evelyn *vis-a-vis*! No one more the fashion than Mr. Evelyn. Money makes the man, Sir.
Frantz :	But de tailor, *de schneider*, make de gentleman!

Lord Goring is a dandy and has made life an art. Wilde's experiences with his family when the scandal broke down the public life of Sir William Wilde are also echoed in Lord Goring's generalisation: "Fathers should be neither seen nor heard. That is the only proper basis for family life. Mothers are different. Mothers are darlings."

An Ideal Husband offers more suggestive parallels with the writer's own life. Sir Robert Chiltern's dual personality is like the dual personality of Wilde, to both the writer and the character of his creation, public and private life are different. Lady Chiltern most resembles Constance Wilde who idolised her husband and then finding him faithless to her, retired to seclusion. To Lady Chiltern "One's past is what one is". To her this discovery of Sir Robert's dual life "wakes terrible memories...And now—oh, when I think that I made of a man like you my ideal! the ideal of my life." Sir Robert pleads that "it is not the perfect, but the imperfect, who have need of love...All sins, except a sin against itself, Love should forgive...Women think that they are making ideals of men. What they are making of us are false idols merely..." Lord Goring speaks the truth: "Women are not meant to judge us, but to forgive us when we need forgiveness." This is the fundamental difference between the Ibsen-Shaw concept of the new woman as an equal of man and claiming superiority over men in their invulnerability agains wrong and Oscar Wilde's concept claiming love of women and not their justice. Constance Wilde could never forgive Wilde for what he had done. How perilously close was the theme of the play running to what was in store for Wilde within the next two years gives *An Ideal Husband* a significant place in autobiographical studies.

An Ideal Husband continues two main underlying themes in Wilde's plays: conversion of the Puritan; criticism of upper-class life. The self-righteous attitude of Lady Chiltern gives way to the hard realities of life. Mrs. Cheveley says: "Morality is simply the attitude we adopt towards people whom we personally dislike." Almost prophetically she says: "Nowadays with our modern mania for morality, everyone has to pose as a paragon of purity, incorruptibility, and all the other seven deadly virtues—and what is the result? You all go over the ninepine—one after the other. Not a year passes in England without somebody disappearing. Scandals used to lend charm, or at least interest, to a man—now they crush him." Lady Windermere, Hester Worsley and Lady Chiltern—the three Puritans meet their moral antipodes in Mrs. Erlynne, Mrs. Arbuthnot and Mrs. Cheveley, respectively. Their conversion shows the tenuousness of their puritanical ideals.

Wilde does not justify corruption and fraud in persons. If, despite the crime Sir Robert committed, he is promoted to a higher status, it is because of the fact that Sir Robert has now undergone a mental expiation of his guilt. True penitence is better than a fake show of it. But by pointing out one case of fraud in the political life, Wilde has only hinted at what was true of many a prosperous politician. The vein of social criticism in *An Ideal Husband* is as deep as in *A Woman of No Importance*. Wilde, who never was an active socialist like Shaw, has not glorified the aristocracy in any of his plays. They are always shown with some glaring defects in their character, but as Wilde said: "No artist has ethical sympathies". Wilde did not expose his subject to attack from the public. Indirectly he suggested their weaknesses and lingered on their interesting qualities.

The limitations imposed by the theme of corruption in *An Ideal Husband* proved too much for Wilde's fancy which broke loose from all such ideas of 'purposes' in drama and his next play *The Importance of Being Earnest* illustrates this best.

To attempt any analysis of the plot would be necessarily otiose as The *Importance of Being Earnest* is the best known play of Wilde's. Yet some of the characteristic situations illustrative of his gift of characterisation and comedy may be noted.

Algernon invites his aunt Lady Bracknell and Miss Gwendolen Fairfax to tea. His friend John Worthing, known as Jack in the country and Ernest in town, comes in. Both are men of the fashionable type. Algernon has a very happy knack for inviting himself to others' parties. He says to Jack "...I wouldn't be able to dine with you at Willis's night, for I have been really engaged to Aunt Augusta for more than a week."

Jack : I haven't asked you to dine with me anywhere tonight.
Algernon: I know. You are absolutely careless about sending out invitations. It is very foolish of you. Nothing annoys people so much as not receiving invitations.

The broad farcical lines on which the play develops further continues Wilde's favourite theme of dual personality. There is a Wilde and there is an anti-Wilde; the contrast built on the two aspects: the external face of a dandy, the sophisticated conversationalist, the wit and the other face, the real Wilde *l'homme moyen sensuel*', the sinner, the seeker of hidden pleasures of mind and body.[1] Jack explains his motives:

When one is placed in the position of guardian, one has to adopt a very high moral tone on all subjects. It is one's duty to do so. And as a high moral tone can hardly be said to conduce very much to either one's health or one's happiness, in order to get up to town, I have always pretended to have a younger brother of the name of Earnest, who lives in Albany, and gets into the most dreadful scrapes. That, my dear Algy, is the whole truth pure and simple.

Algernon calls Jack a Bunburyist. Gwendolen and Jack meet in the absence of Lady Bracknell.

Jack : And I would like to be allowed to take advantage of Lady Bracknell's temporary absence.

---

[1] Arthur H. Nethercot : *Oscar Wilde and the Devil's Disciple*, P.M.L.A LIX, 1944, p. 843

Gwendolen: I would certainly advise you to do so. Mamma has a way of coming back suddenly into a room that I have often had to speak to her about ......

Jack : (nervously) Miss Fairfax, ever since I have met you I have admired you more than any girl......I have ever met since... I met you.

Gwendolen: Yes, I am quite well aware of the fact. And I often wish that in public, at any rate, you had been more demonstrative......

The real importance of being Ernest is revealed when Gwendolen tells Jack that she could only love him whose name was Ernest. Jack loved her in the name of Ernest.

Algernon, who knows the country address of Jack, goes there under the town name of Jack-Ernest. Cecily, Jack's cousin, falls in love with Algernon. Jack arrives with the intention of telling them that Ernest, the city brother, is dead. Instead he meets Algernon. Gwendolen also comes there and there are two girls for the one man Ernest. There is great confusion over the issue.

The conclusion in this fanciful play is reached as Miss Prism, the governess of Cecily, reveals that Jack is the son of Lady Bracknell's sister, and was lost when Miss Prism by mistake put him in a bag intended for the manuscript of a novel she was carrying. She forgot the bag at Victoria station. Thus Jack turns out to be Algernon's brother and is most delighted to hear that his Christian name is Ernest.

Wilde called this comedy "a trivial comedy for serious people" but "for ourselves we prefer to term it extravagant farce."[1] Critics lavished generous appreciation on this play for its "iridescent filament of fantasy"[2] and acknowledged it as a "sublime piece of frivolity[3]" In an interview with Robert Ross which appeared in the *St James' Gazette* on 18th January 1895, Wilde spoke of *The*

---

[1] *Telegraph*, quoted by Harold Hobson: *Verdict at Midnight*, p. 53

[2] The World: in Pearson, p. 256

[3] Graham Hough: *The Artist as a Man of Action, The Listener*, October 21, 1954, p. 666

Importance of Being Earnest as "exquisitely trivial, a delicate bubble of fancy", and a philosophy "that we should treat all the trivial things of life seriously, and all the serious things of life with sincere and studied triviality........."[1] In *The Importance of Being Earnest* both Jack and Algernon are studies in the art of triviality like Lord Goring in *An Ideal Husband*.

Algernon holds queer opinions about marriage: "Divorces are made in heaven" and "girls never marry the men they flirt with. Girls don't think it right." Not only Algernon but even Gwendolen thinks that if Lady Bracknell should "prevent us from becoming man and wife, and I may marry someone else, and marry often, nothing that she can possibly do can alter my eternal devotion to you." Despite the cynicism involved in phrases like "divorces are made in heaven", the irony and sardonic wit reveal a practical truth that attacks pharisaism on one hand and on the other offers the delight of a queer emancipation from traditional bonds. Wilde hits at the hypocrisy of marriage and sentiments. In Wilde, romantic dispositions change with a Gilbertian suddenness. It lends the play a dehydrated intellectual outlook and makes acute the want of real human warmth. The people retain the hard gem-like glitter but remain impoverished at heart. *The Importance of Being Earnest* brought recognition for Wilde as a dramatist with an ingenious comic skill. It was regarded as outstanding among his plays for the 'liberation of genius' in Wilde.[2] Here are no forsaken beloveds, illegal marriages, political corruption or any sentiments. Here Wilde appears in full command of his comic genius. His predilection for passing queer and sensational remarks and his special aptitude for intellectual trifling appear at their best in this play. *The Importance of Being Earnest* while showing the best aspect of Wilde's genius also shows the worst aspect of his literary technique. It is written in imitation of Gilbert's *Engaged*. In his earlier plays also, the illogical arguments and travesty of sentiments followed the lines of the Savoy Operas.

---

[1] Pearson: *op. cit.* p. 254

[2] Stephen William, *Plays on the Air*: A Survey of Drama Broadcasts, p. 9

Here the influence is too clear in the plot construction as well.

In Gilbert's *Engaged*, Belinda is very careful about the money Cheviot has before marriage. Belinda says to Belvawney: "I love you with an imperishable ardour which mocks the power of words......But as I said before, business is business, and unless I can see some distinct probability that your income will be permanent, I shall have no alternative but to weep my heart out in all the anguish of maiden solitude..." In Wilde's play, Lady Bracknell also shows great concern about the financial security of Jack before he is allowed to marry Gwendolen. In *Engaged*, by coincidence, two girls Belinda and Mimie get engaged to Cheviot. In Wilde's play Gwendolen and Cecily are rivals for the man named Ernest. When Gwendolen meets Cecily they like each other. Gwendolen says, "Cecily Cardew: What a sweet name! Something tells me that we are going to be great friends. I like you already more than I can say. My first impressions of people are never wrong." Soon they realize that they are rivals:

Cecily : (rising) To save my poor, innocent, trusting boy from the machinations of any other girl there are no lengths to which I would not go.

Gwendolen: From the moment I saw you I distrusted you. I felt that you were false and deceitful. I am never deceived in such matters. My first impressions of people are invariably right.

and a little later,

Cecily : (to Gwendolen) A gross deception has been practised on both of us.

Gwendolen: My poor wounded Cecily!

Cecily : My sweet wronged Gwendolen!

Gwendolen: (slowly and seriously) You will call me sister, will you not?

A similar situation where two ladies are deceived by one man and who resolve the tangle by clear reasoning occurs in *Masks and Faces* (1852) by Tom Taylor and Charles Reade. After mutual misunderstanding they find an affinity between themselves:

Oscar Wilde

Mabel	:	......Can you trust me?
Woffington	:	And will you let me call you friend?
Mabel	:	Friend! no — not friend!
Woffington	:	Alas!
Mabel	:	Let me call you sister? I have no sister.

In *Engaged* Belinda enrages her rival by eating tarts from the wedding buffet. This rather coarse humour is repeated by Wilde in his comedy twice—first with cucumber sandwiches prepared specially for Lady Bracknell being eaten by Jack and then again with muffins.

In *The Importance of Being Earnest*, Jack presents himself dressed in the deepest mourning:

Chasuble	:	Dear Mr. Worthing, I trust this garb of woe does not betoken some terrible calamity?
Jack	:	My brother.
Miss Prism	:	More shameful debts and extravagance?
Chasuble	:	Still leading his life of pleasure?
Jack	:	......Dead! (Shaking his head)

His supposed brother Ernest is sitting in the drawing room. Algernon is now posing as his brother. In *Engaged* Symperson enters in deep mourning for Cheviot who threatened to commit suicide:

Cheviot	:	What's the matter?
Symperson	:	Hallo! You're still alive?
Cheviot	:	Alive? Yes; why (noticing his dress), is anything wrong?
Symperson	:	No, no, my dear young friend, these clothes are symbolical; they represent my state of mind. After your terrible threat which I cannot doubt you intend to put at once into execution......

Gilbert had insisted that *Engaged* "should be played with the most perfect earnestness and gravity throughout." He only pleaded for the importance of being earnest. Gilbert wanted a trivial piece to be considered in earnest and Wilde also wanted a trivial comedy for serious people. This influence of Gilbert on Wilde spotlights the latter's tendency to plagiarise. Wilde told Robert Ross his opinions on this point: "My dear fellow, when I see monstrous tulip with four wonderful petals in some one else's garden, I am impelled to grow a monstrous tulip with five wonderful petals, but that is no reason why some one else should grow a tulip with only three petals."[1]

The Importance of Being Earnest was Wilde's most successful comedy and it was written in 1895 when Wilde's trial began and ended in his ruin. Wilde's career as a dramatist was the most scintillating and he divided it into prose works and works of poetry. *Salome* and *The Duchess of Padua* were his two contributions to poetic drama. Mention must also be made of two other fragments of plays. *A Florentine Tragedy* was written about the year 1893 and was not completed. A merchant of Florence marries a beautiful girl Bianca. As the merchant is mostly away, she has an affair with the Prince. The merchant and the Prince meet in a duel and the latter is killed. The end of the tragedy is reached when the wife and husband reunite.

Bianca : Why?
           Did you not tell me you were so strong?
Simone : Why? Did you not tell me you were beautiful?

La Sainte Courtisane was also written at about the same time and was never completed. From the fragments available, the story seems to have been modelled on *Salome*, except that the ending in *La Sainte Courtisane* shows the reversal of situation. In this fragment Myrrhina is the temptress, the woman covered with jewels. She comes to tempt the beautiful young hermit: "Where does he dwell, the beautiful young hermit who will not look on the face of woman?" She meets the Saint Honorius and describes to him the luxury in which she rolls. The descriptions are

---

[1] *A Note on 'Salome'*: Translated from the French by Oscar Wilde with Sixteen Drawings by Aubrey Beardsley; p. xviii

highly sensuous, especially of the body. She says of a play-fellow: "He was pale as a narcissus, and his body was like honey." Honorius meets the temptations with coldness: "Thy body is vile Myrrhina. God will raise thee up with a new body which will not know corruption and thou wilt dwell in the courts of the Lord and see Him whose hair is like fine wool and whose feet are of brass." In a similar vein Jokanaan said to Salome: "Daughter of adultery, there is but one who can save thee, it is He of whom I spake. Go seek Him......bow thyself at His feet and ask Him the remission of thy sins."

As Myrrhina leaves, Honorius falls a prey to temptations but now Myrrhina is moved by his words and is changed. The moral of the tale is brought home in an exquisite fashion.

Honorius :	You talk as a child, Myrrhina, and without knowledge. Loosen your hands. Why didst thou come to this valley in thy beauty?
Myrrhina :	The God whom thou worshipped led me here that I might repent of my iniquities and know Him as the Lord.
Honorius :	Why didst thou tempt me with words?
Myrrhina :	That thou shouldst see Sin in its painted mask and look on Death in its robe of Shame.

La Sainte Courtisane, although a fragment, is an exquisite piece of poetic beauty. The spirit of temptation is beautifully embodied in Myrrhina, modelled as it is on *Salome*. The basic difference between *Salome* and *La Sainte Courtisane* is that whereas in *Salome* the spirit of Sin is triumphant and smothers the voice of conscience, in the latter play the spirit of temptation is defeated and transformed. *Salome* was only a poetic display of sensuous passions, *La Sainte Courtisane* is an excellent morality play.

Oscar Wilde's fame now rests only on one comedy *The Importance of Being Earnest* as it is the only comedy that is free from his intellectual preoccupation with sin, and criticism of society, however indirect.

In his comedies Wilde showed a definite |affinity with the

Restoration dramatists. The same picture of vice glorified, the delight in exquisitely decorated sin and the fascination for clever and witty conversation are the chief features of Wilde's comedies and also of the Etherege-Wycherley-Congreve variety. In Wilde's comedies the glamorous aspect of society is presented, but it was the only way out for Wilde if he was to criticize the manners and morals of his age. *Lady Windermere's Fan* touched upon one significant aspect of late nineteenth-century fashionable life. The number of women deserting husbands for lovers was large. In their craving for jewels, scents and champagne they could even blackmail their sons-in-law. Mrs. Erlynne is only one of the many such women. *A Woman of No Importance* dealt with the 'problem' of an unmarried mother. *An Ideal Husband* had for its theme a rather weak appreciation of conjugal happiness. The political intrigue in the play was its main feature. Wilde's only comedy to rise above the usual run of mechanical plots was *The Importance of Being Earnest*. It is here that the artist in Wilde asserted himself.

In one sense Wilde has earnestly kept away from the serious aspects of life, and, in his comedies seems to completely ignore the world beyond the fashionable and the aristocratic. However, it will be a misreading of his work to call it purely fantastic and unreal. Wilde's aim in writing for the stage was different from the aim of his contemporaries. To him entertainment was of supreme value in a work for the stage. Purpose was alien in the context of his comedies. This was, in fact, not always true as Wilde, who appeared apparently devoted to portraying the superficial glamour of society, never lost sight of the weaknesses and lack of morals and never forgave them even when overlooked artistically; the best represented people in his plays are the aristocrats, and they are also the worst in the sense that they are shown in all their weaknesses. While many of their weaknesses have been pointed out, one more may be noted from a scene from *The Importance of Being Earnest*, included in the original first text, but omitted in the stage version given by Alexander. H. Montgomery Hyde has published this scene in *The Listener*, November, 4, 1954. Grisby comes to arrest the so-called Ernest at Jack's country house for debt. Grisby says what applies to the aristocracy in general, "The Officer of the Court ....has arrested in the course of his duties nearly all the younger sons of the aristocracy, as well as several eldest sons, besides of course a good many members of the House of Lord's." The surprise of the scene is hidden here:

Algy : Pay it? How on earth am I going to do that? You don't suppose I have got any money. How perfectly silly you are. No gentleman ever has any money.

Grisby : My experience is that it is usually relatives who pay.

× × × × ×

Prism : £.762 for eating! How grossly materialistic! There can be little good in any young man who eats so much and so often.

Chasuble : It certainly is a painful proof of the disgraceful luxury of the age. We are far away from Wordsworth's plain living and high thinking.

Many such examples of luxurious living can be found in the aristocracy which are certainly not complimentary to them. There are many other instances where Wilde told the truth about the society of his time. Lord Caversham says: "Can't make out how you stand London Society. The thing has gone to the dogs, a lot of damned nobodies talking about nothing." And what is most true of Wilde's own technique, he says in *Conversations*: "To get into the best society nowadays one has either to feed people, amuse people, or shock people—that is all." In *The Decay* of *Lying* Wilde wrote: "What is interesting about people in good society is the mask that each one of them wears, not the reality that lies behind the mask." The truth of these statements can be seen in Wilde's own life in London.

Apart from the comedy of aristocratic manners another main distinguishing feature of Wilde's comedies is the brilliant and witty dialogue. The fluency with which epigrams flow from the lips of certain characters is remarkable. But Wilde depended too much on this feature, and there are scenes where he seems to be deliberately running after epigrammatic conversation; for example, the scene in *Lady Windermere's Fan*, when Lord Darlington retires with his friends at two in the night to talk and delight in phrases and epigrams "much like the Moore and Burgess Minstrels used to sit round to exchange conundrums with a 'Mr. Johnson' at one corner and a Mr. Somebody-else or the other."[1] In *An Ideal Husband* Lord Goring and Lord Caversham's conversation is mostly of this type. The succinctness with which Wilde could express the most intelligent and most idiotic ideas was his singular gift. On this point Wilde came in conflict with Pinero and Jones who were making rapid strides in realistic dialogue and brief pithy conversation.

In the construction of his plots, Wilde shows the influence of Scribe and Sardou, not that of Checkov and Shaw. His comedies are well-made. While everything in Wilde seems to move on easily, the hand of coincidence and surprise in the movement of plot is quite heavy. Here again Wilde was easily surpassed by Pinero and Jones. There is no play of Pinero which can be easily surpassed by Wilde's in matters of construction. The scene in *The Gay Lord Quex* where the hero is caught by the leading lady in his affair with the Duchess and the cross-examination scene in *Mrs. Dane's Defence* are so deftly put together that even Wilde's best does not match them. Yet, on the whole, in his comedies and poetical plays Wilde has displayed "such a sense of the stage that one is inclined to give him the benefit of any doubt."[2] He does not reveal any remarkable advance in technique because his theatrical sense is largely artificial and purposeless.

---

[1] E. T. Raymond: *Portraits of the Nineties*, p. 142
[2] Osbert Burdett: *The Beardsley Period*, p. 147

Chapter IX

English Stage 1865-1900

> "the theatre is irresistible; organise the theatre."
>
> Matthew Arnold

> "the Independent theatre is becoming wretchedly respectable."
>
> George Bernard Shaw

The last three decades of the nineteenth century stage outgrew the decadent and moribund conventions of the theatre. The new stage showed a great advance in different aspects of the theatre, viz. the audience, scenery and costume, actors and management. Together they prepared the ground for a new drama.

The audience played a significant role in the renascence of drama in these decades. The unruly crowds that gathered around the two patent theatres were representative of the huge population of London that clamoured for popular evening entertainments. Unlettered, vulgar working classes wanted spectacular shows and musical extravaganzas—for them existence of a theatre was justified only when it catered to their taste. They never associated any thoughtful matter with the entertainment they expected from the theatre. Their favourites were farces and extravaganzas. The realisation that the stage was different from the music hall, ballroom or fashion parade, that it had a higher artistic and moral purpose and that it could wield a considerable influence in tackling moral, social and economic problems and in reshaping society, was very slow to dawn on the mind, not only of the unlettered audience but even of the producers and playwrights.

English drama was reduced to a popular entertainment. It was necessary that managers and directors should step forward to check further degradation. The responsibilities of a theatre manager and director towards restoring the drama to its proper place were realised first by Marie Wilton and Squire Bancroft. Robertson showed awareness of his responsibilities as a writer under such miserable conditions.

Gradually the audience realised that the theatre was more than a mere evening rendezvous. It was a source of thoughtful and wholesome education. This change in attitude followed the joint efforts of stage managers, directors and authors. Due to an increased number of theatres following the Act of 1843, the worst and the most uncontrollable section of the audience went to music halls which, like theatres, were now no longer obliged to work under pretensions. Only those genuinely interested in drama as an art form came to theatres. The Queen also favoured the theatre by her occasional visits and her presence exercised a salubrious influence.

Chief among the various objectives of the Bancroft's management was the education of the public through dramatic shows. From the beginning they realised that if a new play was to be produced it should come in spite of the wishes of the people. They forced *Society* upon people who hitherto had favoured the various hybrid forms of drama. The movement was begun by Robertson and soon it was followed with greater zeal and determination by the succeeding generations of dramatists. William Gilbert was dreaded both behind the stage and across it. Pinero had no problem with the audience. Jones made great efforts to cultivate propriety in the audience. He made the first efforts to create a bond of understanding between the playwright and the audience. Popular comedies and other plays dealt with some social problems but never involved the audience with them. Jones and Shaw forced on the audience a realisation of their share in the social misery. Of course at first their efforts shocked the audience but there slowly developed a good understanding between the writer and the audience. *Saints and Sinners* was Jones' first attempt in this direction. Shaw carried forward the work started by Jones, and in *Widower's Houses* and *Mrs. Warren's Profession* he introduced a new trend which aimed not so much at making the audience conscious of the higher value of the drama as to make the playwrights themselves realise their new responsibilities towards the audience.

Another factor responsible for a change in the outlook of the audience was the organised paper activity on the part of certain dramatists. People were now given a choice between musical and spectacular shows and thoughtful drama. Jones' efforts did much in this sphere. He ventilated his opinions on the theatre and public through the press. Jones held that :

> The theatre is not the place to save men's souls. It is the place to give us thoughtful amusement, to instil a large and sane knowledge of life, to educate us insensibly in the supreme science of wise living......The theatre at its best is the most potent instrument of 'general' education.[1]

Bernard Shaw's zeal in this sphere was remarkable as from the beginning of his career he sailed against the wind, and assailed the popular, enervating trends in the drama. He thought it was the duty of the dramatist to obey the voice of his conscience and not that of the public. In his first dramatic review, written for *The Saturday Review*, of *Guy Domville* by Henry James, Shaw strongly objected to the idea that "the drama's law the drama's patrons give." He vindicated the truth when he said: "It is the business of the dramatic critic to educate these dunces, not to echo them."[2] 'Dunces' was used perhaps in a comprehensive sense to include not only the audience but also the playwrights. On another occasion, Shaw, while reviewing *Delia Harding* by Victorien Sardou, made observations on the first night audience which incorporated views detrimental to his own interests as a dramatist. He said that the theatre must be cleared of all un-

---

[1] *Patriotism and Popular Education*, p. 46
[2] *Shaw's Dramatic Criticism*, p. 2

desirable elements even with the help of the police as "ninety-nine out of every hundred people in it are incommoded by rowdyism, and are only too glad to be protected from neighbours who cannot express their disapproval or approval decently."[1]

It was the result of such deliberate attention given to the audience by critics and dramatists alike that ultimately produced a sobering effect on the people as regards their behaviour in the theatre halls. In the nineties Jones had no complaint against the audience.

> We have our first nights, interspersed with perhaps a few ticklish but easily quieted elements of mischief, that serried pack of bright earnest intelligent faces in the first row of the pit, lovers of the drama for the drama's sake, whose self-appointed duty it is to give a loud unmistakable verdict of approval or condemnation.[2]

The change in the attitude of the Church towards the stage also had a salutary effect on the audience. Canonical authorities realised the growing importance of the theatre as a social force. Rev. H. R. Haweis in a sermon delivered at St. James, Maryleborne announced that the time had come "when prelates and playactors shake hands."[3] Certain sections of the society which abstained from the stage were now drawn to it. Aristocrats and members of the rich and high class families now perceived the change in circumstances. The new audience did not demand a six-hour programme, a veritable pot-pouri of farce, musical extravaganzas, melodrama and the like. It was well satisfied with a three-hour show which sometimes began with the main play without a curtain raiser. The small cosy theatres were no longer obliged to stage ranting poetic plays of the romantic genre. The gigantic auditoriums of the Drury Lane and the Covent Garden theatres still carried on with romantic plays. The small new theatres depended on the new comedies and sought the cooperation of the audience in a thoughtful appreciation of plays. Gradually the audience of

---

[1] *Shaw's Dramatic Criticism*, p. 2
[2] *The Renaissance of the English Drama*, pp. 18-19
[3] *The Era*, xli, October. 19, 1819, p. 5

the nineties learnt to appreciate realistic comedies and abandoned its old love for romantic melodramas.

Another significant change which altered the contours of the drama occurred in the conceptions of acting. Great romantic actors were the objects of blind admiration for the ordinary theatre-goers. The entry of the polite society in the theatre brought corresponding change in modes of acting. Actors of the older generation depended on passion plays and melodramas but a marked departure from this tradition was made with the advent of Robertson. The Bancrofts, apart from giving tone to management, also inaugurated a new era in acting with the production of *Society*. Previously it was considered the privilege of outstanding actors to have 'parts' written for them with the result that the whole play did not receive as much attention from the writer as certain parts in it that gave an opportunity of feigning and ranting to the stage celebrities. Robertson in *Society* wrote no 'parts'. He paid all his attention to the 'whole'. The heroine of Pinero's *Trelawny of the Wells* complained that she was given no part in plays of the writer-hero, and her complaint was portentious of the new drama. The body of the play as a whole came to be treated with greater care. The great actors who kept the torch of the romantic tradition burning on the stage were Macready, Charles Kean, and Henry Irving. The far-off historical and 'passion' tales which hitherto occupied the stage now gave way to themes of contemporary interest — themes not commanding the prestige of history, yet more important because they were making history. In discarding the romantic tradition of acting, people discarded the one firmly rooted tradition of the stage. Robertson by casting ordinary people in his plays gave a serious jolt to the Irving School of Acting and established a new school of natural acting.

Gilbert discarded the contemporary star system in his direction of the Savoy operas. He gave prominent parts to less known actors, such as Rutland Barrington and George Grossmith with a view to checking the merciless operation of the star system. The dictatorship with which Gilbert ruled his theatrical group earned for him the reputation of being the most dreaded director of his time. Gilbert's selection of unknown players in the leading roles marked a definite break from the established traditions of acting.

When Pinero came to write for the stage, conditions had changed and a group of new actors appeared on the stage. John Hare, George Alexander and Charles Wyndham attained great fame and set new standards in realistic acting. Pinero cast these actors in his social plays. Only Henry Arthur Jones adhered to the old traditions, and made little effort in the direction of realistic acting.

Shaw's contribution in this direction was indirect. He used his pen against the Irving School with great power. A few quotations are necessary here to illustrate its full force. Reviewing a Lyceum production of *Cymberline* he observed: "A prodigious deal of nonsense has been written about Sir Henry Irving's conception of this, that and the other Shakesperian character. The truth is that he has never in his life conceived or interpreted the characters of any author except himself."[1] He was pained to see that "Irving never did and never will make use of a play, otherwise than as a vehicle for some fantastic creation of his own."[2] Shaw's remarks show the evils of the romantic acting at their worst. The Irving School was the most formidable force working against realistic acting. Parts in romantic acting were tailored to fit the talents of certain stars. The main attraction was the performance of a star actor and not the play in which he appeared. Shaw's bitterness of tone was due considerably to Irving's refusal to produce *The Man of Destiny*. The star actors were so averse to unromantic, realistic acting that even Ellen Terry appeared in *Captain Brassbound's Conversion* only after much persuasion.

This, however, does not mean that Irving and his school of acting was trash. He had served the English stage at a critical time in his own way. When he appeared on the London Stage in 1866, the actors' profession was deemed neither respectable nor artistic. It was Irving's powerful personality that lent dignity to the pro-

---

[1] *Shaw's Dramatic Criticism*, p. 212
[2] *Ibid.* p. 183

fession and art to the technique. With him the actor emerged from a mere entertainer into a social figure. But we have to admit that his mode of acting raised the position of the actor at too great a sacrifice of the art of the drama, which could not be retrieved without a reaction against Irving.

The decline of the romantic tradition exercised an indirect influence over English drama. Nearly all the plays in which these 'stars' appeared were tragedies. The transition from the romantic to the realistic drama came through the intermediate stage of melodrama. With the fall in the calibre of the tragic hero and a growing favour shown to heroes of comedies, English drama began its march in a new direction.

Irving was honoured with knighthood in 1897. Later he unveiled a statue of Mrs. Siddons in a public place. This showed the new prestige of actors. Before Gilbert's advent on the English Stage, actresses were treated with contempt by respectable people. There was no self-respect among actors and actresses as they came of very low families. Gilbert supervised his stage with great dictatorial control. He looked after young women 'like a dragon.'[1] He allowed no outsider to contact women members of his team. He always made them feel respectable. Once when in Gilbert's absence, Carte brought The Prince of Wales into the green room, Jessie Bonp annoyed Carte by sitting down and continuing to stitch in the presence of the Prince. Later she explained her behaviour on the ground that she was not presented to him. In a further meeting with the Prince she told him that there are "ladies in our profession". "Miss Bond," the Prince said, "you are perfectly right!" To prove the sincerity of his conversion to her view he made a request.

'May I come to see you, Miss Bond?'
'What for, Sir?' she asked.

At this point the conversation ended.

This dignity among actors and actresses came from the new

---

[1] Pearson: *Gilbert and Sullivan—A Biography*, p. 149

facade that the stage was putting up. As the stage found favour with the higher classes, talented people were drawn to this profession without fear of losing their social prestige. Actresses now came from respectable sections of society. The Prince of Wales patronised the Savoy Operas by frequent visits to the Opera Comique. The Queen also ordered performances of a few plays at court.

The transition from the romantic to the realistic drama was made possible through another subsidiary change in stage management. Production of Shakespeare's and other poetic plays demanded gorgeous stage settings and magnificent period costumes. The antiquated devices of decoration and design hampered growth of realism on the stage. Irving in acting and Charles Kean in stage management kept the old traditions to the total neglect of new dramatic devices. Charles Kean's productions of Shakespearian plays at The Princess's were a great attraction to the average playgoer. At the Prince of Wales' Theatre the Bancrofts fought a battle for survival. Robertson's novelty consisted in his using real doors and real locks as devices towards producing realism on the stage. He broke away from the bondage of spectacle and magnificence.

The glory of the stage scenery reached its peak in the production of romantic plays. Spectacular shows depended on magnificent scenery for their life. Gigantic structures were raised at infinite cost to create an illusion on the stage. With this architectural and archaeological accuracy and minuteness the cost of production was tremendous and yet the stage-reality remained, at best, only an illusion. As the new theatres did not bind themselves to catering to the demands of the spectacle-loving audience, managers were no longer obliged to invest stupendous sums on individual plays. The new audience and the new dramatist demanded no rich scenery on the stage. The new drama depended on the story of the play and acting.

Gilbert alone among the new playwrights needed attractive scenery for his operas. Pinero and Jones depended only on the acting of their plays. They needed little help from the stage carpenter. Shaw and Wilde completed this deliverance from the thraldom of the stage carpenter.

These changes on the stage were related to the contemporaneous developments in the continental drama and stage. France set the standards for the new English drama. Translations of French plays were already in vogue among English stage managers. Robertson, Taylor, Boucicault, Albery and H. J. Byron were fully steeped in the French tradition and technique. The workman-like standards in play construction came through the well-made play. Scribe's influence on the English dramatists made them realise that there was something basically wrong with the English stage. The visiting foreign troupes confirmed this impression. The warm welcome given to the first visit of the company of Comedie Francais in 1871 left them with a feeling of dissatisfaction with their own technique. The visits were repeated in 1879 and 1893, only to confirm the first impression. English critics and authors were deeply impressed by the finish and niceties of production of European theatres and actors.

Successful tours of the Comedies Francais drew other foreign troups to London. The new visiting companies included the Gymnase Dramatique, the Vaudeville, the Palais Royal and a few other companies. Saxe-Meiningen and the Rotterdam Dramatic Company also toured England. Attention given to the minutest details of production gave their performances a new look and English managers soon learned their lessons. Whatever be the direct influence of these visiting companies, it became clear that the English stage badly needed improvement. Ibsen also entered the English scene with a triumph. He left English playwrights agog at his marvellous stagecraft. He relegated the carpenter to the backyard of the stage.

The new consciousness in the people conferred great importance on the drama as a social force and efforts began to be made to rejuvenate it in all directions. The chief enemy of the original and fresh talent was the long run system which prevailed despite many efforts to put an end to it. The long run system was aided by the star system. As an effort to give new authors opportunities to show their talent the matinee system was introduced. Many stage societies were formed with a view to reforming conditions on the stage.

The Dramatic Students, a society of young actors, was founded in 1886. They aimed at producing the little known classics on the stage. It was felt that "these form the very nucleus of a very wholesome revival of interest in the best theatrical writing......By and by this seed will, we do not doubt, bear fruit."[1]

Another venture to set the stage free from old effete traditions was the Independent Theatre Society, started under the leadership of J. T. Grein in 1891. The Bancrofts had started The Prince of Wales' Theatre with a view to improving the conditions on the stage and giving new authors more opportunities of exhibiting their talent. The Independent Theatre was started as a reaction to the flourishing drawing-room drama and particularly aimed at encouraging playwrights, new and advanced in thinking.

Pinero and Jones were the most well-established masters of the drama. Shaw disliked their plays for the mildness of their social criticism. Open criticism of society was a sign of advanced opinions. Shaw said: "The Independent Theatre is becoming wretchedly respectable."[2] He hailed the establishment of the Independent Theatre as "an excellent institution, simply because it is independent. The disparagers ask what it is independent of...... It is, of course, independent of commercial success......The real history of the drama for the last ten years is not the history of the prosperous enterprises of Mr. Hare, Mr. Irving and the established West-end theatres, but of the forlorn hopes led by Mr. Vernon' Mr. Charrington, Mr. Grein, Messrs Heney and Stevenson, Miss Achurch, Miss Robins and Miss Lea, Miss Farr and the rest of the Impossibilities."[3]

The role played by the Independent Theatre in the formation of a new drama was estimated highly by its admirers like Shaw. Independent Theatre started its career with the production of *Ghosts* and followed it up by *Widower's Houses*. Enthusiastic writers like Shaw, who were refused performance by managers

---

[1] *The Saturday Review, LXI,* January 23, 1886, p. 116

[2] *Shaw's Dramatic Criticism,* p. 30

[3] *The Saturday Review, 1 XXIX,* January 26, 1895, p. 126

of the popular theatres embraced the opportunity offered by Grein's venture. Despite the commercial failure which attended Independent Theatre productions, its mere existence was indicative of the people's restlessness for a change.

Earlier in 1875, it was planned to set up an Academy of Dramatic Arts at Stratford. Later, London was actually chosen as the venue of this institution in view of the fact that in it was congregated the best acting talent of the country. But this plan could not materialize. In 1879 came the proposal for founding a Royal Academy of Dramatic Art which "might sit as a jury on unpublished plays and unknown playwrights......In time it might build a theatre...and the National Theatre would be the issue... it would create, organize, and control a complete system of instruction."[1] These various dramatic societies aimed at creating better conditions on the stage suited to the development of the drama in the proper direction. With this view an academy was tentatively established in October 1883 with the cooperation of great personalities and literary figures like Matthew Arnold, Tennyson, Wilkie Collins, Henry Morley and Bulwer Lytton. The academy was, however, closed in 1885.

Efforts to raise the standards of the stage and the drama continued. Writers and critics made good use of the press in educating lovers of the dramatic art. Books were written assessing the contemporary drama by William Archer. *English Dramatists of Today* was soon followed by *About the Theatre*. Magazines gave more space to reviews of the theatrical performances. *The Athenaeum* allocated more pages to such reviews. *The Saturday Review* entrusted Shaw with the responsibility of writing for the drama section. Later Shaw's reviews of the stage were published in book form in three volumes as *Our Theatre in the Nineties*. Frank Harris became actively devoted to theatrical activities. Oscar Wilde joined the group of reviewers as a critic for the *Pall Mall Gazette*. Joseph Knight's reviews for *The Athenaeum* were published as *Theatrical*

---

[1] W. E. Henley: *A Corporation of Actors* (The Theatre, N. S. ii, November. 1880, pp. 274-79)

Notes. Oscar Wilde published his reviews as *Critic at the Pall Mall*. Max Beerbohm succeeded Shaw as dramatic critic to *The Saturday Review*, and later published his reviews as *Around Theatres*. In 1880 there was established *The Theatre* and *The Journal of Dramatic Reform*.

But for certain critics who looked after their job with great earnestness the real zeal for theatrical reform would not have been so pronounced. Critics divided themselves into two fiercely opposed groups. To the first group belonged critics who had faith in the old traditions and were dogmatic in their concern to avoid infringement of these values by new ideas. The second group comprised critics who sincerely believed in novelty and change in the existing form of the drama. The formally recognized leader of the first group was Clement Scott, the favourite critic of the middle-classes. His most noted feature was his contempt of Ibsen and his reviews of *Ghosts* and *A Doll's House* showed a personal and violent protest against the tendency to change the form and technique of the drama. Discussion of the new drama, new woman and sex and economic questions—he regarded as foreign to the province of drama. Clement Scott's was a classic attempt at preventing the renascence of the drama. Leadership of the second group went to William Archer who regarded new ideas as the life-blood of the drama. The ideal dramatist who could deliver the goods was Ibsen. Archer's clear foresight perceived that Gilbert, Pinero and Jones were going to dominate the English theatre in the last decades of the century. His support of Ibsen won him Shaw's appreciation. Shaw on *The Saturday Review*, A. B. Walkely on *The Star* and *The Times* and young Justin McCarthy on *The Sunday Sun* and *The Gentleman's Magazine* continued their efforts in encouraging a new drama.

The zealous mutual attacks among the critics left theatre-goers at a loss to choose between the two—the Ibsen drama and the Pinero-Jones drama. Shaw's contempt of the Pinero-Jones drama was greatly prejudicial as it was due to his inspired Ibsen-worship. Shaw made a very wise suggestion in laying down certain qualifications for the critics' profession. Each paper started a section on the drama and indiscriminately appointed critics to review plays. This had an injurious effect on the quality and standard of criticism. Shaw wrote: "The advantage of having a play criticised by the critic who is also a playwright is as obvious as the advantage of having a ship criticised by a critic who is also a master shipwright."[1] To him the greatness of Shakespeare and Pinero as excellent stage craftsmen was considerably due to their early training in acting. He held that "critics who, either as original dramatists or adapters and translators, have superintended the production of plays with paternal anxiety, are never guilty of the wittily disguised indifference of clever critics who have never seen a drama through from its first beginnings behind the scenes. Compare the genuine excitement of Mr. Clement Scott, or the almost Calvinistic seriousness of Mr. William Archer, with the gaily, easy, what-does-it-matter attitude of Mr. Walkley, and you see at once how the two critic-dramatists influence the drama, whilst the critic-playgoer only makes it a pretext for entertaining his readers."[2]

The last thirty-five years of the century witnessed organized activity in all aspects of dramatic art. The audience, acting profession, theatre organisation, criticism and magazine discussion all passed through a critical period and ultimately yielded to the forces which culminated in the arrival of the new drama. Drama attained new heights as a social force equal to the Church in importance. All these activities were so far limited to the stage only. There were still two obstacles in the way to be cleared before the new drama could establish itself.

Censorship continued to be the enemy of all new ideas on sex, economic questions and religion. The censoring of plays laid its heavy hand on supporters of the new drama. It is surprising the way censorship remained uninfluenced by all movements aimed at reforming the existing conditions of English drama. It still valued high morality in plays clothed in the most provokingly disguised

---

[1] *Shaw's Dramatic Criticism*, p. 116
[2] *Ibid.* pp. 117-18

form. It could not stand clearly reasoned-out immorality. Even the occasional oaths on the stage and references to religion were tabooed. Lord Chamberlain did not read the plays himself. This was done by an Examiner of Plays which made him the most powerful man who could prevent any writer from staging a play on very flimsy grounds of morality. Often the changes which were made according to rule were absurd. For example, an expression like "as drunk as a Lord" was changed to as "drunk as a Heaven", in pursuance of the rule that 'Heaven' should be substituted for Persons of the Trinity without paying any attention to context and to the article 'a'. The conception of morality was so stiff-necked that the censor forced the producer of an English adaptation of *La Tentation* by Octave Fenillet to insert the lines "I sinned but in intention" in the play as the heroine, a married woman, was guilty of indiscretion in her earlier life.

Questions of sex and religion were seriously objected to by the censor. Shaw's *Widower's Houses* and *Mrs. Warren's Profession* were forbidden stage production as they dealt with problems hitherto never openly discussed by writers. Serious and earnest efforts of certain dramatists to enlarge the province of the drama by incorporating new subjects were met with cool indifference by the censor and often resulted in getting doors of theatres closed against public performance of such plays. The censor would object to plays pointing out social evils, it would with pleasure pass plays only thinly veiled over highly immoral themes. Really speaking, the subject matter of the later nineteenth century drama did not differ much from earlier productions; the only difference that now appeared was that subjects of moral lapses in women, of unhappy married life, of social stratification based on money, were all separated from that sweetness of tone, the repentance for mistakes and reconciliation with social values which characterised all earlier dramas.

English drama acquired a new look when it parted company with the Victorian compromise and complacency in matters needing reform. The Censor regarding smugness, hypocrisy and compromise as the true features of the drama faced an uphill task when under the powerful impact of Ibsen English drama changed its complexion rather suddenly. The reason for Pinero's popularity and Shaw's unpopularity is easily found here. Pinero's treatment of moral lapses in women was in keeping with the Victorian outlook. His erring women never had peace and happiness in the end (*The Second Mrs. Tanqueray*) and thus served as object lessons in morality. On the other hand, when Shaw took up Mrs. Warren's case he put the blame on society for her present condition and thus heaped coals of fire on the smugness and complacency with which the Victorians would have damned Mrs. Warren for her degeneration. Pinero's play was passed by the censor whereas Shaw's play was forbidden public performance.

The censor could not stand this new frankness in dramatists of the Ibsen School. Shaw had already begun his campaign against consorship in the Preface to his *Plays Unpleasant*, and now he brought the attack to a head with a lengthy article 'The Censorship of the Stage in England' for *North American Review CLXIX* August 1899. Jones also worked hard against this effete institution. In England censorship was more a matter of tradition, followed on the assumption that "without a censor the stage would instantly plunge to the lowest practicable extreme of degradation —an assumption quite undisturbed by the fact that literature without a censor, behaves far more decently than drama with one."[1] Before the close of the century censorship gave up much of this unwanted severity in matters of licensing plays. It grew more tolerant of the new drama. *The Athenaeum, The Era, the Pall Mall Gazette* and *The Saturday Review* devoted full columns to onslaughts against the pernicious effects of indiscriminate and prejudiced censoring of plays.

The renascence of the drama did not come about merely on account of more favourable conditions for the plays. Dramatic authors now found the profession economically not too disappointing. Fickleness of the public taste and uncertainty of income which

---

[1] Shaw: *The Censorship of the Stage in England*, reproduced in *Shaw on Theatre*, Ed. By J. E. West, p. 73

earlier drove authors of genuine dramatic talent to look for a living in other forms of literature now settled to an increasingly hopeful prospect. Original talent was deprived of just income because cheap translations and adaptations filled managers' rooms. Boucicault, Charles Reade and Tom Taylor lived on meagre incomes. Boucicault having suffered tremendous loss suggested a way out to managers. He did not sell his play to the manager, but proposed sharing the income. The royalty system opened up new prospects of income for authors. It gave them a sense of security from economic distress. Pinero and Jones profited most by this system. In the nineties, Wilde earned flattering sums for his comedies. These examples encouraged authors to devote their talents wholeheartedly to writing for the stage.

Absence of copyright laws had discouraged publication of plays. The Copyright Act of 1843 protected only those plays which had been staged even if only for a single performance. America, where drama became greatly popular, throve on this state of affairs in England. Pirated editions of popular English plays earned a huge income for managers there. Not much was done by an international copyright agreement in 1887. A landmark in the direction of achieving legal protection was the American Copyright Act of 1891. It provided security to the authors against the risks of publishing their plays.

Publication of plays after the American Copyright Act became secure, and those who did not publish their plays within a reasonable time after production invited comments on the merit of their work, that the work was "a thing of the theatre needing to face the calm and cold daylight of print."[1] It was felt that a general reading public be created to show that the drama had come out of the intellectual paralysis that had afflicted it till then. The Copyright Bill offered "an accurate gauge of any individual playright's pretensions, and of the general health and conditions of the national drama."[2] Publication of plays aimed at ending

---

[1] Preface to *Saints and Sinners*, p. vi
[2] *Ibld* p. v

the general misconception that literary and theatrical elements in a play are antagonistic to each other. What was more important about it was the general feeling that "we are never likely to have a native drama of much literary merit without the practice of publication to emphasize conscientious finish and rebuke slovenly writing."[1] Gilbert had earlier started this practice to his advantage. He had been to America to attend the production of *Patience* before it was pirated. Shaw's *Arms and the Man*, also, was performed in New York by Richard Mansfield with little pecuniary gain to the author. In England, Pinero and Jones followed the lead given by Gilbert. Shaw published his *Plays Unpleasant* because of the difficulties created by the censor. Wilde published all his comedies and made huge profits.

Publication of plays set to advantage certain literary elements which could not have been noticed in a stage performance. *The Profligate, The Second Mrs. Tanqueray, The Notorious Mrs. Ebbsmith*, and *The Benefit of the Doubt* were Pinero's contributions to the 'literary' drama. Jones' plays; *Saints and Sinners, Michael and His Lost Angel, Judah, Liars* and *Mrs. Danes Defence* in their published form added greatly to his stature as a literary writer although Shaw and some others never acknowledged Pinero and Jones as such. However, the perusal of their plays in their published form at once brings out the difference between them and the popular theatrical fare of those days.

The English Stage, in the years 1865-1900 witnessed a great change in the temper of the audience, the position of the playwrights and actors, the conception of the drama and the financial aspects of the theatre. These changes were bound to effect a greater and more significant change in drama as a genre of creative, literary writing.

---

[1] *The Era*, i, December 10, 1887, p. 9

Chapter X

A Period of Achievement

> It was through the efforts of Gilbert, Pinero, Jones, Shaw and Wilde that the nineties saw a rejuvenation of drama.

English Drama toward the close of the nineteenth century came to exercise a great social impact and the need to revise old values was realised in all spheres of the theatre. The long-run and the star system, factors regarded with deference by producers, were the two powerful enemies to new developments and originality. The matinee system alone offered opportunity to new authors. The dominance of the scene by the favourite playwright and the favourite actor was found tyrannical and forces to counteract their effect began to make their appearance. Many stages and societies came into being and began to function, infusing a new life into drama. 'The Dramatic Students' (1886) aimed at reviving little known classics. The Independent Theatre (1891) wrecked vengeance against the popular drama and took Ibsen as their guide into new and unexplored regions. Shaw felt in 1895 that "the Independent Theatre is becoming wretchedly respectable."[1] and looked upon the commercial failure of its productions as proof of its artistic superiority over the popular drama.

---

[1] *Shaws' Dramatic Criticism*, p. 30

A Period of Achievement

The nineties were crowded with activities for dramatic reform. The proposal to set up an Academy of Dramatic Art was made as early as 1875. Four years later 'an academy of acting' was in the offing, followed by another proposal to set up a Royal Academy of Dramatic Art. In October 1883 an academy was tentatively established with personalities like Matthew Arnold, Tennyson, Wilkie Collins, Henry Morley and Bulwer Lytton on the committee. It was closed in 1885. However, efforts and proposals continued to be made in an uninterrupted series.

This organised theatrical activity expressed the people's awareness of the need for a new theatre. Writers and critics made good use of the press in educating the masses. Books were written with a view to assessing the contemporary drama. William Archer's *English Dramatists of Today*, appeared in 1882, to be soon followed by *About the Theatre*. Magazines gave more space to reviews of theatrical performances. *The Athenaeum*, *The Saturday Review* with Shaw as its dramatic critic, *The Fortnightly Review*, *The Theatre* and *The Journal of Dramatic Reform* were genuinely devoted to surveying activities in the theatrical world.

Dramatic critics divided themselves into two fiercely opposed groups. The advocates of the new drama were headed by Shaw, and supporters of the old drama found a leader in Clement Scott. Clement Scott's derision of the 'new' element in Ibsen was more than suitably expressed in his reviews of *Ghosts* and *A Doll's House*. He exploited all the resources of his personal force and violent expression to prevent the arrival of the new drama on the English stage, and probably his vehemence, force and violent tone were responsible for the matching vehemence of his critical opponents: Shaw and Archer. His impassioned denunciation of the new drama increased its supporters and gave a keener edge to their advocacy. In his *Saturday Review* articles Shaw answered Clement Scott with equal force. Shaw claimed "that high dramatic art does mean Ibsen." In the academic and theatrical skirmishes fought in the pages of these magazines, Shaw had the advantage of being a critic who was also a playwright. Scott was fighting a losing battle.

Apart from the problem of an irresponsible critical activity English drama faced another difficulty in the prejudicial censorship of plays. The Government had earlier brought into evidence its apparent lack of concern for the national drama by the Licencing Act of 1843. Censorship turned into a personal affair and served as a barrier to advanced and new thinking. References to God and religion, sex and corruption were still taboo. Really it was the frankness with which these subjects were being treated by the new dramatists that enraged the Censor. Shaw and Jones fought against its rigid control. Both looked upon this as the most formidable and exasperating obstacle in the way of a wholesome and healthy development of the drama. Shaw favoured "the entire abolition of the Censorship and the establishment of Free Art in the sense in which we speak of Free trade."[1]

Despite opposition from all sides drama continued to be the most popular of literary forms. Yet the persons with a real talent for narrative and portraiture found drama economically undependable and stayed away from it, probably not by choice but because the stage that flourished on the cheap second hand translations, adaptations, rapid comic drama and stupid farce showed no deference to talented writers. It is not to belittle the service that the Bancrofts and others rendered in encouraging young writers, yet on the whole, the results were far from satisfactory. Boucicault started the system of payment on royalty basis thus providing writers some security against the fear of economic disaster. But it created a group of writers whose names spelled commercial success and thus closed the door on new writers. Pinero and Jones profited most by this system. The absence of copyright laws and the influx of unacknowledged foreign plays discouraged publication of plays by dramatists. The Copyright Act of 1883 did not do much to protect the authors as it only covered plays actually acted on the stage. Plays were pirated to America which was becoming the promised land of dramatic enterprise. Not much could be gained by the International Copyright Agreement of 1887. A

---

[1] *Shaw on the Theatre*, Ed. by E. J. West, p. 11

landmark in the continued efforts to seek legal protection was the American Copyright Bill of 1891. While it assured economic safety it was felt that "there is ......one ray of hope for English authors in the Act......We are never likely to have a native drama of much literary merit without the practice of publication to emphasize conscientious finish and rebuke slovenly writing."[1] Henry Arthur Jones also looked upon the publication of plays as "an accurate gauge of any individual playwright's pretensions and of the general health and condition of the national drama."[2] Publication of plays improved the standard of writing because the authors had now to bear in mind that their plays were being submitted to more leisurely and critical scrutiny. Gilbert, Jones and Pinero gave the lead in this direction and soon had followers like Shaw and Wilde. Jones regarded the publication of plays as symbolic of a progress without which the "stage remains in the same state of intellectual paralysis that has afflicted it all the century."[3]

The new conditions had a direct influence on the contemporary drama. Gilbert's essay 'A Stage Play' gives an idea of how a play was constructed in his times. The author gets 'a general idea' guided by the resources of his company, and arranges 'striking situations for the end of each act.' This is of course written in a satiricial and ironical strain. The conditions he describes prevailed in the seventies and eighties and his originality appears in a striking contrast against the plethora of the stock-in-trade drama. Gilbert never struggled to set himself free of the Victorian tradition, specially its love of sentimentality. His 'Savoy Operas' show great originality in their conception of a topsy-turvy world where he can get an untrammelled view of life. In his own way Gilbert gave a new realism to English drama at a time when it was very greatly needed. The 'Savoy Operas' thus reveal an auriferous vein of social comedy which prepared the ground for Shaw and Wilde.

---

[1] *The Era*, iii, Jan. 10, 1891, p. 15

[2] Preface to *Saints and Sinners*, p. v

[3] *Ibid.* p. vii

The importance and magnitude of Gilbert's contribution becomes clear when he is compared with his contemporary James Albery. *Two Roses* (1870) shows Albery at his best. It also shows the best features of Victorian drama: love of maudlin sentimentality, purity and division of people on the basis of money and similar social stratification. Joseph Knight rightly diagnosed the difference between Gilbert and Albery when he said that "Mr. Albery is the most independent and indisciplined. Mr. Gilbert aims at shapeliness and regularity of composition."[1]

The indirect but forceful commentary on the society which forms an integral part of the 'Savoy Operas', served as the cornerstone of the later edifice of social criticism erected by Shaw and Wilde. Gilbert's endeavours were steeped in sincerity and consistency. Gilbert was the only writer of comedy and extravaganza while he was turning out his 'Savoy Operas' in quick succession The English stage was slowly moving in a new direction, tending towards popularisation of the literary drama.

Pinero made the beginning of his dramatic career by providing the stage with a number of popular farces and melodramas. He established his reputation at the Court Theatre with *The Magistrate*, *The School Mistress* and *Dandy Dick*. Pinero, in writing farces, was only subscribing to the popular trend of comic drama. But he knew what he was meant for and under the impact of the new social movements, he wrote his serious plays: *The Profligate* (1889), *The Second Mrs. Tanqueray* (1893), and *The Notorious Mrs. Ebbsmith* (1895). His plays, wrought with technical perfection and craftsmanship, fell a little below the greatest contemporary dramas of Shaw and Ibsen. Sentimentality was his worst fault. He believed that "the art of drama is not stationary, but progressive. By this I do not mean that it is always improving......a dramatist whose ambition it is to produce live plays is absolutely bound to study carefully, and I may add even respectfully—at any rate not contemptuously–the conditions that hold good for his own age and generation."[2]

---

[1] *Theatrical Notes*, p. 37

[2] 'Robert Louis Stevenson as a Dramatist' a lecture delivered in Edinburgh in Feb. 1903 in *Papers on Playmaking* Ed. by Brander Matthews, p. 57

Pinero made conscious efforts in raising the written drama above the commonplace. He laid great stress on dramatic talent which, he thought, "is the raw material of theatrical talent." While dramatic talent is "the power to project characters, and to cause them to tell an interesting story through the medium of dialogue......theatrical talent consists in the power of making your characters, not only tell a story by means of dialogue, but tell it in such skilfully devised form and order as shall, within the limits of an ordinary theatrical representation, give rise to the greatest possible amount of that peculiar kind of emotional effect, the production of which is the one great function of the theatre."[1] Pinero called 'strategy' and 'tactics' integral parts of a dramatist's skill, and looked upon the dramatic suitability of the dialogue as its sole virtue. These points raised in his lecture on Stevenson very well bring out Pinero's creed as a dramatist. Writing in an age when publication of plays came to be regarded as a test of its literary merits, Pinero gave to drama a new look. The grip over dramatic situations and the realistic dialogues gave to his plays their two sterling virtues.

The success of Pinero's dramas also explains why the new drama was delayed in making its appearance on the English stage. He never acknowledged the influence of Ibsen, although it was suggested by his choice of themes in his serious plays like *The Profligate*, *The Second Mrs. Tanqueray* and *The Notorious Mrs. Ebbsmith*. The audience was still not prepared for a frank and open attack on public morals after the manner of Ibsen. It liked Pinero's plays for their serious problems and maudlin sentimentality which happily solved problems at the end. Shaw was still to make his mark. But despite their apparent lack of concern for supporting any theatrical regeneration movement Pinero's plays rose high above the average staple fare of the London Stage on the basis of their superb craftsmanship, excellent characterisation and originality.

Jones shared with Pinero the reputation of saving English drama from extinction. If toward the close of the nineteenth

---

[1] *Ibid.*, p. 58

century the audience showed a marked change in its behaviour and appreciation of drama, it was due to the tireless campaign of Jones and Shaw to educate the masses. In his zeal for reform Jones left Pinero far behind. Jones writing on *The Theatre and the Mob* expressed great dissatisfaction with the prevailing condition on the stage where amusement was considered as the test of a dramatist's art. The renascence of drama as it appeared in the nineties was no less the result of Jones' efforts in explaining to people his concept of modern drama and its requirements than it was due to Shaw's campaign for Ibsen. Jones pleaded for the following points:

(1) The modern drama must be recognized as a branch of English literature………

(2) The drama must be seen to be in many ways opposed to the theatre, and must no longer be considered by play-goers as a negligible appurtenance to the theatre.

(3) Actors and actor-managers can never reform the drama. It is not their business………

(4) The drama will only flourish when the author has authority and vogue with the great play-going public, and when he is in supreme command of his own work.

(5) The drama must be recognized as something different from popular entertainment,……it must be judged and criticized as a fine art.

(6) The drama must be encouraged and supported by Government and the municipalities…………

(7) Plays must be read by play-goers—a habit of play reading must be cultivated as in France……I do know that I have set forth a few great rules that are the foundations of any possible school of drama……[1]

Jones efforts to usher in a new drama were not limited to lecturing and arguments on paper, but he actually laboured hard to enlarge the province of drama by including within its sphere subjects hitherto tabooed, such as religion and politics. It was in consequence of his efforts that sensational melodrama and cheap farces which held the stage, were forced to give way to

---

[1] *The Life and Letters of Henry Arthur Jones*, op. cit. Letters to Mr. H. H. Spielmann, pp. 81-82

drama with a social mission. Though the work of dramatists like Lord Lytton and Dion Boucicault occasionally touched upon social themes, they were dominated by cheap sentimentality and sensationalism. Lytton's *Money* (1840) and Boucicault's *London Assurance* (1841) and *The School for Scheming* (1847) dealt with social questions only in a symbolic way. Their main concern was to satisfy the hunger of the audience for sensationalism. What was just a casual matter in their plays, became the chief concern of Jones. Jones differs not only from his predecessors but also from his contemporary Pinero. Pinero and Jones picked up their subjects from the same basket. But whereas Pinero was held back by his predilection for themes yielding more emotional stuff, Jones risked his dramatic career by seriously attacking religion in his plays.

In his essay "Religion and the Stage', Jones wrote: "the two chief subjects which are by common consent supposed to be most difficult of stage treatment are religion and politics, because these are the subjects upon which counter opinions are most rife and popular feelings most easily raised......it is quite certain, however, that the existence of such a restriction upon the dramatist forbids the hope of the English drama ever reaching forward to be a great art, and condemns it to remain as it is, the plaything of the populace, a thing of convention and pettiness and compromise."[1]

Even Shaw nowhere made a louder protest in support of his dramatic theories. The force with which Jones hit at the Philistinism in people earned for him Shaw's appreciation. Plays like *Michael and his Lost Angel* and *Judah* showed his control of dramatic situations even under new circumstances. Jones did not merely theorise for the new drama but conforming to his theory readily used the material that the age offered him.

While English drama was slowly reshaping itself, diverse currents were flowing at the same time. Melodrama, popular since the beginning of the nineteenth century, continued to draw large audiences till the end of the century. Jones in *The Silver King*,

---

[1] Appendix to *Saints and Sinners*, pp. 122-26

gave to his age a drama which best showed what newness of theme and mastery of technique could achieve. But what is more important is Jones' use of comedy as a vehicle of social criticism. In *The Liars* and *Mrs. Dane's Defence* he dramatised situations for which even the Restoration dramatists might envy him. His handling of comedy of manners was also masterly and provided Shaw and Wilde with hints for their greatest dramatic enterprises.

The revival of a genuine comedy of manners can be attributed to the works of Pinero and Jones. Their greatness and distinction appear in striking contrast when they are set against dramatists like Sydney Grundy. Grundy's best plays, *A Pair of Spectacles* (1890) and the earlier *The Glass of Fashion* (1893) are mawkish commentaries on contemporary fashionable life. He could not depict serious problems in a controlled and dramatically effective manner, as *In Honour Bound* the wife's infidelity lends seriousness to the play which ends on a happy note. Pinero and Jones had in their minds 'ideas' about drama and in their own ways, tried to give it a certain distinction lacking in contemporary drama. They wrote many kinds of plays but their chief countribution to the renascence of drama comprised their serious plays The true precursor of Shaw was not Ibsen but Jones. Jones' efforts had their natural culmination in Shaw. Shaw made his debut on the English stage under great controversy over the artistic value of of his *Plays Unpleasant*. Like Jones, Shaw also adopted the dual strategy of educating the public mind in true dramatic values through his articles in the *Saturday Review* and putting their taste to test by offering plays embodying his own principles. He had a singular derision of the drama as Pinero wrote it and got a little satisfaction from the fact that J. T. Grein of the Independent Theatre "will shortly be consecrated by public opinion as the manager of the one theatre in London that is not a real wicked Pinerotic theatre, and is, consequently, the only theatre in London that it is not wrong for good people to go to."[1]

With this basic complaint Shaw endeavoured to rid the English

---

[1] *Shaw's Dramatic Criticism, op. cit.* p. 31

stage of its evils. His lecture 'Quintessence of Ibsenism' made it clear that he was championing a drama completely new in outlook and entirely different in conception from the prevailing type. Like Jones, Shaw was chiefly concerned with widening the scope of the drama. Apart from religion and politics for which Jones had said so much, Shaw included economic questions among subjects for stage plays. Principle and precept went hand in hand and he presented the first embodiment of his principles in *Plays Unpleasant* in which his purpose was to show that the stage could also be used as a pulpit to propagate reforms on big economic and social issues like slum conditions and causes of prostitution. Shaw in *Widowers' Houses* and *Mrs. Warren's Profession* hit his fancied target in dramatic reform. He showed no inclination to a truce with the social circumstances—the biggest weakness in his contemporaries. But the influence of Ibsen soon left Shaw high and dry and his pecuniary failure on the stage sadly reminded him of the truth Pinero and Jones had realised from the beginning, and it was this that an author could never completely ignore stage values in his work. *Plays Unpleasant* had good economics but poor drama.

The realist in Shaw who was devoted to unmasking the face of economic wretchedness in *Plays Unpleasant* parted company in *Pleasant Plays* where with a touch of irony and satire he dealt with popular notions of romance, chivalry, moral preaching, heroism and emancipation of women through education and neglect of biological needs. In the second phase of his development as a dramatist Shaw fell back on the principles of Pinero and Jones and carried them farther by the force of his individuality. *Three Plays for Puritans* include a melodrama, a historical character study and a 'passion' play. Except *Plays Unpleasant* which were written directly under the Ibsen vogue, *Pleasant plays* and *Three Plays for Puritans* showed Shaw's unacknowledged debt to his contemporaries, Pinero and Jones.

Shaw's real contribution to the making of a new drama was made not so much through his plays as through his critical reviews and essays in which he set about reforming English drama in three ways: first, by vehemently opposing the Irving tradition of acting on the stage; secondly, by attacking his contemporaries for the note of compromise in their plays; and, thirdly, by advocating the cause of Ibsen which gave an idea of what he wanted others to emulate. His criticism of Shakespeare was greatly misunderstood although he made it clear that he did not "profess to write better plays," as it did not mean "that the right to criticize Shakespeare involves the power of writing better plays". He realised that "it is the philosophy, the outlook on life, that changes, not the craft of the playwright."

Shaw, more than any of his contemporary dramatic critics, was conscientiously devoted to the task of demolishing factors alien to the true spirit of drama. The three volumes of *Our Theatre in the Nineties* form the most enlightened body of reviews of contemporary dramatic productions, Shaw did not directly influence any playwright, nor did he formulate a technique. He himself carried forward the technique of William Gilbert. Actually he gave to drama a realism which appeared in a more effective form in Galsworthy's *The Silver Box*, *Strife* and *Justice* written in the twentieth century. Shaw's influence was limited to a small coterie of writers which looked at the 'Problem Play' with admiration and as a distinct form of drama. His work in a way expressed one important phase of the development of drama in the nineties, but before the close of the century this phase was to decline.

In this sense Oscar Wilde may be said to have caught the real spirit of the times. Realism, as Shaw advocated it, declined soon and was replaced by imaginative literature. In his comedies Wilde gave the best examples of the comedy of manners written in his times. He looked upon drama as "the most objective form known to art", and made it as personal a mode of expression as the lyric or the sonnet; and in his own way, "widened its range and enriched its characterisation".[1] His method was different from that of Pinero and of Jones in that neither like the former did he sneer at the *beau monde* nor like the latter did he moralise. Wilde was concerned with presenting an unfabricated picture of society. What makes

---

[1] *Complete works of Oscar Wilde* p. 657

A Period of Achievement

Oscar Wilde's work truly representative of the nineties is his grasp of the literary modes. He perceived the dramatic possibilities of a poetic theme and gave to the London Stage *Salome, Duchess of Padua, A Florentine Tragedy* and *La Sainte Courtisane*. Their intrinsic merit apart, these plays were symbolic of the rejuvenation of a trend which was forgotten in the clamour for realism. But the tradition of poetic plays had never completely lost its hold on the people.

Wilde's work did not bring poetic plays to the height of artistic development. Poetic plays had to wait for some time before Stephen Philips could come with a lyrical fervour quite unknown to the stage of his time. Poetic plays in the nineteenth century invariably followed the Elizabethan strain. In *Paola and Francesca* (1900), Philips with an uncontrollable weakness for the Elizabethan model showed the charm of word music. James Barrie, whose main dramatic work falls in the twentieth century, had adopted his famous novel *The Little Minister* for the stage in 1897. Barrie's contempt of the serious and intellectual drama found expression in highly comical plays. Realising the impatience of the people with the realistic drama, he substituted subjectivity for objectivity, and instead of realistic pictures gave his own imaginative versions. The revival of poetic drama in the nineties heralded the complete end of the Ibsen vogue on the London stage. The craze for realism petered out in the wake of light comedies and poetic drama. Oscar Wilde's work presented a meeting-point of these two tendencies. Through his light comedies he demonstrated the success of entertaining and intriguing situations as against the heavy weight of economic and social questions that occupied the writers of the problem plays. In *Salome* and other poetic plays he announced the revival of an old strain, that of poetic drama.

What then was the truth about the renascence of English drama towards the close of the nineteenth century? It was in fact a realisation of the truth that a nation could not long survive on borrowed goods, that to have its own life it had to discover its own resources. English drama before the seventies had slumped into such a decrepit state due to excessive influx of translations and adaptations of foreign works that it was feared that English drama had become extinct. But through the genuine and sincere efforts of Robertson, Gilbert, Pinero, Jones, Shaw and Wilde, English drama achieved a new life and truly national character. English dramatists were writing on the same lines and same subjects which appeared with greater force and clearness in Ibsen. The rejuvenation of English drama toward the close of the nineteenth century was the work of English dramatists. Ibsen's abrupt appearance and shortlived influence on contemporary dramatists showed the depth of native talent. It was through the efforts of Gilbert, Pinero, Jones Shaw and Wilde that the nineties saw a rejuvenation of drama.

Select Bibliography

Theatre

Archer, W. *The Old Drama and the New* (N. Y., 1926)

Balmforth, Ramsden *The Problem Play* (Allen & Unwin, London, 1928)

Bancroft, Sir S. W. *Rocollections of Sixty Years* (London, 1909)

Brunstein, Robert *Theatre of Revolt* (Atlantic Monthly Press, Toronto, 1956)

Carter, H. *The New Spirit in the European Theatre* (Ernest Benn Ltd., London, 1926)

Chandler, F. W. *Aspect of Modern Drama* (Macmillan, 1914)

Clinton, Baddley, V. C. *The Burlesque Tradition in the English Theatre After 1660* (Methuen, London, 1948)

Dickinson, Thomas H. *The Contemporary Drama of England* (John Murray, London, 1920)

The Theatre in a Changing Europe (Putnam, London, 1940)

Gassner, John *Form and Idea in Modern Theatres* (Dryden Press, N. Y., 1956)

The Theatre in Our Times (Crown Publishers, N. Y., 1954)

Masters of the Drama (Dovers, N. Y. 1951)

Dramatic Soundings (Crown Publishers, N. Y., 1968)

Hudson, Lynton *The English Stage 1850-1950* (George G. Harrap, London, 1951)

Nicol, A. *A History of Late Nineteenth Century Drama Vols I & II* (Cambridge, University Press, 1949)

Reynolds, E. *Early Victorian Drama: 1830-1870* (Heffer & Sons Ltd., Cambridge, 1936)

Rowell, George *The Victorian Theatre—A Survey* (Oxford University Press, London, 1956)

Sawyer, N. H. *The Comedy of Manners from Sheridan to Maugham* (University of Pennsylvania Press, 1931)

Shaw, G. B. *Our Theatres in the Nineties*: 3 *vols*. (Constable, London, 1948)
Major Critical Essays (Constable, London, 1948)

Social Background

Brinton, Crane *English Political Thought in the Nineteenth Century* (Ernest Benn Ltd., London, 1933)
Buckley, J. H. *The Victorian Temper* (Allen & Unwin, London, 1952)
Burdett, O. *The Beardsley Period* (John Lane, London, 1925)
Ensor, R. C. K. *England 1870-1941* (Clarendon Press, Oxford, 1936)
Gallienne, R. Le, *The Romantic Nineties* (Putnam, London, 1951)
Godwin, Michael *Nineteenth Century Opinion* (Penguin)
Gaunt, William *The Aesthetic Adventure* (Jonathan Cape, 1945)
Halevy, Elie *A History of the English People in the Nineteenth Century, Vol. IV: Victorian Years 1841-1895* (Ernest Benn Ltd., London, 1951)
Reymond, E. T. *Portraits of the Nineties* (T. Fisher Unwin Ltd., London)
Somervelle, D. C. *English Thought in the Ninteenth Century* (Methuen, London, 1950)
Thomson, Patricia *The Victorian Heroine: A Changing Ideal* (Oxford University Press, 1956)
Walter De La Mare *The Eighteen Eighties* (Cambridge University Press, 1930)

W. S. Gilbert

Dark, Sidney and Grey *W. S. Gilbert: His Life and Letters* (Methuen, London, 1923)
Darlington, W. A. *The World of Gilbert and Sullivan* (Peter Nevil Ltd., London)
Hudson, Lynton *The English Stage: 1850-1950* (George G. Harrap, London, 1951)
Pearson, H. *Gilbert and Sullivan—A Biography* (Hamish Hamilton, London)
Gilbert: His Life and Satire (Methuen, London, 1927)
Reynolds, E. *Early Victorian Drama 1830-1870* (Cambridge University Press, 1936)
Barker, H. G. "Exit Planche—Enter Gilbert" (*The London Mercury*, 1922)
Boas, Guy "The Gilbertian World and the World of Today" (*English*, Vol. VII, No. 37, 1948)
Ellehauge, V. M. "The Initial Stages in the Development of the English Problem Play" (*Englische Studien*, 1931)

Select Bibliography

Arthur W. Pinero

Boas, F. S. *From Richardson to Pinero* (John Murray, London, 1936)

Borsa, M. *The English Stage of Today* (John Lane, London, 1908)

Downer, A. S. *The British Drama* (Appleton Century Crofts, N. Y., 1950)

Davies, Cecil W. "Pinero The Drama of Reputation" (*English*. Vol. XIV, 1962)

Fyfe, Hamilton *Sir Arthur Pinero's Plays and Players* (Ernest Benn Ltd., London, 1930)

Hale, E. E. *Dramatists of Today* (Henry Holt & Co., N. Y., 1911)

Henry A. Jones

Cunliffe, J. F. *Modern English Playwrights* (Harper, London, 1927)

Disher, M. W. *Melodrama: Plots That Thrilled* (Rockliff, London, 1954)

Jones, D. A, *The Life and Letters of Henry Arthur Jones* (Victor Gollancz, London, 1930)

Jones, H. A. *A Faith That Enquires* (Macmillan, London, 1922)

    Patriotism and Popular Education (Chapman and Hall, London, 1919)

    The Foundations of a National Drama (Chapman and Hall, London, 1915)

Northend, M. "Henry Arthur Jones and the Development of Modern Drama" (*Review of English Studies* Vol. XVIII. Oct. 1942)

Weales, Gerald, *Religion in Modern English Drama* (Pennsylvania Press, Philadelphia, 1961)

Henrik Ibsen

Bull, Francis *Ibsen: The Man and the Dramatist* (Clarendon Press, Oxford, 1954)

Downs, W. *Ibsen: The Intellectual Background* (Cambridge University Press, 1946)

Northam, John *Ibsen's Dramatic Method* (Faber, London)

Tennant, F. F. D. *Ibsen's Dramatic Technique* (Bowes, Cambridge, 1948)

Williams, Raymond *Drama: From Ibsen to Eliot* (Chatto and Windus, London, 1952)

Arestad, Sverre "Ibsen's Concept of Tragedy" (*PMLA*, Vol. LXXIV, 1959)

Robertson, J. G. "Henrik Ibsen" (*The Contemporary Review*, Vol. 153, 1928)

English Drama 1860-1900

G. B. Shaw

Colbourne, M. *The Real Bernard Shaw* (J. M. Dent, London, 1949)
Dent, Alan, *Bernard Shaw and Mrs. Patrick Campbell* : *Their Correspondence* (Victor Gollancz, London, 1952)
Hamon, Augustin, *The Twentieth Century Moliere* : *Bernard Shaw* (George Allen, London, 1915)
Handerson A. *Bernard Shaw, Man of the Century* (Appleton Century Crofts, N. Y., 1956)
Joad, C.E.M. *Shaw* (Victor Gollancz, London, 1949)
Kaye, J. B. *Bernard Shaw and the Nineteenth Century Tradition* (University of Oklohama Press, 1958)
Krutch, J. W. *Modernism in Modern Drama* (Russell & Russell, N. Y., 1962)
Pearson, H. *Bernard Shaw* : *His Life and Personality* (Collins, London, 1943)
    G. B. S. — A Postscript (Collins, London, 1951)
Stewart, J. I. M. *Eight Modern Writers* (Clarendon Press, Oxford, 1963)
St. John Christopher *Ellen Terry and Bernard Shaw — a Correspondence* (Rheinhardt & Evans, London, 1949)
West, Alick, *A Good Man Fallen Among Fabians* (Lawrence, London, 1950)
Woodbridge, H. E. *George Bernard Shaw — Creative Artist* (Carbondale, 1963)
Batson, E. J. "Geroge Bernard Shaw : Orator and the Man" (*English* Vol. XIV 1962)
    Couchman, G. W. "Here was a Caesar : Shaw's Comedy Today" (*PMLA* 1957 Vol. LXXII, No. 1)
    "Comic Catharsis of Caesar and Cleopatra" (*The Shaw Review*, Vol III, No. 1, Jan 1960)
Duerksen, R. A. "Shelley and Shaw" (*PMLA*, March 1963)
Elliot, R. C. "Shaw's Captain Bluntschli, A Latter Day Falstaff" (*M. L. N.* 1959)
Nethercot, A. H. "The Truth About Candida" (*PMLA*, 1959)
    "Bernard Shaw, Philosopher" (*PMLA*, 1954)
Mc Kee, Irving "Bernard Shaw's Beginnings on the London Stage" (*PMLA*, LXXIV, 1959)
Whiting, G. H. "The Cleopatra Rug Scene : Another Source" (*The Shaw Review* Vol. III, No. 1 Jan. 1960)

Oscar Wilde

Braybrook, P. *Oscar Wilde — A Study* (Studies Publications, London, 1929)
Ervine, St. John *Oscar Wilde — A Present Time Appraisal* (George Allen & Unwin, London, 1951)

Select Bibliography

Larvin, J. *Aspects of Modernism From Wilde to Pirandello* (Stanley Nott, London, 1935)

Laver, James *Oscar Wilde* (British Council, London, 1956)

O'Sullivan, Vincent *Aspects of Wilde* (Constable & Co., London, 1936)

Pearson, Hasketh *The Life of Oscar Wilde* (Penguins, Middlesex, 1954)

Perry, H. T. E. *Masters of Dramatic Comedy* (Harvard University Press, Cambridge, 1939)

Symons, Arthur *A Study of Oscar Wilde* (Charles J. Sawyer, London)

Hough, Graham "The Artist as a Man of Action" (*The Listener*, Oct. 21, 1954)

Nethercoott, A.H. "Wilde and the Devil's Advocate" (*PMLA LIX*, 1944)